Educational Evaluation:

Analysis and Responsibility.

edited by

Michael W. Apple/Michael J. Subkoviak
Henry S. Lufler, Jr.

University of Wisconsin-Madison

McCutchan Publishing Corporation
2526 Grove Street
Berkeley, California 94704

Library of Congress Catalog Card Number 73–17611
ISBN 0–8211–0011–4

Printed in the United States of America
Typography by PBS Enterprises, Berkeley, California

Contents

Preface

The editors of this volume were the organizers of a Conference on Evaluation held in Madison in April 1973, under the sponsorship of the School of Education at the University of Wisconsin. The six papers presented at the conference appear in this book, along with two chapters written by the editors that are designed to introduce aspects of educational evaluation.

In organizing the conference we first picked the topics to be considered and then sought able researchers to address these subjects. We picked topics to reflect the breadth of concerns we felt should be of interest to those involved with evaluation: the concept or philosophy of evaluation, anthropological approaches, empirical methods, secondary evaluation, process evaluation, and the ideology of evaluation. The conference and this book were both designed to present a freewheeling exchange among individuals approaching evaluation from such a variety of perspectives.

Each paper was responded to by one or two of our University of Wisconsin colleagues, who had prepared their remarks ahead of time by reading the conference papers in advance. These faculty critiques appear after each of the chapters in this book, and the informal reply of the paper's author to his critics is given next.

The conference audience, students and faculty from several universities, also joined in the debate over the issues raised. Following each of the papers we have included part of this discussion, without substantial rewriting, so as to give the reader a taste of the lively exchanges that took place. Perhaps a more elegant product would have resulted had we thoroughly edited the proceedings, but this would have been at the cost of sacrificing the breadth of the concerns presented. Subtitles indicating the topics discussed should help the reader locate items of particular interest.

Donald J. McCarty, Dean of the School of Education at the University of Wisconsin, Madison, made the conference possible, providing both wise counsel and practical assistance. The School's Multimedia Instructional Laboratory provided its full support as did its Business Office. The editors would not have finished without the help of their editor, Susan A. Niles, who provided sound advice while typing, which made the completion of this work possible.

Michael W. Apple
Michael J. Subkoviak
Henry S. Lufler, Jr.

Madison, Wisconsin
September 1973

Contributors

Michael W. Apple is Associate Professor in the Department of Curriculum and Instruction, School of Education, the University of Wisconsin, Madison. He has written numerous articles and monographs in curriculum theory and development on such topics as ideology and curriculum thought, the hidden curriculum, and students' rights. He is the author of the forthcoming *Schooling and the Rights of Children*. Professor Apple is currently working on the 1975 ASCD Yearbook, *Schools in Search of Meaning*.

Thomas D. Cook is Associate Professor in the Department of Psychology at Northwestern University. During the 1973-74 academic year, he was a Visiting Professor at the London School of Economics. He has conducted studies on the complex subjects of attitude change and research pitfalls in the study of changing attitudes. He is a coauthor of the forthcoming book, *Sesame Street Revisited: A Case Study in Evaluation Research*.

Clarence J. Karier is Professor of History of Education at the University of Illinois. He has taught and conducted research in the area of nineteenth- and twentieth-century educational thought and practice. He is author of *Shaping the Educational State* and coauthor of *Roots of Crisis: American Education in the Twentieth Century*.

Philip W. Jackson is Dean of the School of Education at the University of Chicago. He has studied and reported on the problems of educating both gifted children and those with learning handicaps. He has viewed the teachers of these students in his books *Life in Classrooms* and *The Teacher and the Machine.*

Richard J. Light is Associate Professor at the Laboratory of Human Development, Harvard University, and Assistant Director of the Institute of Politics, John F. Kennedy School of Government, Harvard. Dr. Light has taught, conducted research, and served as a consultant to groups in the areas of statistics, research methodology, and evaluation.

Henry S. Lufler, Jr., is Assistant to the Dean of the School of Education, University of Wisconsin, Madison. He has served as a special consultant to the President's Council on the Education of Disadvantaged Children, evaluating participation of non-public-school children in Title I programs. He has written articles and conducted research on the judicial process, law and education, and the politics of evaluation.

Michael Scriven is Professor of Philosophy at the University of California, Berkeley. The author of numerous works in the areas of philosophy, ethics, logic, psychology, parapsychology, computer science, and education, Dr. Scriven has also been involved in many major educational evaluation projects. He has served as a consultant to the U.S. Office of Education and has directed the training of evaluators for that office.

Michael J. Subkoviak is Assistant Professor in the Department of Educational Psychology at the University of Wisconsin, Madison. His teaching and research interests focus on educational measurement and evaluation. Professor Subkoviak is the author of journal articles, papers, and reports dealing with scaling methodology, teacher characteristics, and evaluation.

Herbert J. Walberg is Research Professor of Urban Education at the University of Illinois, Chicago Circle. Professor Walberg is the author of numerous studies in the areas of teacher and student personality, attitude, and learning.

Faculty Critiquers

Frank Farley is Professor of Educational Psychology, School of Education, University of Wisconsin, Madison.

Vernon F. Haubrich is Professor of Educational Policy Studies, School of Education, University of Wisconsin, Madison.

Lawrence Hubert is Associate Professor of Educational Psychology, School of Education, University of Wisconsin, Madison.

Francis Schrag is Assistant Professor of Educational Policy Studies, School of Education, University of Wisconsin, Madison.

Spencer Swinton is Assistant Professor of Child Development, School of Family Resources and Consumer Sciences, University of Wisconsin, Madison.

Gary Wehlage is Associate Professor of Curriculum and Instruction, School of Education, University of Wisconsin, Madison.

Introduction

This volume is concerned with three problems of major significance in evaluation. First, it aims at broadening the perspectives of educators on the problems of and approaches to evaluation, going beyond the restrictive input-output models that dominate the topic. With this in mind, authors such as Cook (on secondary evaluations), Jackson (on naturalistic studies of classrooms), Light (on models of research design in evaluation), and Walberg (on "process" evaluation and evaluation of open education) focus their attention on important aspects of evaluation that seek to make the field more responsive and sophisticated.

Secondly, the book is aimed at overcoming the limited range of conceptual and historical insights in the evaluation field. Here, Scriven continues his work in clarifying and broadening the conceptual concerns of evaluators. Karier engages in an analysis of the history of evaluation that stresses the fundamentally conservative posture it has tended to take in the past. Karier's paper is unusual in that an analysis that challenges the accepted interpretation of the field is normally not found in evaluation literature.

Finally, the book portrays the intense controversy that any serious discussion of evaluation is bound to raise. All too often, educators who hold distinctly different positions on the value of accepted forms of evaluation do not confront each other. Therefore, the format of the volume, with questions addressed to the authors, preserves the arguments for and against aspects of the positions the authors present. The spirit of controversial give-and-take is also heightened by the disparate positions taken by the authors of the two chapters in the first section of the book. Apple and Subkoviak discuss approaches to the study of evaluation coming out of two distinctly different intellectual traditions.

Apple's analysis in chapter 1 is critical of the modes of evaluation now employed in education and of the basic rationality behind them. He focuses on valuative, conceptual, and ideological assumptions that have problematic consequences. He argues that evaluation research may act to support questionable bureaucratic and institutional procedures and presuppositions rather than actually bringing about needed educational and social changes.

Apple is concerned with illuminating the taken-for-granted nature of the evaluation field and raising serious questions in the reader's mind about the commonsense presuppositions that guide the practice of evaluation. He draws upon recent research in the history of American education to show that it is possible to take a rather critical position on the history of the evaluation movement. He then turns his attention to the dominance of an efficiency or process-product ideology in evaluation and curriculum thought. It is strongly suggested that this is much too limited a framework to use in the complex problem of placing value on educational activities.

Using perspectives based on the sociology of knowledge and the study of deviance, Apple examines how the social role of the evaluation expert, the clinical model employed in evaluation, the acceptance by evaluators of categories and data derived from taken-for-granted assumptions of institutions, and even the basic logic of the methodologies used in evaluation research all contribute to the latently conservative posture of evaluation.

Apple concludes his analysis by advocating that evaluators turn toward ethical modes of valuing. In accord with this, he asks for a shift away from the evaluation of learning and toward institutional evaluation based upon concepts such as justice, mutuality of influence, and constitutional rights. This will require more sophisticated legal and philosophical training for evaluators and will necessitate drawing on models of research developed by anthropologists and ethnomethodologists such as Goffmann (1961).

In chapter 2, Subkoviak introduces concepts of evaluation that recur in later chapters of the volume. He also examines desirable and undesirable methods of grading students, judging teacher effectiveness, and determining the worth of new educational programs.

Test scores can be transformed into the usual letter grades, A, B, C, D, and F, by either norm-referenced or criterion-referenced methods. Most norm-referenced methods award the same, fixed percentages of As, Bs, Cs, etc., in above-average, average, and below-average classes. Subkoviak illustrates a norm-referenced system that overcomes this weakness by assigning different percentages of As, Bs, Cs, etc., to classes having different mean ability levels. He also discusses a practical method of criterion-referenced grading. Teachers examine the test on which grades are to be based and determine the probable scores of hypothetical A-level, B-level, C-level, etc., students. The scores of actual students are then compared to the hypothetical standards, and grades are assigned accordingly.

At present, teaching effectiveness is evaluated largely on the basis of observational ratings of classroom activity, with little consideration given to the cognitive and affective outcomes of that activity. While observational procedures often provide reliable and valid indications of teacher effectiveness, Subkoviak emphasizes that such information should be supplemented by data concerning students' cognitive and affective growth. A paradigm for gathering and using growth data is presented.

Subkoviak believes that the value of an educational program is determined by how well it achieves stated objectives. He discusses a number of criteria for judging the success of a program in reaching its goals, such as the amount of effort expended, the magnitude of the effect produced, the adequacy of the effect relative to the amount desired, and the cost effectiveness. He then considers experimental designs for constructing evaluative research. Emphasis is placed on strict adherence to the scientific method, contrary to the opinion that controlled evaluative research is impossible in the real world.

In chapter 3, Scriven examines a number of logical issues that arise when one begins to examine the nature of evaluation. Scriven is especially concerned with the place of value judgments in evaluation. One of the problems he deals with is that of coping with the arguments arising from the skeptical client or evaluee who believes that evaluation is either entirely subjective or entirely relative. He argues that this basic fact-value dilemma concerning the choice between being completely arbitrary and being merely relativistic lies at the heart of the neglect of evaluation as a social and scientific responsibility.

In his analysis of this issue, Scriven points to a number of conceptual confusions of such a position and argues the importance of a given context in any fact-value controversy. His major assertion is that the argument that value judgments are somehow less objective than judgments of fact is essentially context-dependent, like the distinction between premises and conclusions. He examines this problem within the context of evaluating computer-assisted instruction.

Scriven then analyzes another difficulty with the position that value judgments are less acceptable scientifically than nonvaluative judgments. He is referring to the doctrine of a value-free science. The position that science has no place for value judgments and that value judgments are not as testable and supportable as anything else in science Scriven finds unsupportable.

Finally, based on his analysis of the place of value judgments in evaluation, Scriven argues that all useful evaluation is implicitly comparative. He suggests that recognition that value judgments in evaluation are almost always comparative can lead to important practical improvements in using these values in evaluation.

The respondent to Scriven's chapter raises two criticisms. First, he argues that Scriven does not deal with some of the knotty questions in educational evaluation. How does one choose between competing value premises in evaluating public education? How can the evaluator adjudicate among competing concepts of good schooling? Secondly, the respondent points out that evaluation seems much more complicated than Scriven's examples indicate. He thinks Scriven seems to pass too quickly over the moral nature of schooling, thus tending to flatten out the value problem entailed in choosing the categories one uses to evaluate education.

In chapter 4, Jackson examines the products of a relatively new genre of educational research, naturalistic studies. He focuses on three major questions: (1) Where have they taken us so far? (2) Where are they apt to go in the future? (3) What potential contributions can naturalistic studies of school settings make to the reorientation of our thinking about educational evaluation?

Jackson compares naturalistic investigations with the more common types of educational research and notes that naturalistic studies are characterized by such factors as a large expenditure of time within ongoing school settings, the absence of formal hypotheses as guides to inquiry, an exploratory search for questions rather than answers, and an attempt to be as unobtrusive as possible. All of these characteristics contribute to the fact that naturalistic observers have greater respect for the integrity of the phenomena under scrutiny than their experimental counterparts do.

Jackson argues that the sympathetic treatment such an approach gives to school phenomena illuminates the complexity of schools and their operations. It also reveals the difficulty of making sense of this complexity with the use of simple schemes, as is so often tried in educational research. In this regard, he raises serious objections to the input-output modes of operation that provide the underpinnings for a good deal of educational thought and research. Linear and econometric models cannot do justice to the complexity of life in classrooms and are incorrect metaphors for conceptualizing the educative process.

It may be that many of the more radical critics of schooling have misconceived educational activity as well. Jackson holds that the results of naturalistic investigations have shown that many seemingly artificial constraints in schools are actually functional compromises and may not be so senseless after all. While there are weaknesses in naturalistic approaches, which Jackson notes, and while they will not provide answers to all the questions educators face, he believes such studies enable educators to delineate a more appropriate conceptual framework within which the search for answers must take place.

The respondent to Jackson's paper argues that he has not gone far enough in examining the potential of naturalistic studies in investigating such questions as how commonsense labels are attached to children in schools and how knowledge, traditions, and values are "filtered" through the professional staff of a school. The respondent further notes that naturalistic studies can lead one to take too sympathetic a position on the bureaucratic regularities of educational institutions unless these studies are guided by political and ethical sensitivity.

In chapter 5, Light addresses four basic issues: (1) the use of regression analysis to discover how and why an educational program is successful or unsuccessful, (2) the strengths and weaknesses of various evaluative research designs, (3) the effects of statistical and measurement error on conclusions drawn from a study, and (4) the future trends in evaluation.

Light believes that the emphasis of evaluative research should be on determining why a program works or does not work. If the causes of success or failure are determined, a program can be changed for the better. A program that undergoes a sequence of such improvements over time gradually approaches maximum productivity.

To understand the workings of a program, Light suggests that evaluative research should focus on the relation between activities or attributes of a program (independent variables) and outcomes or effects (dependent variables). Linear regression and curvilinear regression are obvious methods for attacking this problem. However, Light and the respondents to his paper note certain limitations and abuses of regression techniques, such as fitting many curves to the same data or allowing sample data to suggest the form of curve to fit. A randomization test for determining relationships among variables is suggested by one of the respondents as a possible alternative to regression analysis.

Light also considers the strengths and weaknesses of evaluative research designs ranging from comparison of randomly determined experimental and control groups to comparison of unmatched, intact groups. The dangers of equating unmatched groups by analysis of covariance and the detrimental effects of statistical and measurement error on conclusions drawn from a study are discussed.

Light concludes the paper with a discussion of five future trends in evaluative research: (1) increased emphasis on longitudinal as opposed to one-shot studies, (2) analysis of successful versions of a program to determine what makes the program work, (3) further consideration of the interactions between different types of students and different programs, (4) comparison of programs on the basis of both means and variances of outcome measures, and (5) emphasis on studying program activities that can be successfully repeated in the schools.

In chapter 6 Cook provides a comprehensive discussion of basic issues in the field of secondary evaluation. As the term suggests, *secondary evaluation* is a reevaluation of the data reported in an initial evaluation or primary assessment of a program. Cook in fact extends this definition to include analyses that combine data from many independent primary sources to arrive at a conclusion—for example, Jensen's (1969) study of the heritability of intelligence.

The review focuses on three central issues: (1) why secondary evaluations are conducted, (2) the strengths and weaknesses of the research models commonly used in secondary evaluations, and (3) guidelines for improving secondary evaluations. Cook illustrates his points with examples from secondary evaluations of such primary works as Ball and Bogatz's (1970, 1971) evaluations of "Sesame Street," the Battelle Laboratory (1972) evaluation of performance contracting, the Coleman Report (1966), the Westinghouse-Ohio evaluation of Head Start (1969), Rosenthal and Jacobson's (1968) evaluation of teacher expectancies, Jencks's (1972) work on equality, Jensen's (1969) article on the heritability of intelligence, and finally Armor's (1972) study of the effects of busing and school desegregation.

Some of the functions that secondary evaluations perform are: (1) reducing uncertainty about the conclusions drawn from a primary evaluation, by adding more evidence, (2) obtaining the opinion of a second party who is independent of and perhaps less biased toward the program than the primary evaluator, (3) adding the perspective of a second person who has been trained to ask different questions and to use different data analyses than the primary evaluator, (4) teaching others the art of evaluation by contrasting primary and secondary methods of analysis, (5) obtaining multiple indicators of a program's success or failure when there is no single best method of evaluation, (6) discovering trends in various independent bodies of data from separate primary studies, such as Jensen's (1969) organization of intelligence data, (7) replicating a primary finding across other persons and settings, and (8) determining why a program failed. In addition, both Cook and the respondents to his paper note that some secondary evaluations deliberately attempt to discredit a primary evaluation in order to gain notoriety or prestige. Such "academic head-hunting" casts serious doubt on the validity of the secondary evaluation in question.

Cook next considers various secondary evaluation models: (1) limited reanalysis of primary data, (2) simulating data, (3) answering the same questions with the same data using different methods of analysis, (4) answering new questions with the same data and new analyses, (5) combining multiple data sets to draw a conclusion, (6) conducting primary and secondary evaluations simultaneously, and (7) conducting two or more independent primary evaluations. In each case the author considers strengths, weaknesses, and actions to improve the model.

Cook concludes with suggestions for facilitating and improving secondary evaluations in the future: (1) establishment of a central data bank to which all interested evaluators have free access, (2) recruitment of professionals with divergent training and perspectives to form a secondary evaluation team, (3) increasing the speed with which secondary evaluation results become available, by dividing labor and giving quick access to primary data, and (4) collection of additional data needed to answer significant questions left in doubt by a primary evaluation.

In chapter 7, Walberg emphasizes three themes: (1) learning should be examined while it is taking place and especially from the learners' point of view, (2) the milieu (home and classroom) in which learning occurs should be analyzed to obtain a complete picture of the learning process, and (3) standardized achievement test outcomes are not the sole criteria on which the success or failure of an educational enterprise should be judged.

Walberg begins by showing the importance of measures of home environment (parental pressure, parents' education, birth order, and so forth) in predicting cognitive ability measures (numerical, reasoning, spatial, and verbal). He also notes that parental pressure measures account more fully for cognitive development than do more commonly used indices, such as parents' education, parents' occupations, number of siblings, and birth order.

Walberg next takes issue with the Coleman Report (1966), which concluded that classroom environment had little effect on cognitive development. Results of twenty-two smaller studies indicated that educational expenditures, class size, teacher experience, and other classroom variables did make a difference in learning outcomes. Some fifty other studies showed that teacher characteristics such as clarity of presentation, enthusiasm, and avoidance of strong criticism also made a difference.

In the remainder of the paper Walberg uses his own research to illustrate how environmental variables are measured and how they can be used to evaluate educational programs. In particular he discusses (1) the relation of student perceptions of classroom activities to cognitive and affective outcomes, (2) the use of student perceptions in evaluating Harvard Project Physics, (3) the levels of cognitive ability (Bloom et al., 1969) and affective attitudes that students associate with different subject areas (language arts, mathematics, science, social studies), (4) the decline in students' positive attitudes toward learning with increasing grade levels in traditional schools, and (5) the promise of open schools for improving student attitudes toward learning.

At one point in this discussion Walberg pauses to express discontent with the overemphasis given to cognitive outcomes in present evaluative research. He warns that standardized achievement scores and grades largely reflect a narrow range of verbal skills, which should not be the sole criterion for judging program effectiveness or individual worth. Outcomes such as creativity, citizenship, and personal adjustment should also be considered.

The respondents to Walberg's paper note that, since his work is largely correlational, the causal inferences that he draws regarding environmental variables are educated guesses. The effects of manipulating these variables in a true experiment must be studied to verify such conjectures.

In chapter 8, Karier presents evaluators with a historical interpretation of their work. He takes a revisionist perspective on the history of evaluation, one that disavows the interpretation of evaluation that most evaluators share. Karier presents five substantive theses concerning the ideological and political roots of the testing and evaluation movement. First, he analyzes and describes the Enlightenment ideology that provided the operating framework of the American educational state in the twentieth century. Secondly, he points out that this ideology found expression in both an ideal and a real meritocratic system of education. Thirdly, he argues the provocative position that the educational reward system based on this meritocracy was structured in such a way as to control and channel people rather than to provide avenues for substantive social change. Fourthly, he turns to the nature-nurture debates of the past and present to show that these have actually functioned to obscure the real racial, political, and economic reasons for basic shifts in social policy. Finally, his argument stresses that the ideology that testers, evaluators, and educators in general appropriated in the past now "serves more to destroy than to enhance the dignity of man."

Throughout his paper, Karier's theses center around the role played by major figures in the testing and evaluation movement in supporting a class structure that maintained the unequal distribution of wealth and power in the United States. He indicates how the social and racial beliefs of such individuals as Thorndike, Goddard, Brigham, Jensen, and Herrnstein influenced the approaches they took to educational issues and thus influenced the shape of the evaluation movement and schools. Whether this belief system had the effect that Karier asserts it did on the day-to-day reality of schools is one of the questions asked by the respondent. Karier is also questioned strongly on the historical evidence he marshals in support of his basic theme.

Taken together, the chapters, responses, and discussion in this book represent important steps in analyzing and clarifying how evaluation can be made more sophisticated, yet more socially and humanly sensitive. The responsibility for both kinds of improvements remains with all of us.

References

Armor, D. S. "The Evidence on Busing." *Public Interest* 28 (1972): 90-126.

Ball, S., and Bogatz, G. *The First Year of Sesame Street: An Evaluation.* Princeton, N.J.: Educational Testing Service, 1970.

Bloom, B., et al., eds. *Taxonomy of Educational Objectives: The Classification of Educational Goals,* Handbook 1, *Cognitive Domain.* New York: David McKay, 1969.

Bogatz, G., and Ball, S. *The Second Year of Sesame Street: A Continuing Evaluation,* 2 vols. Princeton, N.J.: Educational Testing Service, 1971.

Coleman, J. S., et al. *Equality of Educational Opportunity.* Washington, D.C.: U.S. Office of Education, 1966.

Goffman, E. *Asylums.* New York: Doubleday, 1961.

Jencks, C. S., et al. *Inequality: A Reassessment of the Effect of Family and Schooling in America.* New York: Basic Books, 1972.

Jensen, A. R. "How Much Can We Boost IQ and Scholastic Achievement?" *Harvard Educational Review* 39 (1969): 1-123.

The Office of Economic Opportunity Experiment in Educational Performance Contracting. Columbus, Ohio: Battelle Columbus Laboratories, 1972.

Rosenthal, R., and Jacobson, L. *Pygmalion in the Classroom: Teacher Expectation and Pupils' Intellectual Development.* New York: Holt, Rinehart and Winston, 1968.

Westinghouse Learning Corporation and Ohio University. *The Impact of Head Start: An Evaluation of the Effects of Head Start on Children's Cognitive and Affective Development.* Springfield, Va.: Clearinghouse for Federal Scientific and Technical Information, Sales Department, U.S. Department of Commerce, 1969.

I

The Problem of
Evaluation

1

The Process and Ideology of Valuing in Educational Settings

MICHAEL W. APPLE

The language and slogans of school people provide symbols for key educational ideas and movements. They serve as standards or beacons that attract adherents and often generate vast amounts of literature.[1] Sometimes, though less often than we suppose, they have a significant effect in reorienting educational practice. The language of accountability and evaluation provides an excellent instance of this phenomenon today. While evaluation is not a new concern to be sure, its recent emphasis—some might argue overemphasis—is striking to anyone familiar with the professional journals that indicate the state of the field.

There is reason to believe that the patterns of interaction among people concerned with evaluation affect the types of discourse that dominate the topic. There has been and, unless patterns change drastically, there will continue to be little debate among educators who hold distinctly different positions about many of the valuative and fundamental questions concerning evaluation because of what has been commonly called "invisible colleges." That is, individuals discuss and engage in debate only with others who already share much of their basic orientation. They never have to take seriously alternative conceptions of their activity because this professional activity is not open to challenge by others of a different persuasion. In this way there is little genuine synoptic progress in education as a whole and in evaluation in particular.

Therefore, a number of the arguments in this chapter will be guided by a perspective that might best be called "critical" in that it seeks to illuminate the problematic character of the commonsense reality most educators take for granted. The critical spirit of the chapter should be interpreted as a step toward engaging other members of the field in the essential argumentation over the role evaluation has played and will play in education. Such intellectual conflict and debate are of fundamental importance if we are serious about confronting educational problems in a manner that does justice to their complexity and subtlety. We need to reflect on Toulmin's dictum that any field that seeks to make programmatic and conceptual headway must stand open to even quite basic criticism and change if it is to be more than a pretender to rationality.[2] Unfortunately, curriculum discourse and a good deal of educational thought in general have been more concerned with both conceptual and social stability than with change, more interested in a search for prior consensus than in the critical give-and-take that supports genuine advances. The original papers and debates that this book presents are part of a response to the need for such informed discussion.

A basic aim of this chapter is to suggest the complexity of the problems that so much recent educational thought has tended to ignore. A good deal of what I shall say stresses the conservative nature of educational evaluation. My discussion employs investigations in areas too long ignored by educators. By bringing new perspectives to bear, I hope to illuminate alternatives to the very limited models we now employ. For example, my discussion often draws upon research on the question of "deviance." It seems that schools act to create certain student roles and expectations; groups of students either fill these and "make progress at school" or do not fill them and thus are channeled into other paths, in much the same way that deviants are created and are treated by other social institutions. Evaluation may play an interesting part here. Research on deviance is also critical in examining the place occupied by psychological language and research, and educational evaluation based on them, in upholding bureaucratic and institutional rather than interpersonal and situational norms and values.

This chapter, then, is meant to serve a number of functions: to raise serious questions in the reader's mind concerning educational evaluation; to point to ideological, methodological, epistemological, and ethical issues raised by the current emphasis on evaluation and accountability; and, at least partly, to reorient educational evaluation to what might be called *institutional evaluation* rather than evaluation of "learning."

Historical Interpretation

In the scientific disciplines, new paradigms emerge to offer more fruitful disciplinary matrices for reorganizing and reconstructing previously accepted explanations.[3] Similar "revolutions" occur in other fields of study. Among the foremost of these is the recent revisionist perspective in the history of American education. Critically oriented history has begun to raise a number of potent objections to our usual understanding of the past and the roles schooling and evaluation have played in it.

Educators' interpretations of their history have often reflected a belief that schools have "liberated the individual and opened up opportunities for social mobility to the disadvantaged."[4] Furthermore, the interpretation holds that, while schools have had their problems, they have been steadily moving toward a more egalitarian ethic and have contributed to and been a part of lasting social and institutional reforms. The accepted view sees testing and evaluation in a similar light, taking for granted the notion that they have led to more humane educational environments and will continue to do so in the future.

However, much of this interpretation is changing and cannot be quite so readily accepted anymore. Historian Michael Katz, for instance, states that the structure of schooling has remained basically the same for decades, a fact that is given more warrant by studies such as Sarason's recent investigation of the process of change in schools.[5] Katz argues that the past "moments" of schooling have reflected "not the great democratic engines for identifying talent and matching it with opportunity," but rather a treatment of "students as units to be processed into particular shapes and dropped into slots roughly congruent with the status of their parents."[6] Schools, therefore, have been instrumental in confirming the existing distribution of knowledge and power in the United States.

Reassessment of the latent social outcomes of education has not been limited to the broad structural characteristics of schools and society. The focus has increasingly come to rest on basic but quite specific aspects of school life. This historical reappraisal has included the process of evaluation. It is possible to interpret the history of the testing and evaluation movement through just such a revisionist framework. In other words, the quest for efficiency and quantitative "output measures" that the movement embodies has mirrored social interests in stability, human predictability, and ultimately social control, and may continue to mirror these interests today.[7] As Karier puts it:

> Whether it was Terman calling for special education for the gifted, or Conant calling for "national educational assessment," or E.T.S. striving to develop, in the name of "accountability," performance-based teacher tests, all served as part of a broader efficiency movement to classify, standardize, and rationalize human beings to serve the productive interests of a society essentially controlled by wealth, privilege, and status.[8]

Evaluators and other school people may find themselves quite disconcerted by such a reconstruction of their past. However, they must not dismiss it casually. A primary reason for taking this perspective seriously is the fact that education is through and through a valuative enterprise. The proposals educators make for organizing and evaluating school activity are usually derived from slogan systems (such as structure of the disciplines, life adjustment, or social efficiency) with identifiable ideological and epistemological presuppositions.[9] Given this fact, educators really cannot afford to be less than fully aware of the latent tendencies in their work.

Let us take one example. The current goal of assessing "affective" educational programs is usually viewed as a meritorious aim, one that enables school personnel to instill in students respect for self and others, to better teach values concerning human relations, and so on. However, given the reality of schools as bureaucratic institutions, the possible latent function of such programs and the measurement of their outcomes should be clear. They have tended and will tend to bring under the purview of public institutions like schools even the most private of students' dispositions and personal meanings, thereby contributing to their rationalization by placing them under the custodial function of the school. Public behavior replaces private meaning.

This interpretation receives historical credibility from the fact that, by the early part of this century, the increasing industrialization and urbanization of American society "had severely eroded the influence of the family, church, and community on individual behavior." While the potency of these institutions weakened, another—the school—received attention as a critical institution of social control. It became *the* agency charged with the responsibility of maintaining social order and cohesion and of instilling individuals with codes of conduct and social values that would insure the stability of *existing* social relationships. Although a preserving institution, the school was viewed as a form of internal control—and therefore more in the "democratic" tradition than such external forms as law, government, and police.[10]

Thus, in response to the conflicts created by the perceived disorder of an expanding industrial economy and a steady flow of immigrants, the school expanded its responsibilities to maintain a social order that seemed to be threatened. It became responsible for the "whole child," increasing its custodial functions to include all of a child's social life,[11] and attempting to homogenize social reality and the different perceptions of disparate groups.

Coupled with the interest in maintaining the stability of the existing market system and social hierarchy was a strong and widespread racist element running through the testing movement and the tests themselves. Early proponents often looked on testing as a truly "scientific" mode by which the "scientific expert could control the evolutionary progress of the race."[12] Thus, another strikingly conservative factor can be uncovered in the roots of evaluation.

If this revisionist interpretation is correct, that the testing movement—the historical roots of the current emphasis on evaluation—often served rather conservative social and economic interests, that it was consistently biased against students who were somehow "different" according to existing institutional labels, and that it acted as an important implement of social control, then school people must examine quite carefully the effects it has today when the movement is supposedly motivated by more "enlightened" sentiments. If these social interests are deeply embedded in the history of evaluation and testing, does use of the methodological fruits of that tradition unconsciously compel educators to appropriate its ideological positions as well? This is a question that cannot be taken lightly, especially when, as I shall note later in my discussion, the logic of the methodologies usually employed in educational research may rest on similar conservative foundations.

Evaluation and Ideological Perspectives

Process-Product Reasoning

One of the tasks of the committed educator is to recognize his own perspective and locate this and its latent implications in relation to competing perspectives extant not only in the past but also now.[13] This task is no less important for those interested in evaluation than for other policy-minded educators.

In order to accomplish this, we should realize that evaluation itself is a process of *social valuing*. It involves one or more groups of people *assigning* values to activities, goals, and procedures done by others, such as students. Furthermore, it involves some particular conception of the types of values to be placed on these activities, goals, and procedures. This sounds rather obvious, but it is especially significant, because it implies that the act of and research in evaluation are not neutral.

Evaluation actually connotes the *placing of value* on a specific set of acts or objects. It not only deals with a form of social valuing but also implies a *choice* among a range of value systems that might give meaning to educational activity. For instance, we can value an activity for its efficiency (its ability to get a student from point A to point B quickly and inexpensively)—a process of valuing that unfortunately is considered the sine qua non of educational evaluation today—or for its human qualities (the extent to which it is an experience that has beauty and form), or for its embodiment of conflict, ambiguity, and uncertainty (its fulfillment of the uniqueness of the human condition).[14] It is also possible to evaluate educational experience politically (the extent to which it increases the power of individuals or groups to make determinations about their own present and future actions). Hence, it is not naturally predetermined that education should be valued only for its ability to reach our goals adequately and efficiently. This is, in fact, a process-product rationality, which Kliebard has shown is actually a factory metaphor.[15] The dominance of this outlook is one of the inherent problems confronting individuals concerned with evaluation.

Let us examine it a bit closer. Evaluation usually fits into a systems management model that looks something like this: we define a program's educational objectives (preferably in measurable terms); proper experiences are developed and organized to bring the student from point A to point B (from not meeting objectives to meeting them); evaluation occurs along the way and at the completion, comparing results to other programs or to the discrepancy between goals and performance; and this evaluation gives feedback to make the system function more smoothly and efficiently. In essence, it is an industrial production model of schooling. However, when systems approaches such as these are applied to education, they bring about political and educational quiescence in a variety of ways. They defuse the important process of political argumentation over what goals educators should be striving for, and they are quite often epistemologically and politically conservative.[16] This conservatism is strengthened by the common sense of evaluation.

Much of the discourse surrounding educational evaluation has been concerned with the development of means to measure the outcomes of schooling. Taken by itself, this is certainly needed. However, the discourse has also been strikingly apolitical (though the way evaluation functions has not), as if the means and ends of education were not context-bound and linked to a specific nexus of institutions, economic interests, and political power.

For instance, the predominance in advanced industrial societies of attempts to rationalize all aspects of intersubjective behavior may lie at the heart of a good deal of evaluation in education. Educators share an unconscious commitment to a form of reasoning that assumes that considerations of instrumental effectiveness when confronting human action are the only ways of generating decisions. In this regard, the current emphasis on systems management, the more vulgar forms of accountability, and the place of evaluation in each are not only "tools toward a more effective educational system," but also symptoms of the absence in our commonsense thought of any appreciation of the necessity of certain factors that are embodied in the human condition. Awe and mystery, uncertainty and ambiguity, conflict and the dialectic of stability and change—all of these are difficult to deal with using an industrial logic, yet all are essential if educators are to appreciate the complexity of their dilemmas and to create institutions that respond to the tension between institutional history and personal biography.

There are a number of difficulties associated with a process-product perspective on schooling. I cannot hope to discuss each fully, nor can I even be exhaustive in listing them in a chapter this size. It is essential, however, that I at least illuminate several of the problematic aspects, so that educators can confront them honestly.

There are two principle problems, one "educational," the other "ideological." First, process-product reasoning can and quite often does lead to consideration of people as "things"—manipulatable abstractions. There is a significant danger in coming to conceive of one's fellow persons as objects: one may begin to treat them as they are conceived.[17] This is a very real problem in schools today and one that is heightened by a number of aspects of evaluation. Along with the possible objectification of individuals, instrumental rationales lead to what sociologists like to call *goal displacement*. For example, efficient institutions obviously should exist for educational purposes; but efficiency may soon become a goal in itself rather than only one consideration in ascertaining the educational worth of an activity. Thus, those items on an educational agenda that are more easily identified and reached seem naturally to become the focus and the actual goals of the institution, although they may be much less important than others.

It is crucial to recognize this danger of efficiency becoming the most important outcome of schooling—the reification of means into ends. It was perhaps best noted by Dewey, who went even further in linking it to the importance of aesthetic experience in any educative event worthy of its name. Bernstein puts it this way:

[Dewey] emphasizes the esthetic consumatory dimension of experience. He criticizes educational and social institutions and practices for neglecting this esthetic dimension of experience. This is evidenced in the separation of means and ends in our educational and social thinking. The quality and content of ends-in-view which we strive to attain depend upon the quality of the means that we use to attain them. When we separate ends and means, when we think of means as *mere* means to some . . . goal, we are in danger of destroying the efficacy of our means and the potency of our ends. Means and ends, whether in education, moral, or political life designate the same experience viewed from different perspectives. Our task is to make all experience more esthetic, funded with meaning, and fulfilling.[18]

One can value, say, predetermined behavioral objectives for their supposed ability to lead to measurable outcomes (their efficiency as means to reach previously chosen ends); however, the very notion that such reductive and atomistic curricular formulations are worthwhile educationally in themselves is an arguable assertion to say the least. It can certainly be argued that they embody an ideology of control, that they place much too high a value on certainty above all else, that they are inaccurate representations of and trivialize the processes of inquiry, and that they are psychologically and philosophically naive.[19] Thus, here as elsewhere, the idea that means are mere instruments to meritorius ends is too limited a concept. This becomes clear if it is examined more carefully than educators are apt to do.

Just as significant a problem with process-product reasoning in education is its ability to hide from school people the political and ethical nature of their acts. It is not an effective language system for disclosing the ideological character of educational valuing. In calling the normal modes of evaluation in schools ideological, I do not wish to debunk entirely the usual means by which professional educators place value on their activity. Rather, my point is to bring into clearer focus the taken-for-granted nature of much that school personnel and others do. An ideology can be defined as a taken-for-granted perspective held by a specific social group. The perspective is not necessarily wrong, but it is necessarily partial and incomplete, just as any accepted perspective is limited.[20] One of my points throughout this chapter will be to argue exactly that—that evaluation as it is currently practiced can give only a decidedly partial perspective on the worth of educational events.

Evaluation is ideological in other ways besides its limited perspective on valuing. In the main, it has tended to be quite conservative with regard to existing institutional structures of education. In his discussion of the latent conservatism of structural-functional social theory and the brand of systems analysis that has grown out of it, Gouldner describes rather clearly the nature of a conservative posture.

What makes a theory conservative (or radical) is its posture toward the institutions of its surrounding society. A theory is conservative to the extent that it: treats these institutions as given and unchangeable in essentials; proposes remedies for them so that they work better, rather than devising alternatives to them; foresees no future that can be essentially better than the present, the conditions that already exist; and, explicitly or implicitly, counsels acceptance or resignation to what exists, rather than struggling against it.[21]

This is an apt description of the latent workings of even rather well intentioned and change-oriented evaluation.

Evaluation as a Social Construct

I should begin by stating that certain types of performance, certain forms of knowledge, certain dispositions, achievements, and propensities are not necessarily good in and of themselves. Rather, they are made so because of specific taken-for-granted assumptions. Thus, their values are relative and temporally conditioned. In order to make this clear, a rather significant but often unrecognized fact should be mentioned here. The guiding principles of evaluation—conceptions of achievement, of success or failure, and so on—are *social constructs*. They are not inherent in individuals or groups of people. Instead, they are instances of the application of identifiable social rules about what is to be considered good or bad performance. Such conceptions are similar to the notion of "deviance" in that just as other people must define an individual's behavior as "out of line" or "abnormal" for it to be deviant, people other than the student define his educational activity as good or bad.

Becker clarifies this in his discussion of deviant behavior.

> *Social groups create deviance by making rules whose infraction constitutes deviance,* and by applying these rules to particular people and labeling them as outsiders. From this point of view deviance is *not* a quality of the act the person commits, but rather a consequence of the application by others of rules and sanctions to an "offender." The deviant is one to whom that label has successfully been applied; deviant behavior is behavior that people so label.[22]

This has important consequences for any analysis of evaluation, since it implies that a complete understanding of evaluation necessitates an investigation into not only the groups of children and programs being evaluated but also the socially accepted rules and assumptions that make certain things important (e.g., demonstration of competence on certain school tests) and other forms of knowledge relatively unimportant. Hence, our focus must be on "evaluating" the school as an institution that embodies these social rules and assumptions as well as on "evaluating" the recipients, the students.[23] Educators must examine the ideological and political *uses* of evaluation and the place of the school in a larger social setting if they are to uncover what evaluation is actually about. And they must engage in the prior examination of what is considered valuable knowledge both overtly and covertly in school settings, why this is considered valuable knowledge, and how this conception of valuable knowledge is linked to institutions in the larger society. I shall sketch some areas that may be worthy of such investigation by examining a number of points: (1) that evaluation is a political language that prevents rather than fosters the questioning of school procedures by people other than professionals; (2) that the power of the evaluation expert is distinctly limited in dealing with organizations like schools by the definition of his role; (3) that the basic clinical perspective of experts contributes to the conservatism of evaluation; and (4) that the interests underlying the basic methodologies evaluators employ may foster the ideology of strict control of human action that guides a good deal of educational policy making.

The Process of Political Quiescence

Any analysis of the political meaning of educational research (and educational evaluation *has* political meaning in terms of the distribution of power in institutions) must occur on at least two levels. First, it needs to examine how evaluation activity gets some groups the tangible results they want, at the expense of others. In the competition for public money, for instance, measurable results are exceedingly important if an institution wants to generate funding. Secondly, the analysis must explore what this research and its results mean to the public at large, and how the general public is "aroused" or "placated" by it.[24] One might want to ask *how and by whom* evaluation data are used. In many cases, evaluation is a means to deflect potent criticism away from the fundamental policies of bureaucratic structures.

It is not too odd a position to argue that the language used for major aspects of evaluation—e.g., accountability, cost-effectiveness, systems analysis, effective schooling—may act to reassure the public that serious changes need not occur in educational settings. This may be especially true in inner-city areas. Like abstractions such as democracy and justice, they are reified by and become identified with existing institutions. The terminology becomes what Edelman has called a "socially pathic" language, a form of language that tends to encourage attachment to existing institutional structures that may actually "deny [individuals] values they prize."[25] That is, because of the bureaucratic complexity and traditional character of the regularities of schooling, it is possible that significant alterations in the structural characteristics of schools and the relative distribution of power to individuals in schools (for example, greater student autonomy and responsibility) must occur if the institution is to perform many of the functions expected of it. In fact, as will be argued later on, it is not inconceivable that schools may effectively create a number of the difficulties they are supposed to solve.

The linguistic metaphors associated with evaluation may act to hide this possibility from the public and especially from minority and culturally diverse groups. By seeming to show the public the undoubtedly real concern of school people to change many ineffective practices in schools, evaluation terminology keeps the populace from seeing the uncomfortable fact that significant alterations in the school environment have been rare and short-lived. Thus, the knowledgeable criticism of a concerned citizenry is deflected.

The Role of the Expert

Not only does evaluation contribute to an often unwarranted sense of well-being on the part of the public, but all too often such research is used to legitimate educators' own commonsense activity rather than to challenge it. This occurs primarily because its practitioners do not very often step back and look at what stands behind their work. Evaluators should be rather cautious about accepting their work at face value for a number of reasons. One of the more important is their failure to see that by committing themselves to the study of officially defined goals and procedures using official categories they may also be giving the rhetorical prestige of science to extant bureaucratic regularities.[26] This offers a prime example of the less than neutral effects of educational evaluation.

An evaluator's or other researcher's basic perspective is quite strongly influenced by the dominant values of the collectivity to which he belongs and the social position he occupies in it. These dominant values *necessarily* affect his work.[27] In fact, his outlook is already sedimented into the forms of language and implicit perspectives found in the social role an evaluator fills. Linguistic, programmatic, methodological, and conceptual tools, and expectations of how they are to be used, are built into his job.[28] It is not very common for evaluators to turn their backs on the institutionalized goals, procedures, and norms that already exist and the storehouse of knowledge serving these official goals that has been collected over the years in the evaluation field.

This congerie of accepted wisdom and value is reinforced by the need of institutional managers for special types of expert advice. This is an exceptionally important point. Educational evaluators are "experts for hire." I do not mean to denigrate the important position they fill. Rather, I wish to stress that the role of the expert in American society is unique and leads to certain expectations that are themselves problematic in educational settings.

Experts are under considerable pressure to present their findings as scientific information, as knowledge that has a significant scientific warrant and, therefore, an inherent plausibility.[29] Not only are experts expected to couch their arguments in scientific terms, but also, because of their very position in the social system, their data and perspectives are perceived as authoritative. The weight and prestige given to their expertise is considerable.[30]

It should be clear, however, that in general educators have appropriated the reconstructed logic of science rather than the logic-in-use of scientific investigation.[31] Their view of scientific activity as the expert and efficient means to guarantee certainty in results has been fundamentally inaccurate. It represents a picture drawn from technological models of thought, whereas accounts of significant scientific investigations show a more sophisticated posture, in which the complex blend of technique, art, and personal commitment is highly evident. This appropriation of an inaccurate model produces considerable difficulty. It leads educators to practice poor research, and, most importantly, it is a major component of their tendency to confirm the conceptual paradigm under which they are working even though substantive progress may require a new disciplinary matrix in place of the current one.[32] The numerous findings of "no significant difference" might just point to this conclusion.

The use of a quasi-scientific or technological perspective is quite unfortunate in other ways. The process of education and the evaluation of educational settings are much too complex human endeavors to ever be totally subsumed under the rubric of science, especially a poor representation of scientific activity. Rather, they can also be illuminated through ethical and aesthetic perspectives and indeed cannot be understood without using these perspectives, if the field is not to lose all sight of the fact that the educational process always ends in a particular act of personal knowing. Walsh puts it well in his discussion of "poetic intelligence" in giving value to educational events.

> In the act of knowing . . . we find engaged two distinct impulses of the mind which are related by a mutual tension and support. They are an eagerness to light on the highest degree of individuality of things and a concern to generalize, to establish an order among the particulars. On the intimacy of union of these two, the richness of the first, the relevance and adequacy of the second, depends the completed act of understanding. It is the nature of poetic intelligence . . . to give us the wholeness of the act of knowing. It is this which makes it so salutory a corrective in education where we fall continually into the error of identifying understanding . . . with one component of understanding, the generalizing, systematizing element, and neglect what it should be grounded in, a sense of the particular, as well as what it should return to, a still more heightened sense of the particular.[33]

The field's use of outdated positivistic models of science to define out of existence these other forms of giving meaning to and evaluating education is indicative of a similar technological orientation throughout other areas of industrialized nations. However, even if we accept the critical power of an elaborated, not reconstructed, scientific rationality to illuminate the consequences of education, giving too strong a scientific warrant to much expert evaluation data does not do justice to the conceptual difficulties that abound beneath the overt assumptions educators make to organize their research. For one example, educators have little cumulative knowledge and only a partial understanding of the process psychologists label "learning." Yet a good deal of evaluation purports to assess this very aspect of human activity. This problem is heightened by the fact that the training of experts in education is usually deep but quite narrow. They are trained to believe in the efficacy of their technical expertise. Thus alternative models of examining problems, models that may come from distinctly different conceptual traditions, are not often considered. Therefore, basic problems with the accepted expertise itself remain unchallenged even when the results of using this framework are poor.

While there are considerable conceptual and technical difficulties with the usual view of what important research looks like, one thing is obvious. Even given these difficulties, school people and decision makers do perceive the information they get from evaluational researchers as "worthy," again because it comes from those who hold the title of expert.

One of the tasks of the expert (read evaluator) is to furnish administrative leaders of an institution with the special knowledge they require before decisions are made. The bureaucratic institution, not the expert, furnishes the problems to be investigated. Hence, the type of knowledge that the expert is to supply is *determined in advance.* Since the expert bears no responsibility for the final outcome of a program, his activities can be guided by the practical interests of the administrative leaders. And what administrators are *not* looking for are new hypotheses or new interpretations that are not immediately and noticeably relevant to the practical problems at hand—the teaching of reading, say. The fact that the expert is expected to work on the practical problems as defined by the institution and not to offer advice outside these boundaries is of considerable moment. It has become increasingly evident that, for whatever reasons (socialization into a position, timidity because of political pressure, a belief that engineering techniques will solve all of our problems, and so forth) the administrative leadership of a large educational organization seeks and is probably supposed to seek to reduce the new and uncertain elements of each complex situation to a practical, safe combination of "old and certain truths" about the processes of schooling.[34] However, there are very few things as conceptually, ethically, and politically complex as education, and educational scholarship has hardly scratched the surface of its intricacies. The fact that these old and certain truths may be less than efficacious, given the complicated nature of educational problems in cities and elsewhere, is not often considered by practical decision makers, for, after all, it is the role of the expert to deal with this complexity. But, as we saw, the knowledge expected of the expert is predetermined; thus, we are caught in a double bind. The evaluator is expected to provide expert advice and services to help solve the institution's problems; however, the range of issues and the types of answers that are actually acceptable are limited by what the administrative apparatus has previously defined as "the problem." In this way the circle of inconsequential results is continued.

This is certainly not new. Expertise has been used by policy makers for quite a long time. It should be clear, though, that from the very beginning, when statistical skills were used to assess social programs, the bulk of official statistics such as evaluation data were policy-oriented, not descriptive. Just as important, these data were determined primarily by and in support of the political goals of officials,[35] often at the expense of an institution's responsiveness to its clientele.

This raises a rather provocative question. Can one study the real outcomes and processes of educational programs when one's research uses categories and data derived from and serving the institution itself, without at the same time giving support to the bureaucratic apparatus these categories and data serve? Can one truly evaluate an institution or a program using such a procedure? If an evaluator's work does latently provide such support on this level, is it possible that other things—the attitudes of researchers and the ameliorative and, especially, clinical perspective that guides them—do likewise?

Clinical Assumptions and Bureaucratic Support

A careful examination of, say, programs to raise the achievement levels of inner-city students might reveal that evaluators have internalized a clinical model. From the outset, three things seem to be striking about this model: (1) the research accepts as given the basic values of the institution that has called these children "underachievers"; (2) the blame is often put on the person or group rather than the institution; and (3) action is taken to change the individual rather than the fundamental structure of the social setting.

In her discussion of the process of labeling groups of mental patients, Mercer makes these points even more cogently.

[The clinical viewpoint] is readily identified by several distinguishing characteristics. First, the investigator accepts as the focus for study those individuals who have been labeled deviant. In so doing, he adopts the values of whatever social system has defined the person as deviant and assumes that its judgments are the valid measures of deviance . . . without serious questioning.

A second distinguishing characteristic of the clinical perspective is the tendency to perceive deviance as an attribute of the person . . . as a lack to be explained. This viewpoint results in the quest for etiology. Thus, the clinical perspective is essentially a medical frame of reference, for it sees deviance as individual pathology requiring diagnostic classification and etiological analysis for the purpose of determining proper treatment procedures and probable prognosis.

Three additional characteristics of the clinical perspective are the development of a diagnostic nomenclature, the creation of diagnostic instruments, and the professionalization of the diagnostic function.

When the investigator begins his research with the diagnostic designations assigned by official defining agents, he tends to assume that all individuals placed in a given category are essentially equivalent in respect to their deviance. . . . Individuals assigned to different categories of deviance are compared with each other or with a "normal" population consisting of persons who, for whatever reason, have escaped being labeled. The focus is on the individual [rather than on the defining agents].

Another characteristic of the clinical perspective is its assumption that the official definition is somehow the "right" definition. . . . Finally when deviance is perceived as individual [or group] pathology, social action tends to center upon changing the individual or, that failing, removing him from society.[36]

All these characteristics, in varying degrees, act in subtle ways to prevent evaluators and the managerial recipients of their information from raising serious questions about the basic qualities of educational life in schools. The phenomenon of mass testing based on unexamined institutional assumptions, the "treatment" language of educators, the acceptance of institutional definitions of normality and deviance all contribute to the problem.

Evaluation expertise, thus, often serves as an administrative procedure that is relatively ineffective in bringing about significant changes in educational processes. To the extent that evaluation fits within the existing factory model of schooling—an input-output model ideally suited to maintain the bureaucratic regularities of educational institutions—it is less than helpful in adequately treating the profound ethical, political, and educational issues confronting educators today. For instance, evaluation as it is practiced does not bring us significantly closer to the answer to one complex educational dilemma school people face: how to design environments that strike the difficult and tenuous balance between a student's desire for a setting that is personally responsive and the professional educator's need to school and control large masses of students. This is as much a moral problem as it is an engineering one.

Large-scale evaluation can in fact be interpreted as one means, latent to be sure, of stereotyping large groups of people. Much evaluation research has had the effect of labeling *students* as the cause of achievement problems and the like, rather than placing a significant portion of the blame on the social rules and assumptions of the institutions that create and impute these labels. By employing testing on a large scale, the educational bureaucracy can maintain a significant social distance from individual students and their perceptions. This is of no small moment, since the greater the social distance between the people doing the stereotyping (with labels such as slow learners, remedial problems, and underachievers) and those having the labels put on them, the broader the type can be, the less evidence educators need to support it, and the more quickly it can be applied.[37] Thus, under the guise of trying to evaluate programs to make them more effective for students, professionals avoid ever having to face large portions of the student population and their specific realities.

This mode of operation, especially as it is carried on in areas drawing, as evaluation does, on psychological and social psychological models of research and practice, has received other pointed criticisms besides those concerning its support of institutional values, its homogenizing effect, its tendency to impute culpability to the individual or the group rather than the defining institution, and so on. Thomas Szasz, for instance, argues that the very perspective of this model of research and practice, when used in large institutions such as mental institutions, clinics, and schools, ultimately serves to harm rather than help those people who are the focus of the particular ameliorative social program.[38] The history of many programs that have sought to improve institutions dealing with youth is instructive. It documents the fact that the social and educational remedies that were supported by research similar to current evaluation practices seemed to aggravate rather than alleviate problems.[39] It is also interesting to note that these remedies almost invariably led to further layers of institutional hierarchy. Hence, the question of giving research support to programs that may have deleterious effects in the long run needs continual scrutiny by evaluators. Without such continual scrutiny, they may indeed be performing merely as data collectors in support of problematic institutional contexts.

One possible interpretation should not be closed off here. Social institutions such as schools may actually be organized to tacitly maintain, if not promote, the problems of achievement and performance that evaluators are called on to examine.[40] The size, relative anonymity, and complexity of the school may prevent meaningful inroads from being made on these issues. This same size and the amount of economic support committed to schools in our society make it less than easy for there to be alternative paths to the goals school people talk about. As long as this set of institutions provides the only real avenue of access to knowledge and power in American society, it may very well be that the problems educators confront not only will not be solved, but also will be continually *created* by schools. This is a hypothesis that must not be overlooked. The social definitions prevailing in schools create the categories that define deviance from educational achievement norms. Evaluation, hence, can be interpreted as giving legitimacy to categories of performance, all too frequently without raising questions about the efficacy of the social definitions themselves.

That we do not see the political nature of this kind of professional work can be partially explained by Mannheim's argument that "the growth of rational bureaucracy decreases the political rationality of the ordinary person employed within a bureaucracy." The same holds true for individuals such as evaluators whose work is generated out of the process-product thought of schools. As Mannheim put it, "the growth of functional rationality decreases substantive rationality."[41] By placing themselves in a position of upholding policy decisions within an administratively predefined context of deliberation, and without also stepping back to examine carefully the possible implications of the position they hold, evaluators are taking a political stance without being aware of it. To paraphrase Mannheim, they run the risk of substituting the search for a smoothly running factory for the critically important debate over the purposes and means of the institution.

The Logic of Research and the Ideology of Control

Not only does a good deal of evaluation research in education often accept institutional assumptions as given and serve as rhetoric to support them, but an even more subtle consequence also occurs. The very logic behind the methodologies employed in educational research may limit us to merely accepting the existing institutional definitions of situations.

The work of the German social theorist Jürgen Habermas illuminates the problem. Modern consciousness in advanced industrial societies centers around forms of logic that tend to make people treat their major problems as technical puzzles that can be solved by the

application of an engineering rationality. That is, process-product
reasoning, or what Habermas calls *purposive-rational action,* domi-
nates to such an extent that political and especially ethical questions
are treated as somehow "metaphysical" or are defined out of existence in some way.[42] They are redefined in terms of the categories of
instrumental logic so that they can be made into technical concerns
demanding a solution based on the application of what Ellul has so
nicely called *technique*—standardized means to get to previously
chosen ends. This effectively vitiates the ethical and political elements involved in argumentation.

Habermas argues that the orientation of purposive-rational action
is guided by certain prereflective (or unconscious) cognitive interests.
These include a fundamental interest in *control* and *certainty.* In the
physical sciences, for instance, this is evident in our attempt to
understand and hence control physical forces and phenomena. However, in the human sciences, the orientation seems to lead to a basic
interest in gaining certainty in the interaction among human beings
and attempting to control (in the strong sense of the term) the
environment to guarantee this certainty. The entire orientation seeks
to eliminate the ambiguity and uncertainty that makes human action
a personal statement, thus also effectively depersonalizing human
interaction. Habermas goes on to argue that such interests, which
dominate advanced industrial society and the knowledge-producing
sciences that support it, tend to break down the symbolic ties that
bind individuals together, lead to alienation and anomie, and ultimately prevent potent ethical and political dialogue from evolving.

Politics then becomes a way of manipulating people, rather than a
primary way in which individuals engage in reshaping their institutions so that these structures are more mutable. Educational thought
becomes an ideology of manipulation rather than a means for providing varied structures that can be made responsive to the needs of
intellectual traditions, social beliefs, and student sentiments. The
growth of the "educational engineering" approach of behavioral objectives and criterion-referenced measures is indicative of these ideological configurations.[43]

Habermas's work is exceptionally abstract, and this is unfortunate.[44] But his points are quite provocative and merit much further
investigation by educators. Educational research has indeed drawn its

models from behavioristic sociology and psychology, fields that have sought to pattern themselves after the strict sciences and that are increasingly under attack for providing support for corporate and bureaucratic interests under the guise of neutrality.[45] Educational research, thus, has adopted the cognitive interests that cohere with these research traditions, those of bringing as many aspects of human activity as possible under technical control and assuring that educators can have surety in dealing with the complex processes of human action.[46] Yet, in the search for certainty of outcome in schools, there is a tendency both to eliminate (or at least not give substantial support to) those portions of student conduct that may somehow threaten the taken-for-granted regularities of the educational setting and to dissolve the elements of argumentation and conflict that enable substantive educational change to evolve.[47]

In saying, then, that a major segment of the educational evaluation that goes on is conservative, the following points should be noted about its latent position. First, there is a tacit advocacy of order and certainty, with little appreciation of the value of conflict and disorder. Evaluation, thus, often can do no more than accept the kind of institutional order it currently finds. Secondly, it has been disposed to put its technical expertise in the service of solving officially and bureaucratically defined problems, even when the official problems offer too limited a perspective. (This disposition may be changing considerably now, however.) Thirdly, it has comported itself in what might be called a quasi-neutral fashion, persistently shying away from social dissent and criticism. It thereby latently gives support to the view that social dilemmas can be dealt with effectively through the application of "modest inputs of centralized administration, along with expert services, research, and advice."[48] This vision of educational issues as modest engineering or technical difficulties does not do justice to the complexity we face in the real world of education. This one-sided vision, though, is not limited to the field of education but is generic to advanced industrial societies. Therefore, any serious criticism of the process-product rationality that stands behind so much evaluation literature must also analyze the economic and political foundations of this commonsense perspective. While that is beyond the scope of this chapter, it is one of the wide-ranging issues educators and others must begin to face.

Analytic Questions

Aside from the ideological issues I have sought to raise, there are certain analytic problems that must be considered when one seriously grapples with the nature of evaluation in educational settings. What one *means* by evaluation is not easily answered when one is pushed beyond surface concepts and slogans. Here I shall note but a few of the more important conceptual difficulties that represent a sample of topics in need of closer scrutiny.

One exceptionally important analytic issue lies at the very heart of evaluation. Educational evaluators are asked to assess "learning," a concept drawn from and warranted by psychology. In fact, much of the entire educational structure and our everyday activities in it rest on such commonsense concepts as reinforcement, feedback, learning, and conditioning. This puts education in a rather difficult position. These are psychological constructs that gain their efficacy within the psychological community. Thus, they can be criticized and corrected by the tradition of scholarly argumentation that exists in that field as in any discipline. However, by borrowing these explanatory constructs, educators take them out of their self-correcting context. They thus risk reifying and misusing them and run the even greater risk of appropriating outworn, surface, or problematic concepts and techniques.[49]

This difficulty is particularly important. Many of the concepts that educators employ are, in fact, being radically challenged within their original communities. Education, without a tradition of careful scrutiny of borrowed constructs, is left out of the discourse that may be crucial to its search for better tools to explain the dynamics of interaction in school settings. Significant examples being questioned include the notion of reinforcement, the basic value of a behavioristic position on human action, and the very concept of learning itself.[50] Hence, evaluation rooted in psychological constructs stemming from these concepts in the long run may be on rather shaky ground. This points to the utter necessity of further philosophical and analytic study of educational problems if we are to make significant progress.

It has become rather commonplace to state that evaluation often deals with those things that can be most readily measured. To be sure, many educational evaluators recognize the problem and seek to rectify it by becoming more technically sophisticated. However, it may also be the case that we are at present dealing with only a limited representation of "knowledge" in more ways than our tendency to stress what can be easily measured. The provocative work of the noted philosopher of science Michael Polanyi seems to indicate that there is a substructure of *tacit knowing* that serves as a foundation for the more explicit types of activities we usually talk about. In fact, tacit knowledge may be more important than explicitly formulated knowledge. This suggests the necessity of a considerable expansion of our investigation of the powers of human comprehension.[51] It also suggests that it may be necessary to reconsider the current emphasis in evaluation on explicit knowledge—an emphasis that can effectively destroy the act of personal knowing that Polanyi argues is the fundamental property of scientific and aesthetic awareness. In our stress on quantifiable achievement we may be negating the very element that makes anything worth knowing.[52]

In addition, the theory of knowledge that underpins curriculum thought, and therefore the aspects of evaluation that are generated out of it, need to be carefully scrutinized in light of positions such as Polanyi's. The basic problems confronting curriculum specialists and other educators may be epistemological as well as methodological, political, and ethical. If it is correct that explicit knowledge is less important than the processes of tacit knowing, then our evaluation efforts are, to a significant extent, misdirected.

Finally, conceptual examinations of the nature of dispositions, propensities, and so forth are of considerable moment in evaluation. If educators are concerned with more than the teaching of information, they have much to learn from investigations that point to the difficulty and danger of reducing these modes of action to atomistic and measurable elements.[53]

Institutional Evaluation

I have said that, while evaluation is considered to be "merely" a technical problem by many educators, it is just as clearly an ethical concern. That is, evaluation cannot be simply a question of assessment, as some might argue. The statement: "After all, didn't this group average such and such a 'score' on our instruments compared to the other group's performance?" simply ignores the fact that the choice of *what* one is to assess is itself a valuative decision. Often this decision is made on practical grounds: "These instruments are available; they may be partial but they are better than not getting any information at all." Or it may be an "ideological" decision: "These are the things we must evaluate because they are exceptionally important in the context of an advanced industrial economy such as our own." These concerns derive mainly from an efficiency rationale that may be important in and of itself but is too limited a rubric to deal with the fact that education is not "just" an interaction among traditions and students but also a profoundly interpersonal act of influence. It, thereby, must be held accountable and evaluated according to ethical norms as well as considerations of instrumental effectiveness. Let us examine what this might mean in terms of reorienting a major aspect of educational evaluation.

All too often, what is ignored in evaluation is what has been called *institutional evaluation*, that is, the assessment of the "quality of life" students experience in schools.[54] The lack of consideration for this quality of life is at least partly due to a factor I pointed to in my discussion of the constitutive interests underlying the dominant forms of consciousness in modern societies. The "goodness" of an educational environment is an *ethical* question; it embodies disparate views on how a group of individuals may treat and influence a younger group. However, the orientation that predominates in much of public policy discourse, and educational discourse in particular, tends to redefine just such a moral question into a technical puzzle, so that it may be dealt with in a means-ends schema, thereby making it less potent.

This obstacle to institutional evaluation could be partially overcome if questions such as the following were raised seriously: Does the basic style of interaction in this institution reflect a commitment to treat individuals *justly*? If roles were reversed and educators were to become students, would they (the educators) consider the basic forms of activity to be morally responsible? These are exceptionally difficult issues and no doubt will lead to only situational rather than general answers.[55] Yet the very posing of the question points out the inherent dilemma of serious educational evaluation. For instance, if it is found that the human engineering techniques of behavior modification and operant conditioning "work" for certain types of "training," will it then be argued that they *should* be used as a primary mode of education? If so, is this ethically justifiable? In other words, what are the moral limits on control of individuals in the name of "efficient" instruction? Here, one is hard pressed to separate the evaluation from the consequences.

Raising questions of this type as a form of institutional evaluation obviously would not require a more rigorous empirical methodology (though such rigor is important, to be sure); rather, it requires a legal and philosophical sophistication that is sorely lacking in the educational community.[56] There are areas of institutional evaluation, however, where a broadened and more sophisticated empirical foundation would be quite helpful. Evaluative research in these areas can be instituted fairly readily.

Among the questions institutional assessment would be called on to investigate here would be the abridgment of legal and constitutional rights of students in schools. The Supreme Court has ruled that students do not lose their rights as citizens upon entering educational institutions, and, hence, anything that is done inside these establishments must be within the bounds of constitutional guarantees.[57] The area of student rights can be a potent focus for evaluation of the patterns of interpersonal interaction in schools.

Norms of institutional evaluation such as these make it desirable that educators engage in much greater descriptive analysis, rather than the means-ends model so often employed. For example, we should examine what Goffman[58] has called the "moral career" of a child to see what effect, say, the labeling process has on his or her life in that specific educational setting. This may tell us much more about what actually occurs in schools and what schools really do value in their day-to-day patterns of interaction than we can presently ascertain using our conventional models of evaluation. This is one reason why anthropological approaches similar to those employed by Jules Henry,[59] Philip Jackson,[60] and others are so important to a serious and *complete* evaluation of an educational program or total institution.

For example, it should be obvious that a fair proportion of what is effectively "taught" in schools cannot be illuminated through our usual process-product forms of evaluation. The literature on the hidden curriculum has made the significant point that many of the dispositions, propensities, and achievements that may make a critical difference in a person's life are internalized by students in the very act of living within an institutional framework for a number of years. The institutional structure itself mirrors and redundantly communicates to students lasting norms, basic ideological assumptions, and models of human interaction.[61] "Teaching" of this sort—and it is effective teaching—may necessitate a searching reappraisal of our accepted evaluation efforts and, perhaps, the training of a different type of educational evaluator.

The implications of the arguments in this section point clearly in one direction. They require an advocacy framework for evaluation, rather than the quasi-neutral approach that has dominated the field throughout much of its history. This need not replace the models now in use, but may be a complementary and essential counterbalance to them. Clearly an advocacy position will lead to extensive conflict and debate in the field. Yet, as I noted earlier, such argumentation is essential if we are to do more than serve the existing and often questionable practices of bureaucratic institutions.

One final point should be made. Shifting the focus at least partly to the institution rather than concentrating on "learning" enables us to see what effect evaluation has on the school and what use the institution makes of evaluative data. Often the data may serve as an excuse to try a program similar to the one first completed but with some slight variation; or they may serve as a socially pathic language, merely to signify to the community that something is being done to change conditions in the schools. If we find that either of these is the outcome, we will have learned a good deal about the role evaluation plays in the process of change. We may be rather disheartened by what we learn.

The Personal Responsibility of Evaluators

What I have been asking throughout this chapter is that evaluators and other educators suspend their judgment of what they usually accept unquestioningly and question what they generally assume as given. In so doing, all of us might begin to shed light on the implications of our activities.

The tendency in the face of the all-too-usual finding of "no significant difference" is to argue for better teacher training, for better science materials, for more sophisticated administrative systems designs, and the like. However, it may well be that more basic questions must be asked, that even the obligatory nature of the institution of schooling may need questioning, or that educators are asking the wrong kinds of questions.

For example, much low achievement on the part of many students could be attributable to a symbolic dismissal of the school itself as a meaningful institution. These students may perceive schools as relatively unresponsive to human sentiments. This is not to argue that schools should be done away with; to take such a position in a knowledge-based economy is somewhat unrealistic. It does signify, however, that educational problems are considerably more fundamental than educators may suppose, and it places responsibility on the individual educator to examine his or her own professional activity in a wider social and political context.

This requires some rather difficult searching, of course. Issues such as the following need to be faced. Why is it important that students learn these particular what's, how's, and to's? Is the reason we continually find little significant difference in our comparative evaluations due to epistemological and analytic as well as methodological problems? What are the *actual* functions of evaluation in educational institutions? What social group does this research support? A final and critically important ethical question can act as a summary of a number that have preceded it: Is my work truly contributing to the reconstruction of educational institutions so that they are more just and responsive?

Only by raising queries of this sort and taking the search for their answers as a personal responsibility can we begin to assume a title that should not be easily bestowed, that of educator.

Notes

1. Israel Scheffler, *The Language of Education* (Springfield, Ill.: Charles C. Thomas, 1960), p. 36.

2. Stephen Toulmin, *Human Understanding: The Collective Use and Evolution of Concepts* (Princeton, N.J.: Princeton University Press, 1972), p. 84.

3. Thomas S. Kuhn, *The Structure of Scientific Revolutions* (Chicago: University of Chicago Press, 1970).

4. Stephan Thernstrom, Foreword to Michael Katz, *Class, Bureaucracy, and Schooling* (New York: Praeger, 1971), p. x.

5. Seymour Sarason, *The Culture of the School and the Problem of Change* (Boston: Allyn and Bacon, 1971).

6. Katz, *Class, Bureaucracy, and Schooling,* p. xviii.

7. Clarence Karier, "Liberal Ideology and the Quest for Orderly Change," in *Roots of Crisis,* by Clarence Karier, Paul Violas, and Joel Spring (Chicago: Rand McNally, 1973), p. 90.

8. Clarence Karier, "Testing for Order and Control in the Corporate Liberal State," in Karier, Violas, and Spring, *Roots of Crisis,* p. 136.

9. James McClellan and B. Paul Komisar, "The Logic of Slogans," in *Language and Concepts in Education,* ed. by B. Othanel Smith and Robert Ennis (Chicago: Rand McNally, 1961); Michael W. Apple, "Models of Rationality and Systems Approaches," in *Perspectives on Management Systems Approaches in Education,* ed. by Albert H. Yee (Englewood Cliffs, N.J.: Educational Technology Publications, 1973), p. 107.

10. Joel Spring, "Education as a Form of Social Control," in Karier, Violas, and Spring, *Roots of Crisis,* p. 30.

11. Ibid., p. 33.

12. Karier, "Testing for Order and Control," p. 112. See especially his discussion of the close link between the testing movement, eugenics, and scientific racism.

13. John Horton, "Order and Conflict Theories of Social Problems as Competing Ideologies," in *The Sociology of Knowledge,* ed. by James E. Curtis and John W. Petras (New York: Praeger, 1970), p. 606.

14. An insightful discussion of various modes of placing value on educational events can be found in Dwayne Huebner, "Curricular Language and Classroom Meanings," in *Language and Meaning,* ed. by James B. Macdonald and Robert R. Leeper (Washington, D.C.: Association for Supervision and Curriculum Development, 1966), pp. 8-26.

15. Herbert M. Kliebard, "Bureaucracy and Curriculum Theory," in *Freedom, Bureaucracy and Schooling,* ed. by Vernon F. Haubrich (Washington, D.C.: Association for Supervision and Curriculum Development, 1971), pp. 74-93.

16. Michael W. Apple, "The Adequacy of Systems Management Procedures in Education," in Yee, *Perspectives on Management Systems,* pp. 3-31. Even such systems procedures as creating pools of

goals among which one can "democratically" choose are quite inade-
quate. See Louis Fischer and Robert Sinclair, "Behavioral Objectives,
Performance Contracting, Systems Management and Education," in
Yee, *Perspectives on Management Systems,* pp. 82-98.

17. Robert W. Friedrich, *A Sociology of Sociology* (New York:
Free Press, 1970), pp. 172-73.

18. Richard J. Bernstein, *Praxis and Action* (Philadelphia: University of Pennsylvania Press, 1971), p. 213.

19. For a more detailed treatment, see Apple, "The Adequacy of
Systems Management Procedures"; William E. Doll, Jr., "A Methodology of Experience: An Alternative to Behavioral Objectives," *Educational Theory* 22 (summer 1972): 309-24.

20. Nigel Harris, *Beliefs in Society: The Problem of Ideology* (London: C. A. Watts, 1968), p. 22.

21. Alvin W. Gouldner, *The Coming Crisis of Western Sociology*
(New York: Basic Books, 1970), p. 332.

22. Howard Becker, *The Outsiders* (New York: Free Press, 1963),
p. 9.

23. See Edwin M. Schur, *Labeling and Deviant Behavior* (New
York: Harper and Row, 1971), pp. 12-13.

24. Murray Edelman, *The Symbolic Uses of Politics* (Urbana: University of Illinois Press, 1964), p. 12.

25. Ibid., p. 190.

26. Jack D. Douglas, *American Social Order* (New York: Free
Press, 1971), pp. 70-71.

27. Curtis and Petras, Introduction to *The Sociology of Knowledge,* p. 48.

28. Peter L. Berger and Thomas Luckmann, *The Social Construction of Reality* (New York: Doubleday, 1966), pp. 34-46.

29. Jack D. Douglas, "Freedom and Tyranny in a Technological
Society," in *Freedom and Tyranny: Social Problems in a Technological Society,* ed. by Jack D. Douglas (New York: Alfred A. Knopf,
1970), p. 17.

30. See the discussion of the role of the expert in Alfred Schutz,
"The Well-informed Citizen: An Essay on the Social Distribution of
Knowledge," in *Collected Papers II: Studies in Social Theory* (The
Hague: Martinus Nijhoff, 1964), pp. 120-34.

31. See, for example, Michael Polanyi, *Personal Knowledge* (New
York: Harper and Row, 1964). Compare this vision of science as

explicated by a member of that "society of explorers" with the sterile and unimaginative reconstruction of it in the field of education.

32. See Michael W. Apple, "School Reform and Educational Scholarship: An Essay Review of *How Effective Is Schooling?*" *Journal of Educational Research* 66 (April 1973): 368, 373, 380-81. An alternative research program is suggested in Michael W. Apple, "Commonsense Categories and Curriculum Thought" (paper presented at a conference entitled "Toward the Reconstruction of the Curriculum Field," Philadelphia, May 10-11, 1973).

33. William Walsh, *The Use of Imagination* (New York: Barnes and Noble, 1959), p. 124.

34. Florian Znaniecki, *The Social Role of the Man of Knowledge* (New York: Harper and Row, 1968), pp. 45-49.

35. Douglas, *American Social Order,* p. 49.

36. Jane R. Mercer, "Labeling the Mentally Retarded," in *Deviance: The Interactionist Perspective,* ed. by Earl Rubington and Martin S. Weinberg (New York: Macmillan, 1968), p. 77.

37. Rubington and Weinberg, "Introduction to the Social Deviant," in *Deviance,* p. 10.

38. Thomas Szasz, *Ideology and Insanity* (New York: Doubleday, 1970).

39. See the excellent treatment of the history of the ameliorative reforms of the juvenile justice system in Anthony M. Platt, *The Child Savers: The Invention of Delinquency* (Chicago: University of Chicago Press, 1969).

40. Schur, *Labeling and Deviant Behavior,* p. 147.

41. Mannheim as quoted in Norbert Wiley, "America's Unique Class Politics," in *Recent Sociology I,* ed. by Hans Peter Dreitzel (New York: Macmillan, 1969), p. 200.

42. See, e.g., Jürgen Habermas, *Knowledge and Human Interests* (Boston: Beacon Press, 1971); Michael W. Apple, "Scientific Interests and the Nature of Educational Institutions" (paper presented at a symposium entitled, "Oppression and Schooling," American Educational Research Association, Chicago, 1972).

43. It should be clear that these are not necessarily "scientific" procedures, but instead *are* ideological elements to a large extent. See Apple, "The Adequacy of Systems Management Procedures."

44. See Trent Schroyer, "The Dialectical Foundations of Critical Theory," *Telos* 12 (summer 1972): 113.

45. Gouldner, *Crisis of Western Sociology.*

46. That action, not behavior, cannot be adequately known beforehand, nor can we have nor should we want certainty concerning it, is discussed quite fully in Hannah Arendt, *The Human Condition* (New York: Doubleday, 1958). See also her discussion of the dangers of attempting to reduce, as educators try to, all aspects of human action to forms of overt behavior.

47. A more complete analysis of this can be found in Apple, "The Adequacy of Systems Management Procedures."

48. Gouldner, *Crisis of Western Sociology,* pp. 161, 335-36.

49. Dwayne Huebner, "Implications of Psychological Thought for the Curriculum," in *Influences in Curriculum Change,* ed. by Glenys Unruh and Robert R. Leeper (Washington, D.C.: Association for Supervision and Curriculum Development, 1968), pp. 28-37; Apple, "The Adequacy of Systems Management Procedures."

50. See Charles Taylor, *The Explanation of Behavior* (New York: Humanities Press, 1964); Maurice Merleau-Ponty, *The Phenomenology of Perception* (London: Routledge and Kegan Paul, 1962); idem, *The Structure of Behavior* (Boston: Beacon Press, 1963); Karl U. Smith and Mary Smith, *Psychological Principles of Learning and Educational Design* (New York: Holt, Rinehart and Winston, 1966).

51. Michael Polanyi, *The Study of Man* (Chicago: University of Chicago Press, 1959), p. 23.

52. It is important to point out that this is *not* a romantic notion or a "do your own thing, kids, with no interference" position. See Polanyi's excellent discussion of the nature of apprenticeship to a scientific tradition in *Personal Knowledge.*

53. Donald Arnstine, *Philosophy of Education: Learning and Schooling* (New York: Harper and Row, 1967).

54. Gary Wehlage, Thomas S. Popkewitz, and H. Michael Hartoonian, "Social Studies Assessment in Wisconsin Public Schools," *Social Education,* in press.

55. For other types of questions institutional evaluation might begin to explore, see the interesting but sometimes analytically troublesome discussion in ibid.

56. The concept of *justice* is critical here. The best recent exploration of the idea in relation to policy making can be found in John Rawls, *A Theory of Justice* (Cambridge: Harvard University Press, 1971).

57. For a more complete discussion of the complex topic of

student rights, see Vernon Haubrich and Michael W. Apple, eds., *Schooling and the Rights of Children* (Chicago: National Society for the Study of Education, forthcoming).

58. Erving Goffman, *Asylums* (New York: Doubleday, 1961).

59. Jules Henry, *Culture against Man* (New York: Random House, 1963).

60. Philip Jackson, *Life in Classrooms* (New York: Holt, Rinehart and Winston, 1968).

61. See Michael W. Apple, "The Hidden Curriculum and the Nature of Conflict," *Interchange* 2, no. 4 (1971): 27-40.

2

Method and Evaluation of Educational Entities

MICHAEL J. SUBKOVIAK

Basic Concepts of Evaluation

Evaluation is the process of making a judgment about the value or worth of an entity with respect to a particular characteristic. Assigning grades to students, rating a teacher as a good or bad instructor, and determining the effectiveness or ineffectiveness of a new educational program are instances of evaluation. The entities in these examples are the student, the teacher, and the program respectively; the characteristics evaluated are the cognitive ability of a student, the instructional skill of a teacher, and the effectiveness of a program. In subsequent sections of this chapter methods of evaluating students, teachers, and educational programs are discussed in greater detail. Here I deal with basic concepts of evaluation.

To gain further insight into the process of evaluation, let us consider how grades might be assigned to students. Table 2.1 shows the scores of ten students on a 100-item objective test scored 1 for each correct answer and 0 for each incorrect answer. Test scores were used to assign the grades shown in the table according to the following evaluation rule:

A = top 20 percent of the class
B = next 20 percent of the class

Table 2.1
Test Scores and Grades of Ten Students on a
100-Item Test

Student No.	Test Score	Grade
1	100	A
2	95	A
3	88	B
4	80	B
5	72	C
6	67	C
7	40	D
8	35	D
9	15	F
10	0	F

C = next 20 percent of the class
D = next 20 percent of the class
F = bottom 20 percent of the class

This example illustrates two points. First, evaluation is usually based on evidence. The evidence in table 2.1 consists of *measurements* (test scores) that indicate the amount of a characteristic (cognitive ability) possessed by an entity (student). Of course, grades could also be assigned on the basis of less concrete evidence such as impressions, opinions, or hearsay regarding student ability. However, serious doubt is cast on such evaluations because the reliability and validity of subjective evidence cannot be readily scrutinized. *Reliability* refers to the repeatability of evidence—does a student obtain the same score each time he takes a test or does a teacher form the same impression of student ability on separate occasions? *Validity* refers to the meaning of evidence—does a test score or teacher's impression indicate a student's true cognitive ability? Concrete evidence, like subjective evidence, may lack these qualities; but the important difference is that the reliability and validity of concrete evidence can be determined more readily.

A second point to note in table 2.1 is that evaluation involves transformation of evidence (test scores) into value judgments (grades). This is accomplished by following a rule or set of criteria for transforming evidence into various statements of worth. A number of such rules can easily be formulated. Here is another:

A = top 10 percent of the class
B = next 20 percent of the class
C = next 40 percent of the class
D = next 20 percent of the class
F = bottom 10 percent of the class

Resulting grades for students 1 through 10 in table 2.1 would then be A, B, B, C, C, C, C, D, D, and F, respectively.
A third rule quite different from the first two is:

A = 81-100 percent of items correct
B = 61-80 percent of items correct
C = 41-60 percent of items correct
D = 21-40 percent of items correct
F = 0-20 percent of items correct

Students 1 through 10 would receive grades A, A, A, B, B, B, D, D, F, and F in this case. The first two rules are examples of *norm-referenced* evaluation because worth (grade) is determined by how much of the characteristic (cognitive ability) an entity (student) possesses compared to other entities. The third rule is an example of *criterion-referenced* evaluation because worth is determined by how much of the characteristic an entity possesses relative to fixed standards. Scriven discusses similarities and differences between these two types of evaluation in chapter 3.

As illustrated above, different criteria result in different statements of worth based on the same evidence. This fact has given rise to the suggestion that all evaluations be abandoned on the grounds that one man's wine is another man's vinegar—that is, value depends on who establishes the criteria. As Scriven also argues in the next chapter, one set of criteria is not necessarily as good as another. But first let us consider methods that have been suggested for evaluating basic educational entities: students, teachers, and programs.

Evaluating Students

Although students might be evaluated on physical prowess, psychological adjustment, or a host of other characteristics, cognitive ability as measured by classroom and standardized tests has traditionally received the greatest attention in education. Walberg in chapter 7 questions whether cognitive skills have been overemphasized, but we will bypass this issue here. Let us assume that we have reasonably reliable and valid measures of a cognitive ability such as vocabulary or mathematics. The question is, how can these measures be transformed into evaluations or grades? In this section both norm-referenced and criterion-referenced methods of grading will be discussed.

Norm-referenced Grading

There are a number of methods for norm-referenced grading, and some are definitely better than others. A shortcoming inherent in all common norm-referenced methods is that even if an entire class does above-average work in a course, Ds and Fs are given to some of the students; conversely if an entire class does below-average work, some members still get As and Bs. In other words, an A in an above-average class generally does not reflect the same amount of achievement as an A in a class of less able students. Later we will discuss a norm-referenced grading system that attempts to overcome this weakness, but first let us consider some less desirable norm-referenced methods.

One method is to assign fixed percentages of As, Bs, Cs, and so forth. The particular percentages that are often fixed are:

A = top 7 percent of class
B = next 24 percent of class
C = next 38 percent of class
D = next 24 percent of class
F = bottom 7 percent of class

This method is referred to as *grading on the curve* if the percentages are based on areas under the standardized normal distribution illustrated in figure 2-1a. When the observed distribution of test scores is not normal, the five letter grades do not represent equal intervals on the score scale as they do in figure 2-1a.

A second method for which letter grades represent equal intervals on the test score scale, and one that allows the percentages of A, B, C, etc., to fluctuate is shown in figure 2-1b. Under this system raw test scores are converted to standard z scores and grades are defined as follows:

A = z score above +1.5
B = z score +.5 to +1.5

Figure 2-1
Three Popular Methods of Norm-referenced Grading

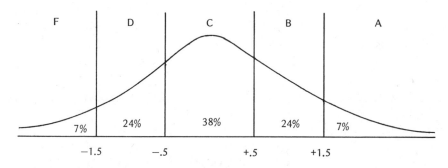

a. Grading on the Curve

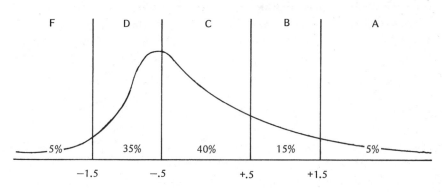

b. Tests Converted to z Scores

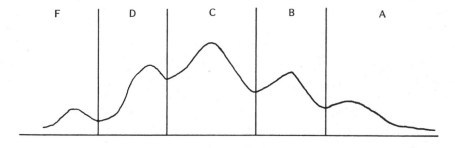

c. Grade Boundaries at Distribution Gaps

C = z score −.5 to +.5
D = z score −1.5 to −.5
F = z score below −1.5

While this is not the best conceivable system, since it does not take into account the possibility that an entire class may be above or below average, it is probably the best of the common systems, since the percentages of A, B, C, etc., are not completely determined in advance and since the letters represent equal intervals of ability.

A third method, which is illustrated in figure 2-1c, locates grade boundaries at gaps in the distribution. This approach has a number of shortcomings: (1) gaps may not occur, (2) gaps are usually chance occurrences that do not represent separations between distinct ability groups, and (3) letters do not correspond to equal intervals on the score scale.

In response to the weaknesses of common methods, Ebel (1972) has suggested a more flexible system, in which an above-average class receives more As and Bs and fewer Ds and Fs than an average class, while a below-average class receives fewer As and Bs and more Ds and Fs than an average class.

Figure 2-2 shows test score distributions that might be observed for classes of average, above-average, and below-average ability. The distributions are normal with equal standard deviations and different means (M). For the class of average ability in Figure 2-2a the lower grade A boundary is 1.5 standard deviations above M, the lower grade B boundary is .5 standard deviation above M, and so on. This results in 7 percent As, 24 percent Bs, 38 percent Cs, 24 percent Ds, and 7 percent Fs. Using the numerical values A = 4, B = 3, C = 2, D = 1, and F = 0, the distribution of grades for the average class has a mean of 2.0 and standard deviation of 1.0. The 2.0 mean is thus the expected grade point average (GPA) for an average class. And since 2.0 falls in the middle of the distribution of numerical values, its percentile rank is 50. This information is compiled in the center row of table 2.2.

Now suppose the same test score boundaries determined in figure 2-2a were applied to a class of above-average ability as shown in figure 2-2b. For the above-average class the lower grade A limit is 1.0 standard deviation above M, the lower grade B limit is M, and so on. As a result the above-average class receives 16 percent As, 34 percent

Figure 2-2
Adjusting Grades for Different Ability Levels

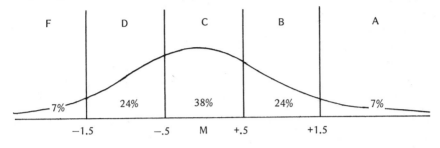

a. Average Class

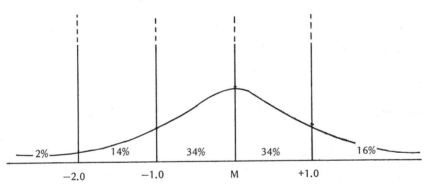

b. Above-average Class

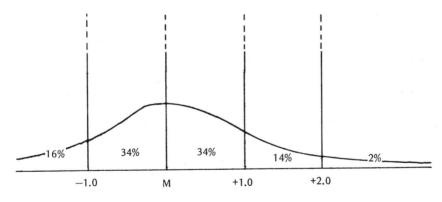

c. Below-average Class

Table 2.2
Statistics for Three Levels of Ability

Ability Level	Lower Boundary of A	Percentage of Grades					GPA	Percentile
		F	D	C	B	A		
Above Average	1.0	2	14	34	34	16	2.5	69
Average	1.5	7	24	38	24	7	2.0	50
Below Average	2.0	16	34	34	14	2	1.5	21

Bs, 34 percent Cs, 14 percent Ds, and 2 percent Fs. The corresponding expected GPA is 2.5, which is .5 standard deviation above the
mean (2.0) in the distribution of grades for the average class. If a
normal approximation to the distribution of grades for the average
class is used, the GPA of 2.5 corresponds to a percentile rank of 69
in the normal class. The information pertaining to the above-average
class is shown in the first row of table 2.2. The last row of table 2.2
was obtained in the same way for the below-average class shown in
figure 2-2c. More rows could easily be added to table 2.2 by considering other above- and below-average classes and making similar com-
putations. Ebel (1972, p. 342) in fact has derived a table similar to
table 2.2 that includes classes at seven different levels of ability with
GPAs ranging from 1.6 to 2.8 and a percentile range from 34 to 79.

Let us consider how table 2.2 can be used to assign grades to a
class such as that shown in table 2.3. The test scores in table 2.3 have

Table 2.3
Test Scores and Grades for an
Above-average Class

Student No.	Score	Grade
1	85	A
2	70	A
3	65	B
4	62	B
5	61	B
6	59	C
7	58	C
8	57	C
9	50	D
10	50	D

a median of 60 and standard deviation of 9.7. School records show the mean GPA for these ten students is 2.55, and their mean percentile on a standardized ability test administered in the school system is 70. In terms of GPA and percentile this class is very much like the above-average group in table 2.2. Thus it would make sense to use the same A, B, C, D, and F boundaries for this class as were used for the above-average class in table 2.2. From table 2.2 we see that the lower A boundary should be 1.0 standard deviation above the mean. Using the data of table 2.3, but taking the median (60) as the measure of central tendency because it is more representative than the mean (61.7) when the score distribution is skewed, we get:

$$60 + (1.0 \times 9.7) = 69.7$$

The lower limits for B, C, and D are obtained by subtracting one standard deviation:

lower B boundary = 6.7 − 9.7 = 60.0
lower C boundary = 60.0 − 9.7 = 50.3
lower D boundary = 50.3 − 9.7 = 40.6

From these lower boundaries the following evaluation rule is determined:

A = test score 70-85
B = test score 60-69
C = test score 51-59
D = test score 41-50
F = test score 0-40

The grades based on this rule are shown in table 2.3. Because this is an above-average group, the grades tend to be high; in fact no Fs were given at all. The primary assumption of this grading system is that classes with high mean GPAs and percentile ranks will have high subsequent course achievement and should receive high grades; the opposite is true for a class with low mean GPA and percentile rank. In practice this is often a reasonable assumption. The outstanding feature of this system is that percentages of As, Bs, Cs, etc., are not fixed but fluctuate with the ability level of each class.

To summarize, the steps involved in this grading system are:

1. Compute the mean GPA and/or mean percentile rank for the class.

2. Select from table 2.2 or Ebel's table (1972, p. 342) the appropriate ability level for the class.

3. Compute the median and the standard deviation of the scores on which grades are to be based.

4. Compute the lower score boundaries for grades A, B, C, and D using the median, the standard deviation, and the lower A boundary factor in table 2.2.

5. Determine a whole number score interval for each letter and assign grades accordingly.

Criterion-referenced Grading

Proponents of criterion-referenced grading believe that the letters A, B, C, and so forth should indicate how much a student knows or what he can do rather than how he compares to his classmates. This is accomplished by defining each letter grade in terms of fixed performance standards rather than class rank or position:

A = 81-100 percent of items correct
B = 61-80 percent of items correct
C = 41-60 percent of items correct
D = 21-40 percent of items correct
F = 0-20 percent of items correct

Under a criterion-referenced system a particular letter represents the same level of achievement in all classes. Also there is no limit to the number of As, Bs, Cs, etc., that can be awarded; an entire above-average class may receive As if warranted by the students' performance, or an entire below-average class may receive Fs. Common examples of judging worth by comparison to fixed performance standards are drivers' tests for motorists, flight tests for pilots, and certification examinations in some medical schools. Also since the advent of mastery learning (Block, 1971), criterion-referenced pass-fail grading has become increasingly popular in schools at all levels.

The most difficult aspect of criterion-referenced evaluation is defining the fixed performance standards to which test scores can be compared. Twenty years ago Nedelsky (1954) suggested a practical procedure for establishing absolute performance standards and assigning the usual five letter grades. To illustrate it, let us suppose grades are to be determined by a ten-item multiple-choice test, in which each item contains five options and is scored 0 or 1. Before the test is administered, a teacher or an expert examines each item and determines the probability that a "lowest A" student will pass the item. For example, item 1 might be:

1. The centigrade thermometer is an example of a(n)_____scale.

  *a. interval
   b. ratio
   c. ordinal
   d. nominal
   e. absolute

*Correct option.

If a lowest A student could eliminate options *c, d,* and *e* as incorrect, his probability of getting this item correct by choosing between the two remaining options (*a* and *b*) is 1/2.

The first row of table 2.4 shows the probabilities for a lowest A student correctly answering each of the ten test items. The sum of

Table 2.4
Probabilities of Correct Responses and Expected Scores

Student	|					Item					Expected Score
	1	2	3	4	5	6	7	8	9	10	
Lowest A	1/2	1/2	1/1	1/2	1/1	1/1	1/1	1/1	1/1	1/1	8.50
Lowest B	1/3	1/3	1/3	1/4	1/2	1/2	1/1	1/1	1/1	1/1	6.25
Lowest C	1/3	1/3	1/4	1/4	1/3	1/3	1/3	1/3	1/1	1/1	4.50
Lowest D	1/5	1/5	1/5	1/5	1/5	1/5	1/4	1/4	1/4	1/4	2.20

these probabilities across items is the expected test score of a lowest A student (8.50). This score is also the boundary between A and B students. The other rows of table 2.4 show the probabilities and expected scores for the lowest B, C, and D students. The boundaries in the last column define the following criterion-referenced evaluation rule for assigning grades:

A = test score 9-10
B = test score 7-8
C = test score 5-6
D = test score 3-4
F = test score 0-2

Steps can be taken to improve on such a rule. Nedelsky suggests that a number of teachers each supply data such as that in table 2.4 and that the average expected score for a lowest A student be used as the A/B boundary; the same procedure would be followed for the B/C, C/D, and D/F boundaries. He also discusses adding or subtracting a constant to or from each boundary so as to increase or decrease the number of high grades awarded. Angoff (1971) and Crawford (1970) also discuss this approach to establishing performance standards.

One shortcoming of the approach is that letters do not represent equal ability intervals on the test score scale. It is also interesting to note that the resulting grade boundaries are implicitly norm-referenced (see Scriven, chapter 3) if one's concepts of the lowest A, B, C, and D students are based on relative comparisons of previously encountered students. Scriven argues that norm-referenced comparisons almost always play some part in the definition of absolute performance boundaries or criteria.

Evaluating Teachers

The current approach to teacher evaluation seems to lag behind the better methods of student and program evaluation in certain respects. At present, teaching skill is judged almost exclusively on the basis of observational ratings of teacher activity inside and outside the classroom, with little consideration of the cognitive and affective outcomes of that activity. This is a bit like judging the value of a salesman on the basis of his sales technique and appearance without referring to how much he actually sells. The value of observational ratings of teacher activity is not denied. A recent review by Costin et al. (1971) concludes that ratings of teacher activity do correlate positively with student growth. Certain teacher activities have been repeatedly identified as contributors to desirable student outcomes (Flanders and Simon, 1969): (1) acceptance of student ideas and opinions, (2) adjusting instruction to different levels of cognitive ability, (3) diagnosing student difficulties and providing appropriate remedial work, and (4) using advanced organizers and outlines. However, where research has not established clear relationships between teacher activities and student outcomes, an attempt should be made to assess student growth rather than assume it.

Let us consider the basic aspects of teacher evaluation as it is currently practiced (Bolton, 1973). First the purpose of evaluation must be specified, such as elimination of inferior teachers or improvement of instruction. In the former case a norm-referenced evaluation would probably be called for; in the latter case criterion-referenced evaluation standards might be defined. In either case the next step would entail the development of measuring instruments. A good source for rating scales, checklists, and other observational procedures is published by Educational Research Service (1969, 1972). A teacher's score is usually obtained by totaling the ratings of an observer (principal, other teacher, students, etc.) across all items or scales. Next, criterion scores defining different levels of teaching ability such as "good," "average," and "poor" must be determined. Norm- or criterion-referenced cutting scores can be obtained using the methods discussed earlier in conjunction with student grading. For example, good, average, and poor could be defined in terms of deviations from the mean of the distribution of scores for many teachers; or ratings could be obtained for hypothetical teachers on the good/average and average/poor boundaries following the Nedelsky approach. Finally each teacher's score is compared to the criteria, and he or she is categorized as good, average, or poor.

Let us now consider how measurements of students' cognitive and affective growth might be added to the ratings of teacher effectiveness. In order to evaluate a group of teachers meaningfully in terms of student growth it is extremely important that they all be given the same raw materials to work with, i.e., that each teacher begin with a class of students whose ability, motivation, prior learning, etc., are the same as other teachers' classes. As shown in figure 2-3 this can be accomplished by randomly assigning students drawn from the population of interest to teachers and to a self-instructional control group if desired. Before assignment, students are given the same or equivalent pre-tests to provide a baseline for measuring growth. These instruments might assess cognitive or affective traits; as Walberg implies

Figure 2-3
Flow Chart for Evaluating Teacher Effectiveness

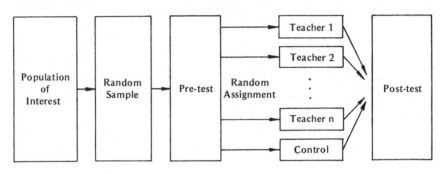

in chapter 7, it may be desirable to measure both. Following the pre-tests, each class is taught a course under conditions that are equivalent except for instructor. No course or teacher should receive more outside support or assistance from school staff than any other. Courses are most likely to be equivalent when they contain the same content and are taught in the same school. To the extent that courses are not equivalent, growth differences may be attributed to factors other than the instructor. Finally at the conclusion of the course each class takes an equivalent post-test. A post-test minus pre-test difference score can then be computed for each student, and the mean difference score for a class can be taken as an index of the corresponding teacher's instructional ability. Teachers can then be evaluated in norm- or criterion-referenced fashion on the basis of these class means. Differences between means can be tested for significance, and post hoc analyses may also be used.

It is obvious that the ideal design illustrated in figure 2-3 is difficult to realize. However, this does not justify ignoring student growth as an indicator of teacher effectiveness. Teacher effort cannot substitute totally for effect. The responsible evaluator will attempt to verify student growth.

Evaluating Programs

In chapter 7, Walberg discusses his evaluation of Harvard Project Physics. The purpose of the program was to teach physics to high school students in a more palatable way than the usual approach. High school teachers from across the nation were randomly selected to teach their physics courses by either the new or the traditional approach. Attitude and achievement measures were obtained for students under both conditions, and comparisons were made. There were no significant differences between groups with respect to achievement or attitude. What is striking about this evaluation, as Walberg notes, is that it is one of the few true experiments in the area of educational evaluation with a national sample. The cost of a national random sample is admittedly prohibitive except for large-scale programs; but this fails to account for the lack of relatively simple controls in numerous small-scale studies, such as the inclusion of comparison groups or random assignment of subjects to experimental and control conditions. Even more disturbing is the fact that weak studies are sometimes defended by professional evaluators on the grounds that evaluative research has to be conducted in the real world, which impedes the use of common laboratory controls. Some authorities stress that program evaluation must develop its own methodology to cope with the real world. To what extent this new methodology might deviate from strict scientific methods is not often made clear. On the other hand, there are evaluators seeking new ways to deal with the real world without sacrificing the scientific method in the process. Suchman, one of the latter group, feels that "evaluative research has no special methodology of its own. As 'research' it adheres to the basic logic and rules of scientific method as closely as possible" (1967, p. 81). This does not rule out planned compromises in areas where limitations of time or money prohibit ideal methodology. After all, compromises are also made in the laboratory. However, it does mean that program evaluation should consider the strongest possible design and analysis and make compromises grudgingly, rather than assemble a methodological "lemon" at the start and rationalize it on the grounds that one can do no better in the real world.

Suchman (1967) provides an excellent overview and organization of the basic aspects of program evaluation, although his examples are drawn from the area of public health rather than education. First, an evaluator must consider the objectives of the program being evaluated. Objectives are often arranged in three hierarchical categories—long-range, intermediate, and immediate objectives. Each level contributes, or is assumed to contribute, to the accomplishment of objectives at the next higher level. For example, in Harvard Project Physics a long-range objective was to keep the United States among the front-runners in technology. An intermediate goal was to increase the proportion of knowledgeable people who choose careers in science. An immediate goal was to increase the knowledge and interest of high school students in physics through a novel method of teaching.

An evaluator should also examine the validity of assumptions that underlie the objectives at each level. The long-range objective in our example assumes that United States technology should be a front-runner. This may require some verification, considering the ecological mistakes that sometimes accompany new developments. The intermediate objective assumes that more people can be motivated to choose careers in science. In light of research on behavior modification, this assumption requires less verification than the first. The immediate objective assumes that a particular teaching method will increase a student's knowledge and interest in physics. This was the assumption that Walberg attempted to verify through his evaluation.

The success or failure of a program to achieve a particular objective may be judged according to a number of different criteria. Suchman (1967, pp. 60-68) lists five possible criteria: (1) *effort*—the amount of activity expended toward accomplishment of the objective, (2) *performance*—the magnitude of the outcome, result, or effect procuced by program activity, (3) *adequacy of performance*—the ratio of the magnitude of observed effect to the total amount needed, (4) *efficiency*—the ratio of output effect to input costs for various methods, and (5) *process*—the determination of why a program worked or did not work. Project Physics was evaluated with respect to performance criteria and was not found to be significantly better or worse than traditional teaching. If the evaluation were done with respect to effort or some other criterion there might have been significant differences.

Let us now turn to evaluative research design. The weakest and yet most widely used design in current evaluation involves a single group, which is measured after the program. It is represented:

$$X \, O$$

Here X stands for exposure to the program and O for measurement of effort, performance, or the like. There is no pre-treatment measure to determine whether any change has taken place, nor is there any control group to determine whether an observed effect is attributable to the program.

A much better design would include the following controls: (1) a random sample of subjects from the population of interest, (2) random assignment of subjects to treatment and control groups, and (3) pre- and post-treatment measures to assess change. Such a design could be represented as follows:

$$O_1 \; X \; O_2$$
$$O_3 \quad O_4$$

The change for the experimental group is:

$$d_E = O_2 - O_1$$

That of the control group is:

$$d_C = O_4 - O_3$$

One would then look for significant differences between d_E and d_C values

Other designs are available that add further control, examine specific program components, permit longitudinal study, and so on. The interested reader should refer to Campbell and Stanley (1963) and Suchman (1967, chap. 6).

References

Angoff, W. H. "Scales, Norms, and Equivalent Scores." In *Educational Measurement,* edited by R. L. Thorndike, 2d ed. Washington, D.C.: American Council on Education, 1971.

Block, J. H. *Mastery Learning.* New York: Holt, Rinehart and Winston, 1971.

Bolton, D. L. *Selection and Evaluation of Teachers.* Berkeley, Calif.: McCutchan, 1973.

Campbell, D. T., and Stanley, J. C. "Experimental and Quasi-experimental Designs for Research on Teaching." In *Handbook of Research on Teaching,* edited by N. L. Gage. Chicago: Rand McNally, 1963.

Costin, F., Greenough, W. T., and Menges, R. J. "Student Ratings of

College Teaching: Reliability, Validity, and Usefulness." *Review of Educational Research* 41 (1971): 511-35.

Crawford, W. R. *Assessing Performance when the Stakes Are High.* Paper presented at the annual meeting of the American Educational Research Association, Minneapolis, March 1970.

Ebel, R. L. *Essentials of Educational Measurement.* Englewood Cliffs, N.J.: Prentice-Hall, 1972.

Educational Research Service. *Evaluating Teaching Performance.* Washington, D.C.: American Association of School Administrators and Research Division, National Education Association, Circular No. 3, 1969; Circular No. 2, 1972.

Flanders, N. A., and Simon, A. "Teacher Effectiveness." In *Encyclopedia of Educational Research,* edited by R. L. Ebel, 4th ed. New York: Macmillan, 1969.

Nedelsky, L. "Absolute Grading Standards for Objective Tests." *Educational and Psychological Measurement* 14 (1954): 3-19.

Suchman, E. A. *Evaluative Research.* New York: Russell Sage Foundation, 1967.

II

Concepts, Values, and Methods in Evaluation

3

The Concept of Evaluation

MICHAEL SCRIVEN

It may be appropriate for us to look at some basic logical questions at the start of a major conference on evaluation. There is now a considerable literature on the methodology, practice, and politics of evaluation, and we shall hear more about these dimensions later today and tomorrow. I shall focus on a couple of logical issues that seem to me to lead to some practical payoff, although there are others of equal interest for the logician in this area.

The Ultimate Problem

One of the main problems in practice is coping with the skeptical client or evaluee who believes that evaluation is entirely subjective or at least relativistic. That is, he or she is convinced that value judgments are intrinsically purely subjective and can be rescued from that state only by conversion into judgments of the value of a particular means for achieving an externally given end. In the latter form they are of course relativistic in the sense that they involve no judgment of the merit of the end itself. This basic dilemma—the choice between being completely arbitrary or merely relativistic—is the source of much indefensible neglect of evaluation as a social and scientific responsibility. Who can feel very much obliged to go through the motions of passing a judgment that is either entirely arbitrary or merely relativistic—let alone spending project funds to get someone else to do this?

Apart from this consequence, which we might call a sociological consequence of the subjective doctrine, a much more specific consequence affects the practice of educational evaluation, namely the widespread use of what might be called the goal-achievement model of evaluation. According to this procedure, the task of evaluation is simply to determine the extent to which a project has succeeded in attaining its goals. After all, it is often said, one could hardly defend the view that the evaluator ought to impose his or her own goals on the project, or the goals of some other project that is trying to achieve something quite different! Again we find ourselves faced with an awkward dilemma.

I want to state as strongly as possible my view that the concept of evaluation that is implicit in these dilemmas is totally, indeed pathetically, wrong. Value judgments are simply a species of scientific judgment; they are sometimes as easy to verify as an observational claim in astronomy and sometimes as hard to establish as a theoretical claim in cosmology. When correctly supported they are totally objective. When inadequately supported, they can be exactly as subjective as any other questionable judgment or assertion of a mere opinion or a matter of taste.

How does one escape the basic dilemma? It is necessary to dig a little deeper, rather than confront it head on. It is necessary to attack the very concept of a value judgment that is implicit in the persuasive formulation of the dilemma. Let me offer a battle plan first, to show where the effort is to be expended. The challenge arises in the premise that value judgments are either assertions about the merit of a means to a given end—in which case they are supportable but relativistic—or assertions about the merit of the ends themselves—in which case they cannot be supported. My response is to say either that there are no "ultimate," i.e., arbitrary, ends, and hence that all value judgments can perfectly well be treated as judgments of means, which (it is agreed) *can* be substantiated, or that judgments of the merits of ends exist and can often be given a rock-solid foundation, sometimes by appeal to definitional truths and sometimes by using indubitable inferences from empirical evidence. The first of these responses may seem to be a debating society point, but I think I can be persuasive that it is not. Which of the two one should adopt depends on further specification of the meaning of some of the terms used.

Let us suppose we can agree that the paradigm case of a value judgment involves the imputation of value or merit or worth to something, and we can agree that educational evaluation normally involves or should involve the production of documentation of one or more value judgments as the major conclusions. You might think that the preceding definitions are obvious enough, but they are not: Jim Wardrop's espousal of "exploratory evaluation," for instance, is for me just an example of confounding research with evaluation. The line is not sharp, indeed; but we should adhere to it as closely as possible or else we find ourselves expecting the evaluator to answer research questions that are far beyond his or her means, interests, and responsibility (e.g., Sam Ball in the "Sesame Street" evaluation went after several costly research questions and left some basic evaluation questions unanswered, as Professor Cook points out). But you will notice in Professor Cook's paper (chapter 6), on the other hand, many cases where the line between research and evaluation has not been carefully drawn, I would say that he tends to include far too much straight research under the heading of evaluation. Conclusions about the relative power of genetic and environmental factors over IQ are not value judgments at all.

Value judgments are judgments of value, worth, or merit. The normal use of grades for student papers is an example of evaluation, of the production of value judgments. Even the use of grades by someone who uses a curve to grade is an example of *comparative* evaluation, not a merely descriptive exercise, for the abscissa of the curve represents an ordering by merit, not by height, weight, or other such factors.

Notice, then, several confusions. Estimates, readings, or calculations of values for a variable, and normative data are not examples of value judgments. But the judgment that the estimate made was the best estimate; the judgment that the calculation was well done; the judgment that someone did far better than the norm; or the judgment that the norm identifies good or fairly good performance—these are value judgments.

One can cast the net a little wider by taking account of the notion of context-dependence. There are certain contexts in which a judgment that would normally be entirely value-free in fact carries a value judgment. There are contexts in which the judgment that someone is very intelligent has the implicit force of a positive evaluation. There are other contexts in which it has the force of a negative evaluation, excluding the individual from consideration for a date or a job, for example. Is the notion of intelligence *intrinsically* evaluative? Couldn't one say it means "the mental quality of being good at problem solving"? It is, then, intrinsically evaluative *with respect to problem solving,* but not with respect to the merit of the person as a person. Here lies the importance of context. One may see that the statement "He is under 125 pounds in weight" carries the force of a positive (or negative) value judgment from its context, even though it is not intrinsically evaluative. Similarly, "His IQ is under 125" may have positive, negative, or no evaluative force in a certain context (i.e., with respect to certain criteria, whether or not it has some intrinsic evaluative force with respect to other criteria). One might thus say that the judgment of intelligence is intrinsically valuational whereas the judgment of weight is not. But hold on: isn't intelligence (however badly we may measure it) just a property of an organism, like weight? Isn't it simply a property of the brain instead of the body? Isn't its value something we read into it? True—and also false. Reflection on just this example will unlock the mystery of the fact-value nondistinction. Values are indeed *relational* properties of entities—but then so are colors and other objective or observational properties. There is nothing subjective about relational properties. We are not overlooking the difference between "valued" and "valuable"; both are relational properties, but they are not the *same* relational properties. The one refers to what is *believed* to be need- or want-fulfilling, the other to what really or "in fact" has that property.

The difference between pounds of weight and IQ points is only that IQ scales were constructed to reflect a prescientific concept that has a valuational direction built into it. "Better at problem solving" is a prescientific notion; and it is a matter of definition, not a matter of taste or opinion, that someone said to be better at problem solving can solve more problems than others, or solve them faster or more completely or neatly. Hence the judgment of intelligence—not an easy thing to judge, any more than atomic weight or planetary weight is easy to judge—is in principle totally an objective matter resting only on definition and performance. Difficulties of implementation do not alter the logical characteristics of a claim. Of course, judgments of intelligence are often clouded by emotion and thus in particular cases may be merely subjective. Judgments of weight are the same—sometimes easy, sometimes hard, sometimes matters of great emotional impact, as when a jockey or a welterweight or a dieter is weighed in—except that there does not happen to be any evaluative component in them. There *is* external reference—usually to a measurement of weight. But there is no reference to a scale whose definition involves the notion of merit.

The way in which merit enters the judgment of intelligence is still only secondary; that is, one cannot infer from the assertion that someone is intelligent (or has a very high IQ) that that person is good or likely to be good, only that they are good at something. Using Aristotle's example, it doesn't follow from the fact that someone is a good thief that he is—even slightly—a good person. By contrast, if one asserts of a beam balance that it is well-damped, one *can* put that down as a plus in evaluating it *as a balance*. We can call such cases, cases of primary evaluative claims. (Note that "well-damped" is not the same as "heavily damped.") It is as straightforward to establish that a balance is well-damped as it is to establish that Jones is intelligent or that Smith is an excellent typist. The whole idea that value judgments are somehow less objective than judgments of fact collapses when one realizes that the very distinction between judgments of value and judgments of fact is essentially context-dependent, like the distinction between premises and conclusions. There is nothing about a premise or a conclusion that distinguishes one from the other *except* their relationship in a particular context or argument. There is nothing about value judgments that distinguishes them from facts except that the facts, like premises, are what we accept as true in a particular context; usually they include dozens of judgments that can be treated as value judgments in another context. Like the distinction between fathers and sons, or between theoretical and observational properties, the fact-value distinction is thought to be better than it is because there are some facts that definitely are not value judgments, just as there are some sons that are not fathers and some theoretical entities that are not observable. But the distinction is no good for the skeptic's purposes because there are plenty of value judgments that are properly called factual, even in the most critical context. It is a fact that Smith is an excellent typist if he makes less than one error per thousand words of copy, typing at seventy-five words per minute. If the world were a different place and people's performances very different, that might not qualify; but in this world it does (and, in a different world, sulphur would not melt at 444.6 degrees centigrade). Facts are facts only in the world as it is—and that goes for value facts, too.

Let us emerge from these subtleties to see what good they are doing us. They enable us to reject yet another concept of value judgment, this one the most deeply entrenched and vicious of all, for it begs the very question at issue. Often one finds the term *value judgment* used to mean "dubious claim" or "mere matter of taste or opinion." The explanation lies, no doubt, in the contextual distinction we make between the data and the evaluation, the facts and the evaluative conclusion. But, as we have pointed out, what are regarded as the facts in a given context usually include a number of value judgments. That is, there is no categorical distinction between facts and value judgments as far as certainty goes. If I want to support the value judgment that computer-assisted instruction (CAI) is not worth what it costs at the moment, I make factual assertions such as the following:

(a) The delivered cost of CAI is higher than that of any other educational support system.

(b) The learning gains attributable to CAI have never been shown to be greater than those attributable to tutoring or programmed texts.

(c) The attitude toward learning evidenced by CAI students does not appear to be superior to that shown by students using competitive systems.

(d) Even the very best CAI hardware, that used in PLATO IV, is subject to substantial downtime because of transmission line faults and is quite intrusive, marginally mobile, and technically troublesome to repair.

As we move from (a) to (d), the evaluative component increases—but there is no decrease in reliability.

There is another source for the idea that value judgments are less acceptable scientifically than nonevaluative judgments, and it is a far more powerful one. I refer to the doctrine of value-free science, particularly value-free social science, and its support. The doctrine was proposed by Max Weber as a sensible political precaution for the fledgling social sciences in the politically sensitive situation of the German universities of his time. It never had any logical foundation, and the feeble efforts to give it one have all the earmarks of rationalization rather than reason.

Not only is it a plain fact of common sense that value judgments, like the ones in the preceding discussion, are as testable and objective as anything else in science, but the supposed logical foundations for the doctrine are also a sham. Take the doctrine that one can never infer value judgments from facts alone, the so-called Humean doctrine. Combine it with the view that science is legitimately able to establish only facts, and we can conclude that science has no place for value judgments. The power of this argument involves four colossal errors. Taking them serially, we can see first that the power vanishes if we notice that value premises need not always be established by scientific investigations in the usual sense but may be established as definitional truths. It is a definitional truth that a good typist is someone who makes very few errors and types quickly; that a superior watch keeps better time than most; that machinery is no good for its job if it constantly breaks down; etc. And those are the only value premises one needs in order to infer conclusions about merit from facts about the performance of individuals and groups.

The second error is the failure to see that the argument is so powerful that it would immediately destroy science as we know it, since a similar "logically unbridgable gap" exists between the observation language and the theoretical language. One cannot *deduce* theoretical claims from any combination of observation statements; but it would be absurd to suggest that scientific theories are not founded on facts. Legitimate inference includes inference to the best explanation or the best conceptualization. And that is precisely how we infer from facts about what is valued—plus other facts—conclusions about what is valuable. For example, we infer from facts about the pleasurable responses of experienced customers (and facts about nutritive value etc.) the conclusion that the food at a particular restaurant is good. We infer from a wider range of facts the conclusion that the Opel Luxus is probably the best buy among small cars in the $3,600 bracket today. These cases are closely related to the ones with definitional value premises mentioned earlier, but, where one could make a case for deduction being the mode of inference in those cases, here the inference is looser. In a general sense of the term one might call this inductive inference. But it is more illuminating to regard it as inference of a prima facie interpretation. This is the standard kind of pragmatic and scientific inference, far more important in science than deductive or purely mathematical inference. One often hears the skeptic attacking a proposed argument in support of a value judgment by saying, "You conclude that this is a good management system from these facts; but there may be something you haven't thought of that would show it had *terrible* consequences. You just can't squeeze the value judgment out of the factual premises!" What we haven't thought of in science is what earns Nobel prizes for the people who do think of it; what we have thought of is what keeps us alive from day to day and what keeps practical scientific and engineering inference in touch with reality. There is no difference between the scientist or the engineer inferring the probable cause of a physical phenomenon and the social scientist or evaluator inferring the probable merit of a particular social or educational innovation.

The third great error in the value-free position concerns the very cases the skeptic uses to illustrate his or her other conception of the subjective status of value judgments. The term "matter of taste or opinion" or "*mere* matter of taste or opinion" is often used here. It is interesting to look at the exact nature of such claims. They are normally expressed in such language as, "I *prefer* Moselles to Sauternes," or "I *believe* Poincaré really had the key notion of relativity theory," or "I *like* working in pure math better than applied math." It is unfortunate that the positivist tradition has long thought of these as exemplars of the subjective—meaning the essentially unreliable and unscientific—when they are simply examples of claims with a restricted range, assertions about an individual rather than all members of a class. There is nothing less reliable about restricted-range claims; in fact they are *more* reliable. The positivists were of course also confused about the verification of such claims, which they took to be necessarily introspective—another term of opprobrium for them. But such claims are subject to entirely external verification and often turn out to be lies, told for reasons of social convenience— a fact we infer from subsequent or prior behavior.

What the positivists really meant was not that claims expressing matters of taste are like value judgments in being unreliable, but that value judgments have *unrestricted* form, which is illicit, and the only related assertion that could be defended is the expression of opinion. Thus, the assertion, "Inquiry teaching has not been shown to be superior even for controversial areas," cannot be scientifically established, and it should be rephrased, "A particular person [perhaps the speaker] *believes* that . . . ." Amusingly enough, the chief problem for an evaluator is the exact reverse. It is considerably easier to establish statements like the first one and much harder to achieve the second!

The skeptic is usually deeply confused about the distinctions between objectivity and subjectivity, reliability and unreliability, individual and general assertions. Usually the skeptical reference to value judgments as matters of taste is meant to imply unreliability, which of course it does not (unless the matter of taste is illicitly expressed in more general terms than are justified). But it is worth remembering that many value judgments are entirely individual (e.g., "this compensatory education program was of considerable benefit to this child"), and many matters of taste are very general (e.g., "most people dislike the taste of castor oil").

The last point I want to make against the value-free position is that it overlooks the essential role of a particular kind of value judgment in science, indeed in the purest of pure sciences as well as in applied science. This is the *methodological value judgment,* such as, "This curve fits the data better than that one," or "Control group methodology is always superior for the evaluation of intervention strategies, if it is socially and logistically feasible." No scientist can be a scientist unless he or she can distinguish good practice from bad practice, good explanations from bad ones, etc. Yet the skeptic is so anxious to reject value judgments that he or she will often do it with a self-refuting claim: "Value judgments have no proper place in science," or "It is wrong for a scientist to suggest that science can support value judgments." Of course, skeptics often think that value judgments are typically *ethical*; for that reason they do not notice the self-refuting character of their condemnation of value judgments. But moral value judgments are just one species of value judgments: they happen to be verifiable by appeal to social facts concerning the effects of social rules rather than physical or natural facts, but that is not a difference of logic. It is, however, a difference of topic, and, since the moral dimension is usually quite a minor consideration in educational evaluation, I will bypass the excitability usually aroused by the suggestion that morality is objective and get back to ordinary value judgments.

How *do* we get values from facts? By realizing that a value judgment is analogous to a theoretical claim in that it is a generator and organizer of facts, not *just* a fact, though it may be that as well. This leads me to a general view of educational evaluation that I call the pathway comparison model. What we have done so far covers the term *pathway* in the title. I now want to say something about the *comparison* part of it.

The Comparative Problem

I claim that all useful evaluation is comparative and that in fact all nontrivial evaluation is at least implicitly comparative. The difference between explicit and implicit comparison can be illustrated by considering two possible conclusions of evaluation. On the one hand one may conclude that product A is better than product B; on the other hand, one may simply conclude that product A is excellent or very good. The first is explicitly comparative; let us see how the second can be said to be implicitly comparative. The point can be made in terms of the following assertion: no matter what the actual performance of a product is, by comparison either with its function or with the goal set for it by the producer, one cannot reach a legitimate conclusion about its merit or excellence unless one can support the views that (a) the goal or function is itself meritorious, and (b) most efforts to obtain this goal or function are—or could be expected to be—considerably less successful than those of this product. (Correspondingly more modest comparative claims are required to support more modest evaluative conclusions.)

Is it possible to show that functions or goals are meritorious without any comparative considerations coming in? Suppose one shows that the function is to fulfill a crucial educational need. Wouldn't that prove that something meritorious had been done? That would depend on how the claim about need is defended in this context. If it is defended by showing not only that fulfillment of the need will be beneficial but also that previous efforts have failed, then we can justify our claim of merit—but only because there is an implied superiority to the previous effort. If the defense of the claim of need does not make any reference to other efforts, then we cannot justify the claim of merit, because the possibility remains open that the need could have been met by a simpler and more economical effort than that involved in the production of the present product. Until that possibility is ruled out, there is no merit in it. One cannot even support the modified claim, "It does an excellent job while fulfilling this function or goal," for—in the usual educational context—it does not do an excellent job if it is excessively expensive. And the criterion for excessive expense is essentially a comparative one; that is, we normally ask whether the cost is greater than that of other, equally effective, products. One may, of course, try an a priori approach to the question of excessive cost; that is, one might check on whether any of the costs actually incurred was apparently unnecessary. This would not be a comparative procedure, but it is an unreliable one. What we really need is evidence that a product of equal merit can be produced without incurring these costs, and the way to get that evidence is by trying to do it—which gives us a basis for comparison.

So, in order to show that achievement is meritorious, one normally has to show that it meets superior goals in a superior way. Is this really just a complicated way of saying that the evaluation vocabulary is an ordered one, i.e., that it contains a range of the terms good, very good, excellent, etc.? I think that I am going beyond this and pointing out that hard-nosed evaluation requires that the evaluator definitely establish the propriety of the term that he selects from the scale. Doing this essentially requires showing that there are other entrants in the competition and that they were located in the appropriate places relative to the candidate under consideration. Sometimes these other entrants are obvious unrealized alternatives, sometimes they are not obvious but demonstrably feasible alternatives.

The practical payoff from this point is very considerable. It runs entirely contrary to Lee Cronbach's position in that it *demands* a search for and information about comparative products. When necessary, it demands the creation of such products. For example, if the evaluator's task is to consider the merit of computer-assisted instruction, then he or she will not simply ask whether the performance is up to expectations or such as to satisfy a clear educational need on the part of the students using the CAI installation. He or she will not even accept a comparison with previous years' performance, which may show great superiority for CAI, for this comparison is not the critical one. What I call the *critical competitor* here is not last year's standards, for it may be extremely easy to improve on those, and no merit (or at least no substantial merit) should accrue to an educational procedure that does something that any educational procedure could have done. (One might be able to justify a claim such as, "It did better than nothing.") In the real world, there is no free lunch. As soon as we begin to talk about the realities of cost, we realize that the evaluator must be looking at cost-effectiveness and not merely effectiveness. Hence, only some rather unimportant evaluative conclusions arise from a comparison with the no-treatment control group. The important evaluative conclusions, such as "It was worth its cost," "It was the best choice," "It is the best choice for next year," "Its achievements were exceptionally meritorious," all require looking at other promising educational procedures that cover roughly the same territory at the same cost level and at different levels.

Conclusion

The ultimate problem about evaluation is where the values come from. I have suggested that they come from a context of desires, needs, and performance, and that *value* is a complicated theoretical term that implies and follows from various combinations of these conditions in a way analogous to the way in which *explanation* comes from observations and logical relations. I have also suggested that evaluation be thought of as a process of compressing complex data in the vise of these contextual constraints so as to squeeze out the water and leave behind the meaty residue of directed information that is a value judgment. Finally, I have suggested that these value judgments are nearly always implicitly comparative if not explicitly comparative, and a clear recognition of this leads to important practical improvements in the utility of value judgments.

Faculty Critique

by GARY WEHLAGE

In view of the short time I had to prepare a response to Mr. Scriven's paper, I cannot offer a systematic critique of the logic of his position. Basically I agree with the position he has developed. In my judgment he has made a useful analysis of the presumed fact-value dichotomy. He has done us a service by pointing out the fallacies and problems connected with arguments that assert a sharp distinction between factual and value judgment claims. My criticisms of Scriven's paper are directed toward several implications of his position that, when spelled out, tend to weaken its practical effects, especially when applied to the field of education. He passed rather quickly over several problems that arise when one enters the world of schools as an evaluator.

In general, my criticisms focus on what I see as potentially an oversimplified approach to evaluation. While Scriven's analysis and logic are certainly not simplistic, he did not caution his audience on the difficulty of applying what seems to be a very elegant and precise approach to evaluation to the real world of schools. Some of the examples he gave could serve to lull us into underestimating the difficulty of making evaluative judgments in schools. Several of the examples dealt with education, but others were concerned with automobiles, typists, or other mechanically conceived functions. This brings me to two specific criticisms: First, questions about what is a "good automobile" or "good typist" call for nonmoral evaluations. By offering such examples, Scriven tends to pass over the fact that schooling is essentially a moral-value undertaking. Secondly, I contend that the development of evaluative categories is much more complicated than Scriven has led his audience to believe. There is a crucial problem of selecting from among alternative categories before data can be gathered and interpreted. How does one choose these categories? What criteria guide an evaluator's choices? These questions were not explored in the paper.

Let me deal with the second criticism first. If one sets out to evaluate the performance of typists, automobiles, basketball players, or automatic dishwashers, some evaluative categories tend to be obvious, and consensus on them can sometimes be reached. Thus, the assumption behind consumer research is that most people agree on most characteristics of a good automobile, or whatever. But even in the most oridnary areas of evaluation there can be sharp disagreement on which characteristics are most significant. Is it better, for example, to have at the center position in basketball a high scorer or a good playmaker? People simply disagree over the relative worth of such players when focusing on specific situations.

In the world of schooling, the problem of evaluation is compounded because the evaluative categories are not always apparent. If one is charged with the responsibility of evaluating a school program, what categories should be selected as nets to collect data? Does one count the number of books in the library, look at the won-and-lost record of the football team, examine the standardized test scores of graduating seniors, or find out the vandalism rate in the community? While each of the categories could be used in assessing a school, it is not apparent that they are good categories to use.

The crucial question is not whether one can objectively evaluate schooling, but rather what categories does one choose and how are they chosen? For example, in evaluating the effects of a school program on students, one might have to choose between the categories of "self-esteem" and "reading comprehension." How does one decide to look at one rather than the other? Even if one assumes a rather extensive set of evaluative categories, it is still necessary to make choices about how much weight each category will carry in the final evaluation. On what grounds is an evaluator justified in looking at "reading comprehension" rather than "self-esteem" or weighing one more heavily than the other? It is obvious that such choices or weights are also value judgments, and it is not clear where they came from.

In the world of schooling, evaluation is complicated by the fact that students, parents, teachers, and the general public have differing and often competing categories into which they want data placed. The competing categories arise from different assumptions and value premises about the qualities of good schooling. In the real world, time and resources are limited, and not all possible valued outcomes concerning schooling can receive adequate attention. Many educational controversies occur because some group feels its goals are being ignored. In other words, some people want schools to stress the teaching of the three Rs, others want the schools devoted to vocational training, and still others want the focus on interpersonal and human relations. Correspondingly, of course, each group feels schools are to be evaluated in terms of how well they do in its key area.

To get some sense of how crucial evaluative categories are, one need only look at the merciless criticism leveled against the schools in the post-Sputnik period. The "soft pedagogy" of the forties and early fifties fared poorly when the new value choices (categories) of the late fifties and early sixties were applied. Similarly, on on the contemporary scene many schools are going through the difficulties of shifting priorities and goals as parents and students change the premises from which *they* evaluate schooling.

The shifting and competing nature of the evaluative categories was not brought out in Scriven's examples. Using his example of evaluating an Opel Luxus, it is soon apparent that some people want maximum acceleration and good handling; others want maximum gas mileage; others seek maximum luggage capacity and interior room; still others want minimum size for maneuverability and parking. To some extent these are competing categories into which data are placed in the process of making evaluative judgments. As long as each person may buy the car he judges to be the best, there is no problem. However, the automobile analogy is helpful as a tool for analyzing the evaluation of schooling only if a number of people with competing value categories must buy a single car. In a sense, that is what happens in the realm of public education (despite efforts of school systems to offer a wide variety of curricula). A knotty question is: how does one choose between competing value premises in evaluating public education? How can the evaluator adjudicate among competing concepts of good schooling? This is a difficult problem for both professional educators and the public.

This brings me to the other major criticism I have of Scriven's paper. It concerns the moral-value nature of schooling. My position is that education involves much more than trivial choices between (say) a car that handles well and one that has a large luggage capacity. When educational evaluations are made, based on certain value premises, there are also tacit assumptions behind these premises about what constitutes the good society and the good life. In his paper Scriven passed over the moral nature of schooling very hurriedly. His main point was that when an evaluator goes through the process of arranging data into categories, he is essentially engaging in a definitional act; the evaluator simply defines what a good automobile is and then proceeds to match the data against the criteria for "good automobile."

Again, I find the case of evaluation in public education more complicated than this example implies. In fact, the decision to evaluate a school on the mathematical achievement of its students, for example, is also *tacitly* an assumption that mathematical achievement is an aspect of the good society and the good person. This may or may not be the case. My caveat to educators is that the categories chosen to be evaluated explicitly determine the public concept of good schooling and implicitly determine the notion of the good person. While this will be true of any scheme of evaluation one chooses, a serious problem develops when evaluators consistently and pervasively choose value categories that concern only a narrow range of possibilities.

Typically, evaluation has dealt with a narrow range of academic and cognitive skills. The evaluation categories and hence the moral-value premises behind them have not usually reflected a concern with the social roles children are asked to assume in the school. That is, evaluators have not been concerned with evaluating the school in terms of the sense of initiative and responsibility children acquire, or the sense of personal worth they have, or the moral development that takes place. There are, of course, some prominent exceptions to this. For example, Philip Jackson, Jules Henry, and Lawrence Kohlberg have explored these areas. I believe it is important that the field of evaluation move beyond mere technical and logical problems to a recognition of the implicit social, political, and moral dimensions of this work.

Conclusion

While I agree that there is no logical difference between value judgments and factual claims, I also believe the problems of evaluation are more complicated than Scriven's analysis implies. In this vein, I contend that evaluators need to be more concerned with the character and assumptions of their craft. Just as they should look for the unintended learnings that occur in schooling, they should also ferret out the hidden or implicit dimensions that accompany evaluation as a discipline. There will always be moral and value baggage carried along with human enterprises, and certainly the various dimensions of education are no exception.

Author's Reply to Faculty Critique

I agree with the general thrust of the two criticisms that were offered. Morality does indeed enter in many important ways into the evaluation of schools; and there is a serious evaluation problem involved in identifying the proper way to conceptualize the data that you're looking at. Let me say just a word more on both these points.

You gave a fairly specific example about the problem of which dimensions to pick, when there seem to be conflicting demands from various areas on how to select means for evaluating schools. I'm inclined to think that you can generally handle that problem by providing rather comprehensive evaluations; there doesn't seem to be incompatibility between evaluating schools on their basic reading and math teaching ability and also evaluating their vocational education offerings and their interpersonal relations offerings. I think evaluators have to treat their product—the evaluation—by looking at the audiences to which it is addressed, in the same way that a producer has to try for audiences when he's developing a product. The evaluator has to be willing to face the fact that there are conflicting demands from different audiences and be willing to provide an evaluation for each of the audiences in response to its particular interests. I don't mean these will be incompatible; they should be supplementary. Bob Stake's concept of responsive evaluation centers around this idea of identifying audiences and providing them with the kinds of things they're interested in; I don't mean the kind of *answer* they want, but the kinds of things they're interested in.

You do have to make choices among ways of conceptualizing the data. Those statistical conceptualizing steps may be important. They can give you a completely distorted perspective of the whole picture, and of course you then go on to the credentialing step on the wrong foot. You've got to be very aware of the different ways of conceptualizing the information.

On the morality issue, I think most of what you say is correct. I've written many papers on that topic, and I'm very fond of it, so I'm glad to hear you stressing it. It just wasn't something that could be handled in this paper. I think there are many features of process that are under moral constraints in the schools. Let me make a distinction that I think is helpful, however: moral constraints on what goes on in the schools are distinguishable from moral imperatives on the curriculum. You must not think that because there are definite moral limitations on the way in which children can be treated in a classroom, for example, that morality dictates exactly what you have to do with children in a classroom. What follows from morality is what you cannot do with them. It would be good to have some serious discussions on key moral issues in the curriculum instead of the uninteresting issues that usually characterize curriculum discussions on the grounds that anything else is going to be controversial.

Audience Discussion

Questions Evaluators Must Ask

Q: Mr. Scriven, Mr. Wehlage made the point that one of the basic issues confronting the evaluator is choosing how one understands the outcomes and processes of schooling, and that these choices are in fact moral choices. An example might be looking at schooling from an efficiency rationale, which implies certain types of decisions. I was wondering what insights you could give us into how one makes authoritative choices between areas of expertise for comprehending the interactive processes that go on in schooling.

Scriven: Well, I think I'd look carefully before jumping into that kind of thing. People tend to say that you should use transactional analysis of a certain aspect of the school. This tends to be a kind of holistic response. My judgment is that cost-effectiveness is really essential for a responsible evaluation of educational activities that involve substantial public funding. And it doesn't show prejudice. If, in analyzing effectiveness, I ignore all questions of interpersonal interaction, then I am showing a bias. But I'm not showing a bias by talking about effectiveness; I am showing a bias by omitting something in my judgment that would be important to it. It seems to me you have to look at the choices with a slightly finer, higher-powered lens than I used at first. And similarly, if someone says you ought to do it in terms of interpersonal relations, I would say that that, of course, deserves to be mentioned. The important question is how heavily you weigh it. The interpersonal interpreters say it's the only thing that matters; that's insane, because if it *were* there wouldn't be any schools.

There can't be schools without economics; there can't be economics without people to run the system; and there can't be people to run the system unless they learn something about how to read and write. You've got to look at the attendant costs very carefully—"costs" meaning not simply dollars, but what you lose or gain. When you start to look at it that way, you begin to achieve some overall perspective on the schools. I think, in a way, that Phil Jackson also was suggesting ways in which anthropologists—or let's say socially oriented critics of schools—might get different perspectives: they might see schools as acculturating agents or vocational training programs. I think those are two different sorts of tasks, both very important, that could be done in that area of socialization. But in terms of individual perspectives, I don't think you can say, "Aha! Now I've got to make a choice between seeing the school as an acculturation agent and seeing it as a means of training the proletariat." I don't think that choice is required. I think the proper thing to do when you discover new perspectives is to create an n-dimensional drawing instead of an n-minus-one-dimensional drawing. And you enrich what you're doing in the evaluation.

Anthropological Studies

Q: What role do you think in-class anthropological studies will play in the evaluation of schooling?

Scriven: Well, from the point of view of hard-nosed evaluation, it seems to me that we're getting a bit lost in the bogs of classroom process. It may be enlightening about something—the reality of the classroom, for example, or the process of the school—but relevant to evaluation it typically is not. Such studies have the status of being pure research in the field, and interesting things have come out of them, but they never turn out to be important. I hope they will be, sooner or later, but I want to remind you that not every interesting turn in the woods leads us toward whether we wasted money last year on a learning center.

Ideal Evaluation

Q: How do you deal with the following complications: (a) incomplete data; (b) data that are known tacitly by the decision maker; and (c) decisions that have to be reached in less time than it takes for a full flowering of your rational model.

Scriven: You're going to be able to do something with less. We have said before here that we could perhaps summarize the literature and make special observations from it. You just have to do it, in certain circumstances; it means that you get across less than you really want to get across. The way I try to train my people is by giving them lots of time to begin with, and then cutting it and cutting it and cutting it, cutting here and cutting there, until finally a guy calls you up on the phone and says, "I want you to evaluate United States higher education for me," and you say, "Okay—it's not very good." It takes an awful lot of talent to be able to do that in a way that can be justified. But you must also be willing to do it in any degree of expansion that he cares to finance. So you're in the compression game. I think all of us have to try to get the unconscious conscious and the explicit routinized and the conscious calculations unconscious; it's a kind of trade-off deal in which we get the routine stuff back into the unconscious so it becomes a snap judgment and still reliable, and we pull out from the unconscious the possibly embarrassing fact that we've got to look at that set of data that we began with.

Values and Evaluation

Q: Let's use one of your own examples about evaluating a typist. I think you said that a fast, accurate typist is unequivocally superior to a slow, inaccurate typist, and I'd certainly agree with that. Now the difficult problem comes up when there is a choice between a fast, inaccurate typist and a slow, accurate one. Do you or do you not provide some basis for choosing between these two?

Scriven: Sure, there are always two bases that have to be considered. One is the market parameters, and the other is morality, which overrides the market parameters. In this case the question is, are you the person hiring the typist—are you the audience for the evaluation?

In that case, I work out from you how much trade-off in speed you're willing to put up with for how much gain in accuracy. That's the answer; the moral dimension doesn't really come in. But, in cases like that, there might be a moral dimension, such as a fast, inaccurate, but badly crippled typist or Vietnam veteran typist against another. Then you've got a dimension that is tricky, but you proceed in the same relatively systematic way. That is, you try to order the relevant principles in terms of priority, and then select on the basis of the most important among conflicting principles.

Q: Aren't we then taking precisely the relativistic position that you said at the outset to avoid?

Scriven: No, because I didn't say that we do it in terms of the goals. I said we do it in terms of what you do in fact want or need, whether or not it's what you explicitly recognize. For example, in doing a market survey, you can proceed by asking people what they would like to see on the shelves, which will give you some kind of an answer, and then you produce that product; that's goal-directed. On the other hand, you can try to do something more serious—to find out what they would buy if it were on the shelves, which requires pilot runs, dummy packaging, and so on. The results always turn out to be substantially different from the answers to the first kind of survey. Similarly, with respect to the typist, if you think a person is a perfectly good judge of what he needs, you can depend on just his say-so. But if it got at all tricky, you'd have to make an analysis of his work schedule, the load of the work, whether a little inaccuracy is really going to hurt him, whether he thinks it is going to, and a whole bunch of questions like that. So you don't look at goals—or you look at them but don't take them as the last word. No, you're not in a relativistic situation. You could put it this way: if everything else fails, and there are no facts in conflict with the goals, use the goals. But otherwise, since that's practically never the case, you practically never use the goals—at least you never emphasize them very heavily.

Educational Goals and Evaluation

Q: It sounds to me like what you're saying is that these educational goals are relatively objectively ascertainable and self-evident. But some groups feel the need for arithmetic and other groups feel the need for openness and sensitivity. Now if their needs were as objectively ascertainable as they might be in the case of hiring a typist, it would be okay. But I don't see it as all that simple in terms of societal needs.

Scriven: Nobody said it was simple. The question is whether or not it can be done. But it seems to me you're falling into the same tendency of assuming that you have to pick up one of these answers and reject the others, instead of saying there are *these* needs, which these people feel very strongly, and there are *those* needs, which other parts of the clientele feel very strongly. It seems to me that's the usual situation, and you can provide composite solutions. You evaluate against a compound mix, instead of simply picking one rather than the other.

There was another thing in what you were saying that bothered me. I am saying that the needs are the determining question. There are certainly cases in which lots of vociferous groups are yelling for one thing and the other, these things being conflicting, and there is a limited supply of resources, so you can't satisfy them all. Now, in that situation often there isn't really any difference, and when you can identify that you can provide the same mix for both sides. You're going to get a lot of flak when you do it. You always have to settle; you always have to make a deal. But if you want an answer in terms of the logic of the situation, frequently you can ignore all the yells and find out what the need is and fill it. That's what you ought to be doing in an ideal sense of order. Everything you do besides that costs the society.

Q: Professor Jackson, do you agree with Mr. Scriven?

Jackson: Well, I don't think I realized it until I heard Mr. Scriven describe it, but yes, I suppose I do. Earlier I was thinking about one of those little homey pieces of advice I give to school people: "Never trust an administrator who has dry palms." Administrators—all decision makers—ought to have sweaty palms. If they don't, either they don't understand the complexities of the problem, or they're just brash and brazen people whom I wouldn't trust to be administrators. I think I understand Mr. Scriven to be saying that the complexities are such that one must always compromise in some way. I hear him encouraging us to make decisions that are as rational as we can make them within the constraints in which we operate. I don't know whether that's distorting it.

Scriven: No, that's not.

Time Constraints and Evaluation

Q: Mr. Light, do you agree with the gentleman telling us that we can make accurate decisions without complete analysis?

Light: No, I guess I don't. But I think it is one of the hardest problems we face. James Coleman gave a paper recently, at the American Sociological Association, I believe, in which he argued that one of the major difficulties with social science as he perceives it today, is simply that we search for the true answer for so long that we're paralyzed at making policy decisions. Mr. Coleman basically said, "If we have to make a decision now on partial information, that's what we really ought to be worrying about, rather than trying to get at the full information after the decision has been made." It would be silly for me to say we shouldn't make any decision unless we have perfect information. But I worry a lot when I see various analyses, scholarly analyses, being done that are the "sort of" variety. It strikes me that getting the rough, ballpark estimates may, in fact, be a very bad idea, because very often these estimates turn out to be wrong after policy has been made on the basis of them. Urban renewal might be the best example of this.

Scriven: Well, suppose you are faced with exactly the kinds of constraints you mention. What are you going to do—refuse to make a decision?

Light: Oh no. Realistically, if we're going to run a school, we have to make a decision. What I had in mind was the number of scholarly analyses that have come out of many universities—many from my university—in the last few years, that have rushed to make a decision. Perhaps the Coleman Report is a good example. Retrospectively it turned out to be quite a fine piece of work; yet, as Mr. Coleman himself was the first to say, it was terribly rushed. And you can see there's a real risk: think of the policy that has, in fact, flowed from the Coleman Report. A lot of people from all sides—conservatives, radicals—argue that current policies are largely based on Coleman. Advocates both for and against busing quote Coleman in various ways. So I just say that I find a real risk in that. In the real world, sure, we have to make fast decisions.

Scriven: There isn't any doubt there's a real risk in doing it, but sometimes you're stuck with it.

Student Grades

Q: The typical evaluations of students are made now in terms of grades. You have the dissertation, you go through the process, and you come up with an A-minus at the end. How do you evaluate the evaluation—that is, what does that A-minus mean? How can you test the validity of your evaluation, which is reflected in that A-minus?

Scriven: I just gave you a model of what happens. Through some process, which varies a great deal from evaluator to evaluator, we finish up with an A-minus. Sometimes the process isn't worth anything at all, and the A-minus is absurd; there isn't any validity to it. Sometimes it is extremely carefully thought out and is done in terms of a norm that is extrapolated from comparable theses done by people of comparable levels and comparable backgrounds. Then it tells you that the paper is better than roughly half the others, but not much better. Sometimes it is done in terms of an abstract conception of quality, and I guess that's what I use when I'm evaluating advanced work. I simply work from the top down: if it scores very well on originality, thoroughness, the extent to which it is expressed clearly, and so on, then it is A-plus, and everything it lacks that is significant knocks off something from that. It can get down to an A-minus in several different ways, but I can explain the way. I likewise have to explain the mensurational scale I'm working on and what it is meant to convey, in the same way that I have to explain the IQ scale.

I remember at Indiana there was a course for graduate students in sociology, called, "Introduction to Research Methods in Sociology." It was a semester-long compulsory course, the only one that was compulsory. There was only one requirement for the course, namely a research paper. And when the student got it back—it was sometimes a fifty-page paper—there was a small letter at the end, and that was it. That was it. You're training research workers on research methods, and what you do is give them a one-letter grade at the end of a long paper at the beginning of their careers as graduate students.

Well that's fatuous. It's not even clear what the letter means; there's no implicit explanation of that in the course. But it certainly isn't an educational experience, or very little of one. So it is often very badly done. But it can be done quite well.

A very interesting problem arises in the following situation: a state college in California last year had a grade point average, on a five-point scale, of 4.8. That is, out of 17,000 grades, there were about a dozen Ds or Fs. Now, in my view, that's a very bad system of evaluation. There has been a long fight going on at that college about the issue, as you can imagine. My general reply is that we should compress information, not throw it away. Suppose I say that we should use a new length scale: everything that is less than sixty feet long is "short," and everything that is more than sixty feet long is "long." Okay, the system does a lot of compressing, but it destroys its information content. On the other hand, suppose I say, "Let us be precise. We'll use nothing except microns to measure length. You've always got to give the length in microns," which means seven decimal places for a thing that is a foot long. That's equally ridiculous at the other end. You don't have the utility for that precision, even if you could give it objective reliability. So the business of evaluation at the end-product stage is the identification of merit as informatively as possible on a scale that is neither so refined that it represents an unreal capacity to measure differences of merit, nor so crude that it fails to distinguish between what can clearly be distinguished.

Those are the ground rules for grading systems. My grading system used to consist of putting a big rubber stamp with six category divisions on the paper. I gave a grade on each of the six categories first, and then I gave an overall grade. That seemed useful to me. It's always informative to grade on originality, coverage, expression, and presentation. You know, I don't weight presentation much, but it's worth mentioning because it can interfere with the communication process. If the paper is badly written, that has a very marked effect on the reliability of grading and a generally bad effect on the grade itself, from the evidence that we have available. It's a cost to the student, but it doesn't affect his overall grade in my thinking. Originality affects it a lot. So it's more informative if I grade him on six dimensions first, and then sum them according to a weighting system, which I indicate in the right hand column of the stamp.

I'm off on a big reform-of-teaching exercise at the moment. All of my early exams in the course are given on the following basis: every student invents a six-figure identification number, which he puts on his exam and writes down in his notebook or somewhere. None of the exams then carry the students' names. I grade all the papers. Now I know where the class is, which is what I need from the exam. I leave the classroom ten minutes early, and leave the papers arranged numerically on the table, so the students can find their papers by the numbers. Now they know how they're doing, but I don't know who did what, so I can avoid a halo effect in my later grading of them. They can treat this exam as a genuinely useful way for them to learn how they're doing, and I can treat it as the same thing, without all of us getting involved in the other part of grading, which is the record for the external audience. When we come to the final, I give them an option: they can hand in only the final, or the final and the two earlier graded papers, or the final and one of these.

I have discovered that there are different audiences: there's the parent audience, the student audience, the registrar and future employer audience, my chairman who wants to know if I'm giving all As or all Fs or something, and me who wants to know if I'm talking over their heads or making it too simple for half of them. Those audiences all ought to be served with an evaluation done in different ways. In some cases it needs a grade, in some cases it doesn't. Where it doesn't need one, don't give it one, because it's always costing you. So, by being more analytic about the process of evaluation, it seems to me I've come up with some procedures that are more useful.

General Conclusions from Particular Evaluations

Q: Do you essentially agree with the claim that the supplies we have available for a certain methodology are not powerful enough, or very seldom powerful enough, for us to make a generalizable statement about the effect of given variables on a program, whether you're talking about Head Start or any other particular program like that?

Scriven: Let me agree with you to this extent: it is often much easier to handle a problem if it is made very particular. Certainly true. But on the other hand, I don't think I'd buy your general argument. For example, I've spent a lot of time evaluating computer-assisted instruction lately, and I don't have any difficulty making the statement that I used as an example earlier, which is that there isn't a cost-effective installation of CAI in existence, nor has there ever been one. And at the moment there isn't very much prospect that there will be one. That's an evaluation of absolute generality, although it is temporally bounded.

Q: Excuse me, but I'm talking about evaluation, and you're talking about cost effectiveness.

Scriven: That doesn't matter; they're two parts of the same thing.

The great thing about backward subjects, like the social sciences, is that negative results are rather easily established, and they are just as general as affirmative results, so that one can confidently assert things about the nonworkingness, or the failure, or the poor value of large numbers of educational activities and social activities, with good support. However, you can do it in the other direction, too. For example, good programmed texts, that is, the best of the programmed texts (defined by a formula, describing the number of iterations or reductions there, independent criterion tests, and things like that), can teach a number of subjects better than anything else, including almost all teachers. That's a positive evaluation of programmed texts. So I think you can produce general evaluations.

Light: I just want to add one note: I think your question is a very good one. There has been a lot of discussion among people who have looked at the results of some of the major evaluations recently, trying to decide what we have been doing wrong. We seem to be constantly finding no effects of any kind. And that has led to a discussion of the different roles of experimentation or post hoc survey analysis. I'm sure Mr. Scriven would agree that in an ideal world we would actually like to run a real experiment, right out of the textbook, with randomized treatments, or subjects to treatments, or treatments to conditions, or whatever. I suspect most people here who know about experimental design would agree. To your specific point, then, when studying one school that seems to be doing something right, there's a real question about replicability and generalizability, and that's what makes it very hard. According to some of the recent literature, exhortation literature, we should be doing more social experimentation. My point is simply that for large-scale evaluations you might, in fact, want to do more experimentation.

Let me conclude with a quick, true story. About four years ago there was a post hoc analysis of some Head Start centers in the

Boston area. It was not done with an experimental design; rather, it was done just as an after-the-fact survey. And it found that the children in this series of Head Start centers being studied seemed to do enormously better than a group of comparable children one and two years before that, who were not in Head Start. It was assumed initially that this difference was due to the effect of Head Start. A little further analysis showed that that happened to be 1970-71, which was the first year of "Sesame Street." And it turned out that, in general, something like 85 to 95 percent of all small children watch "Sesame Street." So children both in the new Head Start centers and in the control group watched "Sesame Street." My point is that, had a real experiment been done, we would have noticed that both the Head Start children and the control group did better than the previous year's children, none of whom had "Sesame Street" available.

Goal-free Evaluation

Q: Mr. Scriven, you apparently suggest that all evaluation ought to be goal-free. Is that correct?

Scriven: No, just that you should do it goal-free if you can. But there are two or three types where you can't. For example, perhaps you're a staff evaluator working with a project from the beginning. That project might consist of you teaching French for the first time. In such situations you can hardly avoid the evaluation of goals, since you can't do any planning without the goals and you've got to start evaluating. And there are other cases like that in evaluating proposals. It looks as if you're evaluating goals; usually the panels evaluate goals, and then they evaluate personnel and amount requested. Actually what they're doing is making a prediction as to the effect in evaluating a topic. But there are some cases where evaluation of goals is okay. It's just that you shouldn't do it unless you have to, because it's too untidy and it doesn't benefit you. The main thing to remember is that if you start goal-free and do an evaluation goal-free, you can always go back and redo it knowing the goals. But you can't do the other. You can't reverse once you know the goals. Therefore, it's always worthwhile to try to do it goal-free first, and then go back and do it again, hearing about the goals, and see if you have to change anything.

4

Naturalistic Studies of Schools and Classrooms
one reader's digest

PHILIP W. JACKSON

Within the past decade or so the products of a relatively new genre of scholarship have made their debut on the educational scene. These documents, which now comprise close to a dozen books, several unpublished doctoral theses, and a few privately circulated papers, contain descriptive accounts of a school or a classroom (sometimes more than one) based on the author's extensive firsthand observations.[1] Though there is considerable variety in this collection of writings, ranging as they do from an intensive analysis of an urban classroom to a case study of an experiment in open education, they are sufficiently alike in design and methodology to warrant treating them as a group for the purpose of considering the potential impact this form of scholarship might have on educational thought and practice.

Because the focus of this appraisal is more on form than on substance and has more to do with the *promise* of an investigatory approach than with its accomplishments to date, no attempt will be made to provide a detailed look at any of the studies in question or to point out particular strengths or weaknesses. On the contrary, having read all these reports, I have tried to allow my recollections of them to fuse until the details of each have been lost or blurred, leaving only a collective image, a set of general impressions, on which

these remarks are based. The underlying questions to which my remarks are addressed have to do with the value of naturalistic studies
as a form of educational research: Where have they taken us so far?
Where do they seem to be headed? Finally, in keeping with the
theme of the conference for which this paper was written, I shall
consider the potential contribution of naturalistic studies to the reorientation of our thinking about problems of educational evaluation.

First, a word about the overall features of naturalistic investigations. Methodologically, as noted, these studies have as their data
base the on-site observations of one or more schools or classrooms.
The author-investigators, often aided by one or more assistants, have
spent from a few weeks to more than a year—a relatively large
amount of time compared to the time spent in gathering more conventional research data in schools—looking at what goes on in these
educational settings, talking with participants, and in some instances
becoming participants themselves. To capture what they have seen
and heard, they have taken field notes, kept diaries, tape-recorded
interviews, collected memoranda and other pertinent artifacts, and
on occasion even administered paper-and-pencil tests and questionnaires of a conventional sort.[2]

This methodological eclecticism, if it may be so called, is consonant
with another distinctive feature of this form of investigation: the
absence of formal hypotheses as guides to the inquiry. Typically, the
person conducting a naturalistic study does not start with an elaborate theory from which he has deduced hypotheses that are then to
be tested. Instead, at least in the early stages of his work, he tends to
meander, looking about the school setting with a naive eye, letting
the natural flux of events guide his vision. In short, he follows his
nose.[3]

The seemingly directionless and somewhat opportunistic character
of this approach does not mean that the final product lacks structure
or that in the course of his work the investigator eschews the customary goal of seeking to bring order out of chaos. The difference, in
part, is one of timing. The naturalistic observer, in contrast to the
more traditional experimenter, spends more time looking over the
lay of the land before he decides on the direction in which to move.
During this exploratory period he might be described as seeking questions rather than answers. Once he has settled on them, his work may

more closely resemble the paradigm of research activity depicted in conventional texts on the subject.

But there is more to this difference than simply a delay in the application of conventional modes of inquiry, for, even after he decides on the questions he wishes to answer, the naturalistic observer typically attempts to interfere minimally with the ongoing operation of the school or classroom. He tries, in short, to be as unobtrusive as possible.

This unobtrusiveness is in sharp contrast with experimental techniques that disrupt the natural conduct of educational affairs. The naturalistic observer is, in a sense, more respectful of the phenomena under investigation than is his experimental counterpart. Figuratively, if not literally, he tiptoes through classrooms and corridors, listening more than speaking, observant more than observed.

An attitude of respect for the integrity of schools as institutions together with the corresponding posture of noninterference with their operation are of course not absent among those who adopt other modes of inquiry. Nor must we assume that those who adopt such an attitude and such a posture are free from criticism. Critics have argued that the naturalistic observer's customary respect for the subject of his investigation covers a flaw of timidity and leads him, in the end, to be little more than an apologist for the status quo. Leaving aside the question of whether such criticism is deserved, it is certainly true that most of the documents under discussion contain what might be described as "sympathetic" accounts of educational practices.[4] Whether this sympathy is simply a cover-up for a lack of ideas about how to improve schools is an issue to which I shall return.

These three characteristics of naturalistic investigation—its methodological eclecticism, its hypothesis-free orientation, and its implicit acceptance of the natural scheme of things—combine to form an approach to educational inquiry that stands in marked contrast to what most of us, schooled in a more psychometric and seemingly tough-minded tradition, have been taught to regard as good research. Whether or not such a "soft" point of view is of enduring worth depends in the final analysis on what it teaches us about the phenomena under investigation. Thus, the sixty-four dollar question, for the future of this research strategy, is: What picture of schools and their operation is beginning to emerge from these descriptive accounts?

A full and objective answer to this question obviously calls for a detailed report of the findings of each investigation, a requirement far exceeding the scope of this paper. Instead, you shall have to be satisfied with an answer that is at best partial and impressionistic, based, as it is, upon the backward glance of a person who has steeped himself in these writings—or, as the title of the essay puts it, one reader's digest. I suspect, however, that other readers of the same material would come to similar conclusions.

At the outset it must be admitted that there are few surprises in these accounts. One does not emerge from reading them with a radically different perception of what schools are like and how they operate, but rather with a confirmation of knowledge already held, even though it might have been little more than a lurking suspicion before the reading.

Certainly the most general statement that can be made about these reports as a group is that they reveal, often in painstaking and sometimes in boring detail, the complexity of schools and their operations. They also reveal some of the difficulties involved in making sense of that complexity. Both the complexity and the difficulty of coming to grips with it are entirely understandable. If we think of thirty children and one adult inhabiting a room for five or so hours a day, one hundred eighty days a year, we instantly realize that the story of what goes on there is bound to be complicated, even if only partially told. Join several of these units together in one building, add an administrative superstructure, including the supportive services of janitors, secretaries, and the like, and the plot thickens. Finally, place this complex institution in its social and physical context, which includes the network of parental expectations, political pressures, and community concerns, to mention only a few of the more obvious forces impinging from the outside, and the chronicler who wishes his description to reflect faithfully that multifaceted reality is faced with a gargantuan task.

Yet a confrontation with this complexity is essential if we are to understand some of the troubles that beset schools. For the second inescapable conclusion left with the reader of these reports is that educators themselves often fail to appreciate the tangle of forces in which they are enmeshed. As a consequence, they often are lured by simplified schemes and the promise of miracle cures for our educational ailments. The result, almost inevitably, is frustration and a sense of disillusionment. That slow curdling of initial optimism is dramatically revealed in several of these reports.

As might be expected, many observers have chosen to work in novel educational settings—schools or classrooms in which new pedagogical ideas are being introduced. Thus, some of the most informative studies that have been carried out so far contain descriptions of open classrooms, parent co-ops, schools-without-walls, free schools, and other innovative practices. Sadly enough, most of these reports turn out to be accounts of experiments that failed or at least fell far short of the expectations of both participants and onlookers. Educators, it seems, are continually relearning the wisdom of Burns's well-known adage about the best laid schemes of mice and men.

What goes wrong? Why do our dreams of educational reform so often come to nothing? There seems to be no easy answer to these questions, for the complexity that has already been mentioned affords many points of slippage between theory and practice, dream and reality. In some instances the plans of innovators are based on unrealistic assumptions or rely on false facts. Other schemes flounder because they demand more of participants than is humanly possible. Still others come a cropper because of poor planning or political naiveté. Always, however, it is evident that the would-be reformers failed to take into account some aspect of the complexity of school life; some crucial part was missing.

Although these missing parts are by no means the same in each tale of unsuccessful reform, at least two interrelated sources of difficulty are mentioned sufficiently often to warrant thinking of them as recurrent blind spots in our educational vision. The first has to do with a tendency to idealize the human condition, and particularly the nature of childhood, in such a way that plans based on this idealization are doomed to failure almost from the start. The second, which is in some ways the exact opposite of the first, has to do with a corresponding tendency to undervalue and even to denigrate the importance of institutional form and management, all of those arrangements that might be lumped under the somewhat pejorative label "bureaucratic structure." The first tendency leads to an overzealous celebration of all that is "natural" in man; the other to an overharsh condemnation of all that is "artificial" about his institutions, particularly schools.

An ennobling view of man and an inspiring depiction of those who work on behalf of such a view are no doubt essential if we are to recruit sufficient numbers of people to what have come to be referred to in occupational terms as "the helping professions." The feeling of having contributed to a noble cause is probably also important in retaining people in these lines of work. Indeed, as financial rewards and other benefits, such as social status, diminish from one occupation to another down the occupational scale, we might expect the motivational role of such an ideal vision to increase in importance.

While they may provide the practitioner with a sense of mission and may fire his energies, such idealized conceptions also have a negative effect. They often leave him unprepared for the harsher and more mundane realities of his work. Shock, disillusionment, and, sometimes, cynicism are the results. Confronted with such rude awakenings not a few teachers leave the classroom for some other form of work. Such an extreme reaction is reported time and again in observational accounts of educational reform efforts. Moreover, though beginning teachers, like newlyweds, are naturally more vulnerable to what might almost be thought of as a posthoneymoon letdown than are their more seasoned colleagues who have weathered some storms, the latter are by no means immune to the same malaise. The experienced teacher or administrator who launches a new practice based on a glowing description of how it should work is often as badly burned as the neophyte. Repeated accounts of such experiences raise interesting questions about the functional and dysfunctional roles of idealism in educational affairs. A certain amount of idealism is obviously necessary, but it is equally obvious that there can be too much of a good thing. How to strike a proper balance seems, as always, to be the problem.

If starry-eyed views of what students are like and how teaching should proceed sometimes lead to trouble in the classroom, so too does an excessive disdain for the standardization and regimentation of organizational life, particularly that form of it that has come to characterize our graded school system. As mentioned, many observational studies focused on schools or classrooms in which new educational practices were being tried: free schools, open classrooms, parent co-ops, and at least one secondary school of the schools-without-walls variety. With minor exceptions these reform efforts have been stimulated by a dissatisfaction with more conventional educational practices, such as grade level divisions, the compartmentalization of the curriculum into various subject matters, the division of the school day into time periods of equal length, and the general proliferation of rules and regulations that govern the conduct of both teachers and students in most schools.

While acknowledging a basic sympathy with the goals of most of these reform efforts, I must confess to a mild feeling of amusement as I read accounts of would-be reformers in action. For, despite their best efforts, so the reports tell us, the reformers found themselves reinstating discarded organizational arrangements and routines—from achievement testing and attendance records to the raising of hands during discussions and the invoking of "no talking" rules—practices that they had specifically disavowed using in the beginning. This slow reemergence of traditional practices is much more, however, than a source of mild amusement for those of us seriously interested in the future of educational reform. It calls attention to a topic about which we need to give much more careful thought than we have in the past, one whose empirical manifestations are especially well illuminated by observational accounts of the sort being considered here.

In broadest terms the topic to which I refer is the dysjunction between the enterprise of education, conceived of as planned intervention in the release of a person's potential, and the institutional manifestation of that process when applied to large numbers of individuals. It concerns, in other words, the mismatch between what we would like to do as educators and what we are forced to do as designers and managers of social institutions. Some might think of this as nothing more than the age-old gap between theory and practice, but the cleavage is deeper and more profound than we might reckon.

Schools are more, much more, than collective attempts to put educational theory into practice. We could ponder for a lifetime the process of education as something that happens to an individual, without hitting on the design of schools as they have evolved in our society. It is only when we contemplate the requirements of social, economic, and political reality that the form schools have taken, with all their seemingly meaningless and artificial constraints, begins to emerge as a reasonable compromise between what the world would be like if there were only one willing student (and presumably one

omniscient teacher) in it—the starting point and often the finish line
for much of our educational theorizing—and what actually confronts
us when we enter the crowded classroom.

This is not to suggest that in our schools as they are presently
designed we have come up with the perfect solution to the problem
of how to educate large numbers of people. It does mean, however,
that there is a functional utility to most, if not all, of the practices
that have endured in our schools for any length of time, a utility that
is often overlooked by those who would rid us of what they take to
be the unnecessary evils of a bureaucratic structure. Interestingly
enough, this utility is not always apparent, even to those who feel
comfortable with current practices. As a result, they are hard put to
defend much of what they do, ascribing it to mere custom or tradition. But even custom and tradition are functional, as every anthropologist knows, in the maintenance of a social institution. The baring
of what might be thought of as the tacit rationale underlying many
current practices may be one of the chief contributions of
naturalistic studies to the field of education. We need help in seeing
that many apparently senseless ways of doing things in schools are
not so senseless after all.

This brings us back to the sympathetic stance of the naturalistic
observer. As has been pointed out, most serious observational studies
to date have an understanding, if not exactly forgiving, tone when
reporting on what the observers saw and heard in schools. The question is whether this sympathy, which often comes across as content-
ment with the status quo, is anything more than an implicit confes-
sion of the observer's own ignorance about how to do things better.
Have most naturalistic observers "copped out" of the serious business of trying to improve education, as Kohlberg,[5] for one, has
charged?

That such a charge may be true cannot be gainsaid, for most
observers clearly seem more fascinated by the "is" than the "ought"
of educational practice. But it would be a mistake to see their work
as nothing more than an attempt to defend the status quo. Their true
goal, as I see it, is a deepening of our appreciation of the functions
served by current practice, an effort to help us understand why
things are as they are. Their studies themselves reveal the penalty
paid for the lack of such an understanding.

In the process of describing what goes on in schools, observers inevitably pass judgment on what they see and hear, though that judgment, as we have seen, is not always as negative as some critics of education would like it to be. But judgment it is, nonetheless. What, then, will the contribution of naturalistic studies be to solving the many problems of evaluation that plague the field of education? Naturalistic observers may have neither the temperament nor the skills to plant and nurture the seeds of educational reform, but can they at least help us at the time of harvest to separate the wheat from the chaff? To answer such a question it is necessary to consider briefly what the practice of educational evaluation is like today and where it seems to be headed.

Broadly speaking, evaluation involves making a judgment about the worth of something, but in the field of education the term has taken on the much narrower connotation of measuring the effectiveness of a given procedure or set of procedures. The techniques of measurement typically involve paper-and-pencil tests of scholastic performance, and the unit by which effectiveness is determined is some form of score on those instruments. Given the fact that education is an instrumental activity, consuming time, money, and human energy in its enactment, this narrower definition is understandable. We obviously want to know whether what we are doing is having its desired effect. And we are also interested in achieving that effect in the most economical way.

Yet despite the common sense appeal of this line of reasoning it has led to practices with which many of us, as educators, are vaguely unhappy. Typically the finger of blame for this state of affairs is pointed at the crude state of the art of educational measurement. If only we had better tests, so the argument goes, our evaluation problems would be solved. Acting on this premise, test makers by the hundreds have set about refining instruments for assessing what are increasingly referred to as "outcome variables" in education, or more simply "outputs."

The deficiencies of this linear and econometric model of educational evaluation are now becoming clearer, even to the test makers, thanks in part to the writings of scholars like Michael Scriven, who has done as much as anyone to expand the narrow conception of evaluation that has dominated the thinking of both policy makers and practitioners for decades. Though Scriven's ideas about evaluation are too elaborate even to summarize here, at least three of his notions are worth mentioning in order to give some sense of the direction in which the field is moving today. All these ideas, in my judgment, bring professional evaluators closer to some of the realities faced by practicing educators.

First, Scriven distinguishes between what he calls *formative* and *summative* evaluation, between judgment of a work in progress and judgment of a final product. The function of formative evaluation, in this view, is to enable corrective adjustments to be made while a plan is in action. It employs the notion of continual feedback of information that is used to guide the course of pedagogical action.

Secondly, Scriven calls for a form of evaluation that he terms *goal-free*, by which he means looking at what is happening in a school or a classroom independently of what the planners of a program claim should be happening. In some ways this admonition is like the more familiar entreaty to look for concomitant learnings and unwanted side effects. It is a plea for a broader vision that extends beyond declared ends and goals.

Thirdly, in his more recent writings Scriven has argued for including goals themselves as objects of evaluation, rather than limiting our evaluative concern to the means by which goals are reached. This suggestion involves the evaluator directly in the many value decisions that lie at the heart of education. It makes him more of a critic of current practices.

These three suggestions clearly take us beyond the narrow confines of measurement and effectiveness as we have known them in the field of education. In so doing, they return us to the more general task of judging the worth of our educational efforts, a task whose dimensions become clearer, if also more complicated, as we reflect on the picture of schooling provided by naturalistic studies.

If there is one thing these studies communicate, loud and clear, it is how unlike factories with their inputs and outputs schools really are and how deficient are the metaphors that lead us to think of the two types of institutions as at all comparable. Among people who profess to be educational evaluators it has become commonplace to talk about learning outcomes and to think of those outcomes as being revealed by scores on an examination of one sort or another. But when we actually look at teachers and administrators it is hard to think of them as producing those outcomes. Indeed, if we take seriously the implicit message contained in these naturalistic studies we would call into question the idea of educators "producing" anything. To think in these industrial terms is probably to take a wrong turn in our efforts to conceptualize the educative process.

This is not to deny that much learning takes place in school. But evidence of its having taken place, particularly when expressed in test scores summated across groups of students, offers at best a very crude measure of how well the educators in charge are doing their job. If we look at teachers carefully and watch what principals do, we cannot help but conclude that to teach well or to administer a school properly involves much more than having students who score highest on a final exam or a school that boasts the largest number of Merit scholars per budget dollar. The real measure of educational merit, as naturalistic studies make crystal clear, is the extent to which teachers and principals make decisions that fit the situation, do things that make sense, given the myriad variables at work. It is the extent to which they act in ways that are at once ingenious, artful, shrewd, compassionate, and sometimes even wise. It is, in short, the extent to which we give thought to what we are doing as educators.

These studies also reveal, however, how difficult such advice is to take. They show us in vivid detail how few teachers and administrators manage to maintain a high level of thoughtfulness in the daily business of juggling the many components of their educational world. This is not a criticism per se as much as it is a statement about the human condition and the complexity of those institutions we call schools.

Given this condition and this complexity how are we to proceed in improving on the way things are? Naturalistic studies do not provide answers as much as they delineate the conceptual framework within which the search for answers must take place. In this sense they are more closely akin to critical treatises than to manuals of style. In short, they reveal in concrete terms what has been done. It is left to the reader to deduce what he, in his setting, must do.

This may seem like a meager contribution to the art of educational evaluation, and so it is; it is even more meager, perhaps, than the contribution of literary criticism, art criticism, and musical criticism to our ability to judge performances in those areas. Moreover, even if the number of such studies were to be increased manyfold we could not expect to obtain a careful and judicious look at all or even most educational settings, any more than we can expect to obtain from our art and literary and music critics a careful judgment of every painting set on canvas or every book written or every musical performance. At best we can hope for a close critique of only a very few of our educational "works."

Yet progress in art, so history tells us, is due in part to what thoughtful critics who look and listen carefully say about it. Why, then, should the same not be true in education? If we can talk sensibly and helpfully about the spread of pigments on a square of canvas or about the arrangements of sounds in a musical composition, why is it not possible to talk with equal sense and in a way that is equally helpful about what happens in schools and classrooms? I think it is possible. So do the authors of the studies I have read. Read them and judge for yourself.

Notes

1. The published writings on which this essay is based include Louis M. Smith and William Geoffrey, *The Complexities of an Urban Classroom* (New York: Holt, Rinehart and Winston, 1968); Louis M. Smith and Patricia M. Keith, *Anatomy of an Educational Innovation* (New York: John Wiley, 1971); Harry L. Gracey, *Curriculum or Craftsmanship* (Chicago: University of Chicago Press, 1972); Philip A. Cusick, *Inside High School* (New York: Holt, Rinehart and Winston, 1973); David H. Hargreaves, *Social Relations in a Secondary School* (London: Routledge and Kegan Paul; New York: Humanities Press, 1967); Calvin Wayne Gordon, *The Social System of the High School* (Glencoe, Ill.: Free Press, 1957); Edgar Zodiag Friedenberg, *Coming of Age in America* (New York: Random House, 1965); Jules Henry, *On Education* (New York: Random House, 1971); Roland S. Barth, *Open Education and the American School* (New York: Agathon Press, 1972); and Philip W. Jackson, *Life in Classrooms* (New York: Holt, Rinehart and Winston, 1968).

Unpublished sources include a set of working papers prepared by Fritz Ianni and his associates at Teachers College, Columbia University, Steve Wilson's doctoral study of Chicago's Metro School (on which I served as an adviser), and two studies in progress—one by William Firestone, which focuses on parent-operated "free" schools, the other by Marki LeCompte, which concerns the tacit socialization process taking place in classrooms.

2. These data-gathering procedures resemble, in general, those of the anthropological fieldworker, a fact that has led reviewers and a few investigators themselves to speak of this genre of writing as though it were a form of anthropology, sometimes referring to it as "educational anthropology." Without getting into the question of what constitutes an anthropological study, besides its reliance on field work as a source of data, I think it is fair to say that the resemblance between most of these educational studies and standard anthropological field studies is not very great. Few, if any, of the investigators have had formal training in anthropology, they typically do not cite anthropological studies as sources of ideas or as points of reference, and they do not share the anthropologist's interest in cultural comparison, macroscopic social organization, kinship structure, institutional evolution, and the like.

To the extent that these investigators have their roots in any discipline within the social sciences, sociology seems to be the most likely intellectual heritage. In this connection it is interesting to note that Willard Walter Waller's classic *Sociology of Teaching* (New York: Russell and Russell, 1961) is far and away the most frequently cited reference in the bibliographies appended to these reports. Other references to sociological literature are abundant, in particular to the writings of Howard Becker, Severyn Bruyn, Charles Bidwell, and Robert Dreeben. Roger Barker and his associates at the University of Kansas are among the most frequently cited psychologists.

3. The intellectual justification and methodological elaboration of this approach is most clearly and persuasively presented in Barney G. Glaser and Anselm L. Strauss, *The Discovery of Grounded Theory* (Chicago: Aldine, 1967), a work that is cited frequently by the investigators under discussion.

4. This is in sharp contrast to another class of writings that have a superficial resemblance to those under discussion—the books and articles written by the so-called radical critics of American education, a group that is also sometimes referred to as the romantic critics of our schools. Many of these writers, like those discussed here, have

based what they have to say on firsthand observations of school life. In a sense, then, they may be said to have undertaken naturalistic studies of educational affairs.

The differences, however, between these two classes of reportage are great, even though they are frequently differences of degree rather than kind. The critics, for the most part, are just that: critics. They make little or no pretense of trying to give an objective or balanced account of what is going on in the schools in which they have visited or worked. Instead, they concentrate on exposing what they take to be the weaknesses or, in extreme cases, the evils of our educational system. As a result, their writings tend to be much more evaluative and much less analytic than those discussed in this essay. Given their avowed goal of arousing public awareness and, I suppose, indignation, they understandably employ a prose style that is more journalistic and strident in tone than that found in the writings of the more academic investigators. In sum, the writings of the critics might be called "hot"; those of the academics, "cool."

The attention paid these differences is not intended as a criticism of the critics of our schools. Indeed, there is nothing inherently wrong with educational exposés, and much to be said in their favor. There is, however, a danger in confusing educational journalism with serious studies of how schools and classrooms operate. It is to that danger that this caveat is addressed.

5. Lawrence Kohlberg, "Moral Development and the New Social Studies," *Social Education* 37 (May 1973): 369-75.

Faculty Critique

by MICHAEL W. APPLE

Let me begin my comments on Professor Jackson's paper with a fundamental premise: Educational thought has by and large wedded itself to inappropriate perspectives. It has been apt to search for simple means to deal with unsimple problems. It thus is relatively ineffective in confronting the day-to-day reality of classroom situations and in engaging in the imaginative yet disciplined inquiry that would enable a significantly new educational reality to evolve. This is especially true of the styles of research that dominate the literature on evaluation. Therefore, I welcome the current growth of naturalistic studies that Professor Jackson describes. However, I do believe that his presentation is limited in that it may ignore some important aspects of naturalistic models of research, especially their ability to bring out in the open what schools actually *do* value, something that may have little relation to the school's goal statement.

Also his presentation runs the risk of negating the importance of the disaffiliation and outrage many students, parents, educators, and others express about the process of schooling as it is practiced in a large segment of our educational institutions. Professor Jackson's paper, though, does present an articulate and honest appraisal of the state of the art of naturalistic studies. I would briefly like to explore both the strengths and a few of the weaknesses of his analysis here and point to further possible uses of the research he describes so well.

All too often, research in education is of the "horse race" type, and it has led to an overabundance of "no significant difference" results. One reason for this is our lack of understanding of the density of the situations in most classrooms. Researchers often approach educational institutions with predetermined notions about how "scientific" inquiry must look and with a conviction that this basic model of research—a strict-science model—will ultimately lead to a thorough understanding and control of educative environments. Aside from the fact that this conviction is probably misplaced, naturalistic studies are helpful counterbalances to the tendency to approach classrooms with preconceptions. As Matza puts it, "The commitment to naturalism is *to phenomena and their nature; not* to Science or any other system of standards."[1] In this way naturalistic investigations provide a partial corrective to some of the more vulgar forms of scientism that prevail in educational research.

The notion behind a naturalistic model is to render the phenomenon cogently in a manner that preserves its integrity—not the integrity of any theoretical viewpoint.[2] Thus, it can tend to disavow or at least raise serious questions about educational research that is tied so strongly to an input-output ideology. Jackson's discussion of just this point is particularly useful. Schools are not factories, and we misperceive the ongoing dynamics of the institution and the transformational qualities of students if we continually couch our questions in that language form.

In this regard, one idea should be mentioned that is made strikingly clear in Jackson's points. If naturalistic studies do nothing else
(and they can accomplish much more than this), they show the
profound human complexity in classrooms, the wealth of types and
styles of interaction, the dilemmas of influence, freedom, and responsibility. To assume, as most educators have, that the language of
psychology is an adequate descriptive device to deal with this welter
of events is not to take this complexity seriously enough.

Professor Jackson is quite correct in asserting that naturalistic
studies will not answer all the questions one might want to ask about
school evaluation. However, in saying this, it is possible to overlook
some of the very real contributions they can make, contributions he
does not actually bring to the fore.

Naturalistic research may be the most potent tool we have for
seeing the effect that commonsense definitions have in school settings. In schools, "play" activity is commonsensically differentiated
from "work" activity, "academic" from "nonacademic," "teachers"
from "students," and so on, and it is quite important that we begin
to illuminate how this occurs, what effect it has on the tacit teaching
to children of what is predetermined as valuable knowledge in our
commonsense thought, and how this confirms existing preconceptions outside of educational institutions. Naturalistic models also enable us to see how knowledge is *used* in institutions. How are traditions and knowledge filtered through teachers?[3] What happens to
curricular formulations when they "pass through" the individuals
involved in schooling? How is this knowledge then transformed by
the children themselves?[4] These are important questions, and we
have made little progress in even asking them properly, much less
answering them.

Naturalistic research can also show how institutions create and
attach labels to individuals and groups of students and teachers.
These labels then help to distribute educational goods and services
differentially by class, race, and sex. For example, as Goffman and
others have shown so well, commonsense labels are not necessarily
neutral categories that are used for therapeutic purposes.[5] When a
child is labeled a remedial problem, a slow learner, or the like, this
may *not* ultimately help him or her. Rather, it can and most often
does have a decidedly harmful effect. The labels have an essentializ-
ing quality: the student is considered "this and only this" in most if

not all of his or her future encounters in schools. Just as important, the distribution of labels by educators is a moral act, primarily because the child then is quite often seen as "different and inferior." Thus, the tendency is to impute culpability to the student once a label is applied rather than to examine the regularities of the institution that creates and distributes these categories in the first place. Naturalistic studies can most certainly enable us to get a more complete understanding of this process.

One thing Professor Jackson certainly does is see the existing reality of schools. This is both a strength and a weakness. He says that statements that embody an "enobling view of man" and that argue against the current basic forms of schooling, though they should not really be frowned upon—after all, they are helpful in bringing committed recruits into the teaching profession—ultimately do not enable educators to face reality. The educators therefore become cynical and disillusioned. While there is no doubt that too much educational literature has an overromanticized view of the human condition, the rest of the statement, it seems to me, ignores the fact that shock, disillusionment, and perhaps even cynicism, may be quite warranted. If Jackson means that we must prepare teachers to face what schools are "really" like, so that they are not totally overwhelmed, all well and good—though I must admit I do not quite understand what the programmatic implications of such a position are if we are serious about what has been called the naturalistic fallacy (the "is to ought" problem). If he also means that this reality should be accepted without some sense of serious disquietude, he is on rather shaky ground. One need only walk into many of the ghetto schools of Chicago or New York or the schools of some of our more affluent suburbs to realize that something is *basically* wrong with these institutions. We may have to face the fact squarely that "realistic tinkering" may not suffice to make them effective educational settings.

In his arguments, then, Jackson does seem sometimes to be a bit too sympathetic to the existing regularities of, say, large schools. He argues that even seemingly meaningless bureaucratic practices are not really senseless in that they relate to other practices and goals of the school. This is undoubtedly true, of course. But that is exactly the point. Any attempt at substantive change in an educational setting must begin with the full realization that things *are* so interconnected,

and, thus, if changes are to be effective, even more extensive alterations in the basic forms of interaction may have to be attempted.
One gets the impression that Professor Jackson might anticipate with
some foreboding the disorder that such alterations could create, and
I find this understandable. It is possible, though, that the conflict
and disorder will have educative effects that significantly outweigh
their difficulties.[6]

Professor Jackson puts his finger on an interesting and rather crucial point when he notes that descriptive research can signify a covert
commitment to maintain the "status quo." This need not be the
case, however. As his excellent book *Life in Classrooms* so vividly
shows, "mere" understanding can go a long way in enabling concerned educators to create more responsive educational institutions;
but this is true *only* if it is coupled with and guided by an informed
ethical and political sensitivity. This is what makes any process of
understanding or any hermeneutic act so ambivalent. It can be used
as a mode by which one can understand and hence insert oneself in
the critical struggle to overcome institutional reification and the industrial consciousness that pervades educational thought, or it can
lead to bringing human activity under even more institutional control.[7] Even with my criticisms of his presentation, I have little doubt
that Professor Jackson favors the former not the latter.

Notes

1. David Matza, *Becoming Deviant* (Englewood Cliffs, N.J.: Prentice-Hall, 1969), p. 3.

2. Ibid., p. 6. The fact that curriculum thought has contributed to
this problem by having a rather abysmal record of relying on *one*
theoretical viewpoint to guide its research and practice is discussed in
Joseph Schwab, *The Practical: A Language for Curriculum* (Washington, D.C.: National Education Association, 1970).

3. See Nell Keddie, "Classroom Knowledge," in *Knowledge and
Control,* ed. by Michael F. D. Young (London: Collier-Macmillan,
1971), pp. 133-60.

4. See Robert MacKay, "Conceptions of Children and Models of
Socialization," in *Childhood and Socialization,* ed. by Hans Peter
Dreitzel (New York: Macmillan, 1973), pp. 27-43.

5. The chapter by Apple in this volume has further discussion of this point.

6. See Richard Sennett, *The Uses of Disorder* (New York: Random House, Vintage Books, 1970).

7. Important here is the discussion of three modes of "sciencing," each guided by different practical interests, that can act to support or deny the process of reification, in Trent Schroyer, "Toward a Critical Theory for Advanced Industrial Society," in *Recent Sociology II,* ed. by Hans Peter Dreitzel (New York: Macmillan, 1970), pp. 210-34.

Author's Reply to Faculty Critique

Thank you for your kind reactions to what I had to say. I'm sure you didn't mean it to sound, and I certainly don't want to sound, as though I were opposed to anthropological studies in schooling. On the contrary, I'd like to see more of them, better done, than those already available. I'm inclined to raise in my mind the question of the contribution of such studies to evaluation decisions, the ongoing, on-the-line decisions that all of us, from classroom teachers to state superintendents, have to make. And I do not consider the kind of anthropological studies that deserve the label anthropological as helpful in that domain as some other sorts of investigations, simply because of the compression phenomenon of having to act quickly, with incomplete data. But I didn't mean to speak against anthropological studies at all.

I have been trying to conduct such a study, keeping a diary for the last three years. I don't suppose I'll ever be able to publish what I've learned, because libel laws and other factors would prevent it. I would have to disguise it so badly that it would lose all of its guts, and I don't know what I'll do with all the data I've been collecting. The study doesn't help me decide any of that range of questions I described in my paper, except insofar as it is a part of the large, apperceptive mass (if I may introduce a rather anachronistic term) that affects in some untold way the decisions that I make and the perceptions of the world that I have. I expected to make my perceptions more complex, perhaps, to enrich my understanding of anthropological studies, and maybe more importantly to humanize my perceptions. I think what we see in the best of the anthropological studies is the world as perceived by a human being. All data are perceived by human beings, but what we see in anthropological studies is the human being as an instrument of observation who colors the report in important ways.

As you were talking, I was reminded of a quotation from George Spindler's book *Being an Anthropologist: Field Work in Eleven Cultures.*[1] If you've not read it, you ought to take a look at it. It consists of very personal descriptions of eleven anthropologists working all over the world, including one working in the United States—how they are collecting data, how they got into the culture, where they found their informants, how they kept notes. I love to hear people talk about their craft. The old *Paris Review* used to do a "Writers at Work" series. Spindler's book is that same sort of document, only the people writing are anthropologists. In his introduction Spindler says the following, which I think is interesting:

> Experience, perception, and interpretation occur in a kaleidoscopic relationship to all events past and present in the experience of the observer-interpreter. There can be no "culture," "social system," or "community" in the absolute, transcendental sense. There is culture, social system, and community as perceived and interpreted. Unless the observer is psychotic, the ethnography is never relative only and wholly to the observer. But all ethnographies are partly personal documents, balanced by strivings for objectivity. Attempts are frequently made, by experienced as well as inexperienced field workers, to be dispassionate observers. To be truly dispassionate in a human community would be inhuman—a profound bias that does not enhance objectivity. A great stride toward objectivity is taken when personal involvement is acknowledged, for once acknowledged it can be recognized, to some extent controlled, and even utilized as a source of valuable data and insight. Ultimately we may understand the use of human perception, feeling, and experience as scientific instrumentation appropriate to the study of human life.

I think that is one of the things that make the anthropological work in education exciting to me: there is the quality of a human trying to make sense of the kaleidoscopic qualities of schooling—recognizing the complexities of them and trying to deal with them. One of the questions is whether the anthropologist is writing for the people he studies or for an audience of other anthropologists or consumers of anthropological literature. That is, did the Trobriand Islanders read Malinovsky? I'm pleased that you like *Life in Classrooms,* but I often felt when I was writing it as Dylan Thomas did when he wrote his poem, "In My Dark and Sullen Craft": that he is writing poems for lovers who are never going to read his poetry and who maybe don't even need to. One of the things that makes me uneasy is whether the material that I or other ethnographers, anthropological types, write will really help the people who are making educational decisions. I don't know. I feel a little bit about these anthropological studies the way I feel about reading a novel. Am I different for having read *Crime and Punishment?* Yes, I suppose I really am. I'll never forget Raskolnikov and his problems. Does it affect my decision-making behavior? I have no idea. That's the uncertainty I felt and tried to express in my paper. Am I willing to consume more anthropological studies? Yes. Do I wish everybody that? Yes. Am I at all convinced that there's some kind of direct contribution between that consumption and improved educational practice or decision making? I must end with a question mark.

Audience Discussion

The Value of Classroom Studies

Q: How can we benefit from studies that view closely what goes on in classrooms?

Jackson: I'm going to approach the point I want to make rather obliquely, and I hope I get there. One of the most interesting directions of educational research, in my judgment (speaking now not about evaluation), and maybe one that might be improved or moved along by quasi-anthropological devices or techniques, has to do with looking at what goes on in classrooms in a very, very microscopic way, using a very fine-grained analysis. Rosenthal's work[2] has been badly criticized and perhaps justifiably so. I think one of the reasons his work was so readily accepted was because it seemed to provide empirical support for something everybody already knew, namely that somehow expectations of teachers, or expectations in general, are communicated to people and that they become in some way a self-fulfilling prophecy. Now we find investigators asking about the medium through which these expectations are communicated.

No teacher (except for the few psychotic people who still rattle around in the profession) would come up to a child and say, "You know, I think you're stupid. You really haven't got it," and so forth. Yet we do know that thousands of children come out of our schools every year with that message indelibly stamped in their psyches. How are such messages communicated if it is not done blatantly? What we are beginning to see, although I wouldn't want to put a lot of blue chips on the data at this point, is that those expectations are communicated by very subtle and quasi-unconscious twitches, such as the ones Brophy and Goode talked about.[3] Their data suggest that when teachers are asking questions of high achievers, (a) the teacher and the kid have eyeball contact, and they hold eyeball contact during the few seconds of the interchange; (b) if the child pauses in giving an answer, the teacher tolerates the pause for quite a long time; (c) if the child gives a wrong answer, the teacher rephrases the question. Now, in the case of the low-achieving youngster, all of those are reversed: (a) the kid is picking lint off his pants, and the teacher is looking out the window; (b) if the kid pauses the teacher tolerates a significantly smaller pause in the case of the low-achieving child (and these are in fractions of a second almost, because the pauses are never long), and (c) if the child gives a wrong answer, or fails to answer, the teacher, rather than rephrasing the question, asks the same question of another child, usually a high-achieving child. Now I don't believe that the teachers are doing this consciously. I don't think any teacher is out consciously to destroy a kid or to make him feel poorly.

Well, that kind of fine-grained analysis, which anthropological investigators are good at, may give us new insights into the long-term significance of some otherwise apparently trivial classroom phenomena. I've long been an advocate of the importance of the trivial, the seemingly inconsequential events that become consequential, that become important as a function of their cumulative significance. If you consider the great amount of time people spend in schools, and if you think of the relative stereotyping of the experiences they have there, you get a piling up over many months and years; the obvious analogue is the silt in the riverbed. If you sit there and peer through the water, you really can't see it happening; it's so minuscule. Maybe our anthropological efforts will adjust our vision so that we become more attuned to the microscopic aspects of classrooms and their potential significance. I also think Mr. Scriven's point is well taken, that mere interest in the descriptions of the classrooms can be a bog, insofar as real decision making and evaluation are concerned.

Notes

1. George Dearborn Spindler, ed., *Being an Anthropologist: Field Work in Eleven Cultures* (New York: Holt, Rinehart and Winston, 1970).

2. Robert Rosenthal and Lenore Jacobson, *Pygmalion in the Classroom* (New York: Holt, Rinehart and Winston, 1968).

3. Thomas L. Good and Jere E. Brophy, *Looking in Classrooms* (New York: Harper and Row, 1973).

5

Empirical Methods and Questions in Evaluation

RICHARD J. LIGHT

What is wonderful about science is that one gets such a great return of conjecture for such a trifling investment of fact.

Mark Twain

For evaluators of new programs, the next few years promise a great challenge. In the 1960s, for the first time, both government agencies and vast segments of the public supported the idea of active interventions to improve the cognitive and affective development and the physical health of children. Thus, programs such as Head Start, Follow Through, Upward Bound, and the Community Mental Health efforts were developed and funded.

Yet at the end of the decade, something turned sour. Support for these interventions began to dry up. Perhaps it was because several evaluations of these efforts suggested that "on the average" they were not doing much good. Perhaps it was because of the general political temper of the times. In any case, program developers in education and public health now find it much harder to get new programs started. Just as in the legal profession probable cause must sometimes be demonstrated to get a court hearing, in education probable success must now be argued to gain backing for a new program.

This is where the challenges come. I feel there may be a rough analogy between the situation that education interventions face today and what medical programs in hospitals faced about 150 years ago. Most people recognized the need for them. Most people were willing to finance their development and improvement, to a reasonable degree. Yet, many candid doctors of that time admitted their lack of knowledge about how to go about designing new medical programs.

In one sense, the doctors of 150 years ago even had an edge on today's educators. At least they could tell in a reasonably short time, sometimes within a few days, whether their patients improved or not. We in education generally do not have that luxury. Yet for most large-scale interventions, whether they take the form of activity programs, such as Head Start, or simply the development of curricula modules and materials, public tax money is used. If the public is asked to support various interventions, it is reasonable for funding agencies to require that early versions of a new program be carefully evaluated, and that what is learned from these evaluations be fed back into newer versions of the program, so that "outcomes" for children can be demonstrably improved.

The contribution of evaluators must be to help program developers achieve these aims in the most effective way possible. Thus, evaluators must carefully study each step in their procedures. They must do a sort of "sensitivity analysis," by asking which component of their overall activity, if changed slightly, might lead to substantial changes in their inferences about how well a new educational program is working, or whether it works at all. I believe this most sensitive component lies in the choice of a statistical model to describe an intervention.

Any evaluation of a new program, whether it is a large-scale national effort or a local curriculum experiment, involves several steps. One step requires specifying precisely the goals and then the design of the program, to isolate the dependent and independent variables. A second step is the selection of a statistical model to underlie the analysis of the program. The final step involves choosing the specific procedures for data analysis. Much has been written about the design of educational experiments—there exists a vast literature on natural experiments versus truly designed experiments versus observational studies (see Campbell and Stanley, 1963; Cochran, 1965; Light and

Smith, 1970). Still more discussion is available in quite fine detail on procedures for data analysis (for example, details of sophisticated procedures, such as two-stage least squares to estimate parameters and multiple covariance analysis to adjust for several "disturbing variables," appear in statistics texts such as Winer, 1962, and Kirk, 1968). Yet little discussion appears in the educational literature about the importance, and implications, of the model selected to underlie the evaluation. Choosing a model before specific data analysis procedures are applied may influence the results and inferences an evaluation will yield. In the first part of this essay, I will focus on some conditions under which the choice of a model may have this effect.

I concentrate on five issues. First, after considering two experimental paradigms, I will discuss the implications of building models from theoretical considerations about how a program works, rather than empirically by curve-fitting procedures. Secondly I consider several kinds of statistical errors that can influence the results of an evaluation and some implications of these errors. The goal of minimizing different kinds of errors may lead to conflicting policies on how to build the most useful evaluation models. Thirdly, I illustrate the interactive process of using data analysis to help choose from among competing theories about how a program works. Fourthly, I briefly describe several alternative procedures for conducting evaluations of new programs and note some strengths and weaknesses of each. Finally, I review the impact that errors of measurement can have in influencing the outcome under specific evaluation models. In the second part of this essay, I consider some of the changes I expect to see in future evaluation efforts.

To begin, let us examine several issues facing the evaluator in his initial selection of an experimental approach.

Choosing among Experimental Paradigms

Evaluations of new programs can have at least two general thrusts. The first and most common is the comparison of the experimental program with a control group. In this situation, the general conclusion will take the form: "On the average, the new program has an impact on the experimental group that is better than [or worse than or no different from] the impact of the 'nonprogram' on the control group." This kind of evaluation is in some ways the easiest to conceptualize, because it ultimately compares two means, the experimental mean and the control mean. More sophisticated forms of this approach break the experimental and control groups into identifiable subgroups, to see whether the difference between the means differs for different subgroups.

A second kind of evaluation focuses much less on overall comparisons between the program and the control, and instead examines the particular features of program centers that seem to have the most beneficial effect on children in those centers. Thus, rather than comparing all program centers to all control centers, the second approach looks for variables whose main effects and interactions seem to have positive effects on outcomes. New centers are then set up with the values of these variables extended in the direction that seems to improve outcomes. Thus, by sequentially studying program centers and modifying their features in directions that appear desirable, the evaluation "iterates in" on program centers that gradually become more and more effective. For further details of this procedure, see Light and Smith (1970).

Both kinds of evaluations have at least two sources of errors. One source is an incorrect specification of the model of effects. A second source is the errors of measurement that may underlie both the dependent and the independent variables. An example of the first source would be using a standard linear evaluation model when the most important effects were strongly quadratic. An example of the second source would be the use of tests and measures that are either quite unreliable or biased. When choosing a model for an evaluation, both types of potential errors should be kept in mind. They have implications for decisions that are as basic as choosing the form of the dependent variable. For example, suppose that pre-program and post-program measures of a variable such as achievement or accomplishment are available. Then a classic question in evaluation has been to decide under what conditions the dependent variable should be the raw final score as opposed to a raw gain score or the final score with the initial score as a covariate. Usually this question is examined only in the context of a linear model, with its constraining assumptions (see Werts and Linn, 1969, for a discussion of these constraining assumptions). But other models—curvilinear, multiplicative, exponential—should also be viewed as potential candidates in the model derby. We now turn to some arguments in support of this proposal.

When researchers wish to estimate the value of a parameter from a sample statistic, a generally accepted criterion for the "goodness" of an estimate is its mean square error, as defined in (1):

(1) $M.S.E. = \sigma_s^2 + b'^2$

where σ_s^2 is the sampling variance of the statistic, and b' is its estimated bias. But expression (1) should not be generalized directly from a single statistic to judging a statistical model, as it does not include specification error. Therefore, a more complete criterion for judging a model might be that in (2):

(2) $M.S.E. \text{ (model)} = \sigma_m^2 + \sigma_s^2 + b'^2 + \sigma_e^2$

where σ_s^2 and b' are the sampling variance and bias applied to the dependent variable in the context of a complete model; σ_m^2 is the additional variance component due to model misspecification; and σ_e^2 is the additional variance component due to errors of measurement on the independent variables.

There may in some situations be cross-product terms that should appear together with the primary components in (2). For example, σ_e^2 will depend on the size of the pairwise correlations among the independent variables, when one or more are subject to measurement error. But, in general, an evaluator's goal will be to minimize as far as possible each of the four components in (2). We now relate these several potential errors to the choice of a "form" for an evaluation model.

Modeling Procedures Using a Theory Rather than Curve-fitting

The form of a model depends on several factors. One is the theory about how the program should work. Another is the quality of the data collected on the program. The sophistication of a theory can help us to minimize σ_m^2, the specification error. The quality of the data to enter our model will have an impact on σ_e^2, the measurement error.

Current practice in evaluations can be generally summarized as involving the following four procedures:

(1) Data are collected on a dependent variable (such as students' achievement scores) and a pool of "potentially important" independent variables.

(2) A general linear model is postulated, of the form:

$$Y = a + \sum_{i=1}^{p} b_i X_i + \epsilon$$

(3) A stepwise regression analysis is done, to search for the particular set of independent variables that, when entered in the regression equation, minimizes the unexplained variance σ_s^2 for the variable Y.

(4) The variables that were included in the regression are interpreted, according to either their b or their beta coefficients, as having a certain relationship with the dependent variable.

As a curve-fitting procedure this may be entirely satisfactory. If we do not have any theory about how the world works (related to our dependent variable), this dredging of the data may provide useful hypotheses or insights that should be pursued further. But when used as a procedure to evaluate new programs (such as Head Start, say), this curve-fitting suffers from three obvious and important drawbacks:

(1) No estimate of σ_m^2, the model specification error, is available. If R^2 for the "best" equation is low, we will never know whether this is because the form of the model is wrong (i.e., the "true" model is far from linear), or because we have not taken data on important independent variables, or simply because the process we are modeling is not a highly predictable process.

(2) Even if a moderately high R^2 is obtained from the best equation, we have no estimate of how large a "regression to the mean" effect might be. It is worth recalling that with p independent variables in a pool of potential variables to be included in our final linear model, $2^p - 1$ different models may be constructed. Even if none of the $2^p - 1$ potential models is a good representation of the "correct" model, one of them will by definition still turn out to be a best fit. Further, if p is large, one of these $2^p - 1$ equations will probably also yield a moderately high R^2, even if it is not a good approximation of the "correct" model. This is especially true if not many children have been included in the evaluation. The clear implication

here is that while curve-fitting may yield reasonable results, in terms of the proportion of explained variance in the dependent variable, it offers little reliable insight into *how well* a program is working and even less insight into *why* it may or may not be working.

(3) Suppose an important independent variable has been left out of the equation (that is, no data on it were collected). Suppose further that this important variable is moderately correlated with several variables included in the "best" equation. Then it is quite possible that the coefficients of the included variables will be substantially biased. It is even possible that their signs might flip over from positive to negative or vice versa. Again, in the absence of a theory, an evaluator may well try to explain his results by concocting post hoc explanations for coefficients, and relationships, that are severely biased. We will study this argument in more detail later in this paper.

In conclusion, then, the implication of the drawbacks and risks of fitting linear models is that an evaluator should have some theory of how a program works and use statistical procedures to examine the theory, rather than to curve-fit. This further implies that two aspects of a theory must be developed. One is the form of the model that relates program characteristics to program outcomes. The second, and no less important, is the particular set of program features that should appear in the equation. After all, fitting a quadratic model to a potential pool of p independent variables and choosing a best subset may require more sophisticated statistical procedures than fitting a linear model, but the resulting best quadratic fit still suffers from all three of the same curve-fitting drawbacks.

Alternative Forms for a Model

When constructing a theory of how a new program affects children, the first step is generally conceptual: What happens to the children as they are exposed to various program features? Once a conceptual theory has been developed, however, an evaluator has many options about what form his model should take.

As previously indicated, the additive linear model has been the most frequently used (see Cicirelli et al., 1969; Coleman, 1966). I would like to list just a few other candidates. (See Himmelblau, 1970, for a detailed list of alternative models.)

(3) (a) a linear model with nonlinear independent variables:

$$Y = a + \sum_{r=1}^{k} \sum_{i=1}^{p} b_{ir} X_i^r + \epsilon$$

(b) a log-linear model, of the form:

$$\log Y = \log a + b \log X + \epsilon$$

or more generally:

$$\log Y = \log a + \sum_{i=1}^{p} b_i \log X_i + \epsilon$$

(c) a cross-product-term model:

$$Y = a + \sum_{i=1}^{p} b_i X_i + \sum_{i \neq j}^{p} b_{ij} X_i X_j + \epsilon$$

(d) a product model such as:

$$Y = a(1 + b_1 X_1)(1 + b_2 X_2) + \epsilon$$

Note that this has nonlinear components in both the bs and the Xs.
(e) product models such as:

(i) $$Y = a(1 - e^{-bX}) + \epsilon$$

(ii) $$Y = [abX/(1 + bX)] + \epsilon$$

(iii) $$Y = aX^b + \epsilon$$

These various examples are just a small sample of potential alternatives to the standard linear regression. Note also that several of the alternative models are closely related. For example, the log-linear model in (b) is, without logs, the product model of (e)(iii). At this point the reader may be asking what is to be gained by choosing among several different models, some of them rather forbidding at first glance, to describe the way a program works? I can now give a specific example. Look at the three equations in (e) above. Suppose Y represents an achievement score in a certain subject, and X gives the number of hours per week that a new program focuses on that subject. If the reader plots Y as a function of X, $0 \leqslant X \leqslant 10$, he will find that, except for a constant multiplier, all three equations yield approximately the same *pattern* of achievement scores. However, as X exceeds 10, the three models give differing patterns of responses in achievement scores.

Suppose a program (such as Head Start), currently was operating in various centers, and these centers tended to have several hours per week of instruction in this subject but never more than ten. In this event, all three models of (e) would inform the evaluator of a *similar* "relationship" between hours per week of instruction and student achievement. Yet for policy purposes, such as the question of whether instruction should be expanded in this subject, the three models yield *different conclusions*.

Which model is "right"? That is a central question to the evaluator. Answering it is difficult. Yet, as I have argued, the ideal approach would be to specify one model form from a theory, and then to test it out with actual data. For example, if model (e)(i) is the evaluator's best guess, he should be able to estimate the parameters a and b from data he has collected from centers with $0 \leqslant X \leqslant 10$. Then, if several new centers are set up, he should try, say, fifteen hours a week of instruction in these centers. The previously fitted model will give a prediction of student achievement for $X = 15$, and this prediction can be compared with the observed outcomes to determine how well the postulated model explains observed patterns of student achievement.

Some recent work at the Center for Educational Policy Research at Harvard University has incorporated directly into an evaluation this idea of comparing models. Michelson (1970), in a study that used data from Coleman et al. (1966), found that a linear model using interaction (cross-product) terms as independent variables gave much better explanations of student performance than did either simple regressions or curvilinear models. More specifically, the interaction terms were particularly useful in determining that in order to maximize achievement, certain types of teachers are best matched with certain types of students. The simple linear model describes "on the average" relationships, because it forces simple additive constraints onto the data. Using a model with interaction terms yielded results that were not only in a more useful form, but also actually contradicted the results obtained from simple linear models.

Using Regression Models to Test Theories

Having argued the need to examine different models when trying to evaluate a new program, I now turn to a corollary question: How does a researcher use an evaluation to help him choose among several competing explanatory theories? In other words, the process of evaluating a new or experimental program can be viewed as taking place at some point along a continuum. At one extreme a researcher simply fits many different curves to a collected set of data and announces the curve that has given the best fit. I have argued that this extreme is unsatisfactory. At the other extreme, the researcher has a single specified model that he believes will describe the experiment, and the collected data are used to estimate the parameters of this model. While this is the "ideal" end of the continuum, unfortunately we usually do not know enough about an experimental program, such as Head Start, to specify a model precisely. Thus, we are driven toward the center of the precise theory versus curve-fitting continuum, and when doing an actual evaluation we are forced to use a judicious combination of both ideas. In this section I discuss an example of how such a judicious combination may work.

For the sake of this example I focus on a multiple linear regression model with which I hope to explain student achievement scores. Suppose we have collected data from many students, in many schools, on the following four variables, the unit of analysis being each student:

1. the student's verbal achievement score (VAC).

2. the socioeconomic status of the student's parents (SES).

3. an index of socioeconomic status of all other students in each student's school ($OSES$).

4. an index of school attributes for each school, such as per-pupil expenditures, number of books in the library, and average teacher's educational level (SA).

Even when we limit ourselves to the multiple linear regression approach, note that two options are available for analyzing our data. One is the *forward solution,* in which we examine which of the three independent variables, *SES, OSES,* or *SA,* when entered alone into a simple regression equation, gives the highest value of r^2. After finding this "first" independent variable, we search for the second independent variable that, *given the first independent variable already in the equation,* increases the overall multiple R^2 the most. We then continue this process, always searching for the next independent variable that increases R^2 the most, given all the previously selected independent variables in the equation.

Suppose we were to exercise this first option. What might happen? To see, let us examine the Venn diagram in figure 5-1. It shows the

Figure 5-1

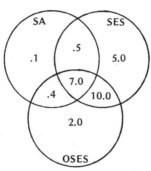

contribution of each of the three independent variables to the total R^2, which is 25 (that is, 25 percent of the variance in *VAC* is explained by the combined effects of *SA, SES,* and *OSES*). Note that the diagram also separates out the *shared variances*. For example, *SES* and *OSES* together share an explanatory 10 percent of variance in *VAC*. Thus, if we were to perform the *forward* multiple regression approach, we would find that *SES* is the single most important variable in explaining variance in *VAC*; it explains 22.5 percent of the variance. *OSES* would enter the equation next, and finally *SA*. Thus, we would conclude that differences among school attributes in our sample explain the least variance in student verbal achievement.

Suppose on the other hand that we believed, from a theoretical point of view, that *SA* was reasonably important as a predictor of *VAC*. We could then have constructed the simple equation:

$$VAC = f(SA)$$

and we would have found a simple r^2 of 8, or approximately one-third of the final multiple R^2 of 25 with all three independent variables. This, then, suggests that school attributes, taken alone, are not such a weak predictor of verbal achievement. The point of this example is to demonstrate that the *shared variance* between and among independent variables can influence the interpretation of which independent variables are important explainers of the variance in *VAC*.

Let us move now to the second option, the *backward solution* to linear regression. This approach begins with the complete multiple regression:

$$VAC = f(SA, SES, OSES)$$

We then ask: If an independent variable is removed from the overall equation, by how much will R^2 fall? Note that by removing SA from the regression equation, the R^2 falls only from 25.0 to 24.9. This is because out of its simple r^2 of 8.0 with VAC, 7.9 is shared with the other two independent variables.

As a general conclusion, we can say that, when dealing with multivariate situations, the forward solution and the backward solution in regression may lead to conflicting inferences about the importance of a particular independent variable. The resolution of this conflict will come from understanding the shared variance among the independent variables.

We can now pursue the example in figure 5-1 to see how data analysis may enable us to choose among competing theories. Suppose that the program evaluator posits the two possible theories of how a program "works" that are shown in figure 5-2. Theory (1) suggests

Figure 5-2

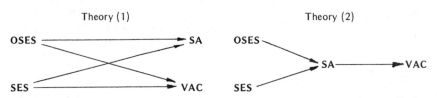

that school attributes are essentially unrelated, or hardly related, to a student's verbal achievement. The variables that "drive" a student's verbal achievement are the socioeconomic status of his parents and his schoolmates' parents. Theory (2) suggests SA should be highly related to VAC, although SA in turn is "driven" by SES and $OSES$. Thus, theory (2) essentially argues that wealthy and highly educated families will create rich schools with many attributes, that in turn will result in high verbal achievement scores by the students. In contrast, theory (1) bypasses the school attributes as a determinant of high verbal achievement scores, and suggests that high scores will result if a child's parents and schoolmates have high socioeconomic status, regardless of the school attributes. Theory (1) eliminates SA as an important "linking" variable.

Using the *backward solution* in regression helps us to choose between these two theories. That is, if we remove *SA* from the complete equation and we find that R^2 hardly drops, we would select theory (1); if R^2 drops substantially, we would have evidence that an arrow from *SA* to *VAC* must exist, and we would select theory (2). Using the actual numbers in the Venn diagram in figure 5-1, when we remove *SA* from the complete equation, R^2 drops from 25.0 to 24.9 percent, so we would select theory (1) as an explanation of how our program was working.

The story can become much more complicated at this point, because the backward solution in regression only enables us to discriminate among certain types of theories, not others. For example, consider theory (3) shown in figure 5-3. That theory suggests that the

Figure 5-3

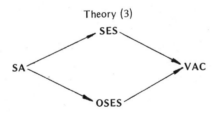

Theory (3)

existence of good school attributes may attract wealthy people or people with high *SES* scores into a program or school, and that these people will then have high verbal achievement scores.

Will the backward solution in regression enable us to test for the existence of theory (3)? The answer is no, because what we need in order to examine theory (3) is a procedure that will tell us if *SA* is a background variable that "drives" the other two independent variables, which in turn are related to the dependent variable. But the backward solution does not enable us to do this, because we are controlling for the two intervening variables. Using our Venn diagram, while the small proportion of variance explained (.1) is attributed to *SA,* it is not coupled directly to *VAC.* Thus, the backward solution would cause us to judge *SA* as being unimportant, whereas in fact if theory (3) is correct *SA* is the primary causal force in the system.

Thus, we may conclude that the backward solution in regression is useful for distinguishing between an intervening variable model such as theory (2) and a spurious variable model such as theory (1). But it is weak in distinguishing between a spurious variable and a prior causal variable that is coupled to the dependent variable only through intervening variables. Thus, if some candidates for primary causal roles—such as *SA* in theory (3)—appear with small unique contributions to R^2, we had better reconsider what might account for this.

While simple curve-fitting with no background theory or model is a bad procedure, the ideal procedure of simply estimating parameters for a perfectly specified theory can rarely be achieved. Rather, an evaluator must judiciously trade off between choosing among several theories and a modest amount of data-fitting, and emerge with what he feels is a reasonable compromise between data-dredging and theory testing.

Simple versus Complex Models

We now turn to a final point about the general form for an evaluation model. As almost any scientist will tell anyone within earshot, a simple model is generally preferable to a complex one. First, a simple model is easier to formulate and to interpret. Secondly, the process of estimating parameters is relatively more tractable. Finally—an important point—a simpler model may lead to lower $\sigma_e{}^2$ due to errors of measurement on the independent variables.

For any model written in the form:

$$Y = f(X_i)$$

the variance in the dependent variable due to errors of measurement on the independent variables can be found from:

$$(4) \qquad \sigma_e{}^2 = \sum_{i=1}^{p} \left[\frac{\partial f(X_i)}{\partial X_i} \right]^2 \sigma_{eX_i}{}^2 + \sum_{i \neq j}^{p}\sum^{p} \frac{\partial f(X_i)}{\partial X_i} \times \frac{\partial f(X_j)}{\partial X_j} \sigma_{eX_i}{}^2 \sigma_{eX_j}{}^2 \rho_{ij}$$

where $\sigma_{e_{X_i}}{}^2$ is the measurement of error variance on variable X_i, and ρ_{ij} is the true correlation between variables X_i and X_j. (See Parratt, 1961, for discussion of this issue.)

The formula in (4) offers some suggestions about general model construction. First, it tells us what we have long known in the context of multiple regression: we should avoid collinear (highly correlated) independent variables. Secondly, it shows us how rapidly errors can accumulate in a model with many independent variables. This implies that if our independent variables may have substantial measurement error, simple models are preferable to complex ones in order to minimize $\sigma_e{}^2$.

However, a minor conflict arises here. Although simpler models reduce $\sigma_e{}^2$, more complex models are generally needed to reduce $\sigma_m{}^2$, the specification error. Few real life programs are highly determined by the settings of only one or two independent variables. This conflict is difficult to resolve, because while $\sigma_e{}^2$ is at least estimable for a given model, $\sigma_m{}^2$ is not. To estimate $\sigma_m{}^2$, we would have to know the "true" underlying model; not only is this rarely possible, but also if we knew it, we would probably use it, and reduce $\sigma_m{}^2$ to a negligible value.

We thus see that an evaluator who wishes to introduce model selection as an integral part of his procedures has to somehow trade off the virtues of elaborate descriptions of how he thinks a program works with the necessity of avoiding a pyramiding of measurement errors. One approach to this problem, which I have never seen tried in a large-scale evaluation, would be for the evaluator to specify several relatively simple descriptions of how he believes a program works, and then to build several different models, based upon these descriptions. The drawbacks are that each of these simpler models might have substantial specification errors and that the interactions of several different aspects of the program do not appear together in any single equation. Yet different aspects of the effect of a program on a dependent variable, such as achievement, could be examined separately. Further, each of the small models would have a small $\sigma_e{}^2$. Then, the joint value of these several models in explaining variations in output could be examined. This may prove to be more useful than a single extensive model, when errors of measurement are moderately large for several independent variables. Alonso (1968) has developed this idea in the field of city planning.

While the discussion in this section has been rather general, I hope it has clarified some of the difficult problems that people who must select a model have to face. Fortunately, although $\sigma_m{}^2$, the specification error, is not usually measurable, some facts are known about the impact of particular measurement errors, for some models, upon the dependent variable. In the remainder of this essay, we will study several of these cases.

Impacts of Certain Errors on an Evaluation

Design Considerations

I focus on regression models, both linear and quadratic in the independent variables for two reasons. First, most is known about these cases in terms of both specification and measurement errors. Secondly, generalized linear regression has been the most frequently used statistical model underlying recent evaluations.

To oversimplify a bit, the general strategy of evaluators who wish to compare a new program's performance with that of a control group (children exposed to some "old" program or perhaps to no program at all), is to take children exposed to both conditions—program and nonprogram. *Ideally,* a group of volunteers for a program should be randomized into halves, the P group and the NP group. The key idea here is randomization, which will eradicate the volunteer effect in comparisons between the two groups, and ideally constitute a true experiment. But lacking an ideal design for evaluating a new program, several alternatives are available, and they can be ranked in order of preference.

The *second* best approach, in the absence of randomization, would be to select children for the NP group who match children in the P group on crucial independent variables. In view of Campbell and Erlebachers' recent work (1970), these potential NP children should be tested *several times* before the program, if pre-test scores are to be entered into the regression. If they are not, the evaluation of the P group's performance relative to the NP group may be biased because the two samples come from populations with different pre-test means, and will both be subject to effects of regression to their respective means in the pre-test-post-test interval. Since perfect matching will be particularly difficult in this nonrandomized situation, covariance analysis should be used to adjust for differences between groups on some of the independent variables.

The *third* best approach is the one post hoc evaluators must follow, because they could not or did not design the new program with advance preparation for evaluation. This procedure, carried out after the P group children have been in the program for a period of time, consists of finding a group of NP children who match them on all important background variables. Unfortunately, not only is the volunteer effect unadjusted here, but the matching occurs on variables whose value is measured after the program has operated for a while, rather than before. A more sophisticated analysis here would try to ascertain changes in values of background variables (such as parents' income) over the program's duration, as well as track down or account for those potential NP children who have moved away from, or into, a geographic area where a program exists. Finally, covariance adjustments should be made on both groups to adjust for differences in background variables that remain despite the post hoc matching effort. This was the general procedure used in the Westinghouse Learning Corporation's evaluation of Head Start (Cicirelli et al., 1969). They did the best they could with a post hoc study, since the design of Head Start did not select groups in advance to facilitate a later program evaluation.

The *fourth* best approach uses no matching of P and NP subjects at all. The NP subjects are simply selected after a program has been operating for some time. Covariance adjustments are the only ones made. This is generally a weak approach, subject to so many errors and potential biases that the results can be seriously questioned. Remember that for covariance adjustments to be fruitful, the P and NP groups must have approximately identical distributions over all independent variables being adjusted. Without approximate matching of the two groups on important background variables, preferably before the program and at a minimum after it, there is a low probablity of this identical-distribution condition being fulfilled.

I will truncate the list of alternative designs here, because under less desirable approaches the P and NP groups are hardly comparable. But note that once the P and NP groups are constituted using one of the four above approaches, there are two ways (at least) of comparing them. One procedure estimates separate equations for the two groups and then sees whether the equations are identical in effects. A second procedure combines all the children into a single equation, with a 0/1 independent variable representing the group to which any child belongs. The *b* coefficient of this variable is then examined, to determine the direction, magnitude, and statistical significance of the program's impact on *Y*, relative to that of the nonprogram. We now turn to a brief discussion of the effects of errors of measurement and specification on these procedures.

Simple Linear Regression

The simplest case is a simple linear regression. Suppose for an independent variable *X*, there exists a normal sampling variance $\sigma_s{}^2$, and an additional variance due to randomly distributed errors of measurement, $\sigma_e{}^2$. Then, defining the reliability of measurements on *X* as:

$$r_x = \sigma_s{}^2 / (\sigma_s{}^2 + \sigma_e{}^2)$$

the "correct" regression coefficient can be estimated as the observed coefficient divided by the reliability r_x. But, since most evaluations comparing two groups involve at some point a covariance adjustment, we can ask further what impact errors of measurement on both *X* and *Y* have on such adjustments. To quote Cochran (1968), "the effect of errors of measurement in *Y* is of course to contribute their variance to the residual variance (of *Y* in the regression equation), while the effect of errors in *X* is to put back a fraction $(1 - r_x)$ of the original reduction in variance, $\rho_{XY}\sigma_Y{}^2$, contributed by the covariance adjustment."

There exists a further problem with using covariance adjustments in evaluation. In the ideal evaluation design discussed earlier, randomization from a group of volunteers was used to separate candidates for a program into P and NP groups. This should ideally result in each *X* variable having about the same mean in both groups. To the extent this is not true, and it will rarely be true in nonrandomized evaluations (i.e., evaluations using the second, third, and fourth best methods discussed above), then the covariance adjustment will be unbiased only if *X* is measured with perfect reliability. The proportion of bias left in the comparison of the means of the two dependent variables, if separate regression equations are estimated for the P and the NP groups, can be found to be $(1 - r_x)$. Thus, if an independent variable has different means for the two groups, and that independent variable is subject to a moderate amount of measurement error, the covariance adjustment will leave the comparison between the means of the dependent variables biased.

Quadratic Regression

If regression equations contain quadratic terms either in $X_i{}^2$ or in X_iX_j, their errors of measurement may have the impact of biasing the constant term a. More serious, perhaps, is that even if the errors of measurement in X_i are normally distributed, the residuals can be shown to be non-normal, as they become a linear function of chi-squares. This may threaten the standard F tests for both the overall effect of an equation describing a complete program and the incremental effect of adding new independent variables.

This non-normality in the residuals due to quadratic terms has a policy implication for the evaluator. One of the unresolved questions in program evaluation has to do with the order of entry of variables into a regression equation. This is a critical issue, as most stepwise regression procedures determine new variables to be entered into an equation based on those already in. Thus, depending on which independent variables are entered first, completely different sets of variables may enter the equation at a later stage. It has not always been clear whether "main effect" variables should be entered first, followed by interaction variables (X_iX_j), or vice versa. A general rule might thus be that main effects should be entered first, simply because they will tend to be the most validly testable effects. As soon as cross-product or quadratic terms are added to the regression, the assumptions underlying their F tests break down. An interesting question for future investigation is how badly the residual errors depart from normality, and how robust standard testing procedures are under such departures. For further discussion of this issue, see Box (1961).

Multiple Linear Regression

In a multiple linear regression:

$$Y = a + b_1X_1 + b_2X_2$$

when variables are subject to measurement errors, the impact on the regression coefficients becomes very complex. Cochran (1968) has found several relationships. First, suppose only X_1 has measurement errors; that is, $r_{x_1} < 1.0$. Then the observed coefficient b_1 equals the "correct" coefficient damped down by the multiplying factor:

$$r_{x_1} [(1 - \rho_{x_1 x_2}^2)/(1 - \rho_{x_1 x_2}^2 r_{x_1})]$$

where $\rho_{x_1 x_2}$ is the simple correlation between the independent variables X_1 and X_2. Since we observed earlier that in simple linear regression the "damping factor" was only r_{x_1}, and for multiple regression it has become r_{x_1} times a ratio that generally is less than 1 (except when independent variables are orthogonal or uncorrelated), we see that adding a new variable to a regression, *even if it has no measurement error,* adversely affects the estimate of the coefficient of X_1, the variable with measurement error. This indicates once again the losses suffered by including collinear independent variables into our evaluation model. Not only is it undesirable from the model specification point of view discussed earlier, but it also distorts estimates of the coefficients of independent variables. A good analysis of this issue is given by Kahneman (1965).

Conclusions about Choice of a Model

I have focused in this essay on what I believe to be the major problem underlying evaluations of new programs. Researchers and statisticians have worked tirelessly to develop more and more refined techniques for data analysis and have produced some highly sophisticated procedures. We have two-stage least squares. We have estimates of the bias in covariance adjustments under certain departures from underlying assumptions. We know and use some of these procedures well. But we know almost nothing about the implications of using a linear regression model to describe a program when the "correct" model is exponential or multiplicative.

Certain basic facts about model construction are known. We do know a little about how errors of measurement are propagated through a model. We also know that when errors of measurement are substantial, a complex model with many independent variables will have a large σ_e^2, although perhaps small σ_m^2. Thus, rather than using a complex model, perhaps several simpler models would be more helpful, as an econometrician uses a set of several equations, with each one kept relatively simple.

But we do not know much about discriminating among families of models, except for straightforward curve-fitting. An important area for future research to investigate is the relationships among models. Sometimes the analysis here becomes extremely difficult. One way to do this research is to specify a model to underlie a set of data, and, for a given fixed set of X_is, to generate some Ys with a specified error distribution (such as normal or lognormal) on a computer. From these simulated data, we fit several competing models (say, curvilinear versus linear versus exponential), and see which model fits best under which conditions. Perhaps different error distributions on the *correct* model will yield differentially best fits for competing alternative models. Ideally, we should work toward devising a procedure to embed a test of comparative models into a program design, before the actual evaluation takes place.

Unless we as evaluators think hard about this problem, we will continue focusing on a particular subcomponent of the overall evaluation process—the post hoc data analysis—and miss the broader perspective. We will continue to try to explain that extra 1 or 2 percent of variance in children's performance by fiddling with an extra term in a multiple linear regression equation, when we should be asking ourselves: If we had chosen a statistical model of a different form, might the outcome of our evaluation have been substantially different?

Future Emphases in Evaluation Methods

Let me now turn to a consideration of some ways in which evaluation strategies may change in the future.

I expect that one major shift in emphasis will be away from the traditional model of a post hoc survey, and toward longitudinal studies of development over time. The reason for studying children longitudinally is well known. If we are to detect detailed developmental changes, a longitudinal study is generally preferable to a series of cross-sectional studies. Only recently, however, have federal and state funding agencies made longitudinal evaluation financially possible. One example of this new emphasis is the Jencks plan for a study of education vouchers (1970), which proposes a five- to eight-year study of the effects of a voucher program on schools. A second and ongoing example is the Huron Institute's study of children who move from Head Start to Follow Through (Smith, 1973).

While it is possible to "pick at" specific details of the ways these studies are designed, their advantage is that if they are well done, trends in both cognitive and affective growth of a group of children can be carefully monitored, and formative evaluation can feed back into the ongoing project any information that might improve a curriculum. In addition, the availability of data over time can help us to choose among social theories about how programs and schools work. To the extent that we conceive of schools as a single element in a large and interconnected system that has effects on children, it becomes critically important to choose among various theories about how schools affect children. The three theories discussed earlier in connection with the Venn diagram in figure 5-1 provide examples.

A second substantive change I expect to see in future program evaluations is a change in goals. Most major evaluations until now have focused on one type of question, roughly stated: Do children exposed to a new or experimental program perform better or no better than a similar set of children who have not been exposed to this program? ("Better" can refer to any criteria a program developer wishes to choose. For simplicity, however, we will focus on cognitive performance.) This question requires the comparison of two means: the experimental group's mean and the control group's mean. Let us consider what we might expect to happen in almost any evaluation of this kind. If the experimental program is one such as Head Start, or Follow Through, or Upward Bound, then it consists of many separate centers, perhaps hundreds, spread over the country. In an evaluation that ultimately compares the means of the two groups, we would have to lump all the hundreds of experimental centers into a single group. What would we expect the evaluation to show? Most likely, we would find that, on the average, the program was not very effective. This is not surprising; after all, in any new program where there is a large amount of variation among experimental centers with respect to curriculum, staffing, and program structure, we could expect a priori that *most* new centers would not do an outstanding job. If an average is taken of all the centers, the many unsuccessful ones will likely swamp the rare handful that are having a significant impact, so that, on the average, the program will be judged unsuccessful.

I believe therefore that evaluators must ask a quite different question: Which versions of a new program seem to be working, and what are the program features that characterize these successful versions? Let us not judge a program on a first round of evaluation by lumping all the unsuccessful centers together with the few successes. Rather, let us detect the few successful programs and try to understand why they were successful. We could then in a second round of program development set up new centers that incorporate these seemingly valuable features, and see if they are in fact replicable and transferable. For a more detailed discussion of how to proceed with this approach, see Light and Smith (1970).

If we attempt to seek out successful program centers, a third issue emerges. This is the rather obvious point that children react to one another. A program's impact on one child or group of children will be substantially affected by the other children or groups sharing the experience. Thus, an important issue in future evaluations will be to study how particular program features interact with different kinds of children in terms of bringing about desired outcomes. The technology for doing this is available (it is called the study of "response surfaces"), and I expect this area of data analysis will soon become much better known to evaluators in education.

We can now put together these several suggestions. We first estimate the interactions between type of student and type of program. By identifying and adjusting for these interactions, we can improve our estimates of the effects of particular program characteristics on particular types of children. For example, assume for simplicity that we have only two kinds of student groups: middle-class children and lower-class children. Assume also that we have tested four versions of our program, and for each of the four versions we have tried three centers: one with only middle-class children, one with only lower-class children, and one with both. Thus, we have tried twelve centers. We would then be able to see whether student performance was affected by the characteristics of the other students in their centers. For example, we would compare the scores of the four groups of middle-class students who were isolated to those of the four groups of middle-class students who attended mixed centers.

We will draw one of the following conclusions: (1) there were no differences in the middle-class group due to isolation or mixing; (2) there were differences but only in the sense that the mixed (or the isolated) middle-class children did better in all program versions; or (3) the isolated middle-class children did better in one version of the program, while the mixed children did better in a different version. We would then repeat this entire pattern of analysis for the lower-class children. Finally, if neither lower-class nor middle-class children showed any interaction with their social context, we could make an overall comparison of how the program has affected both middle- and lower-class children, looking for interactions between the type of child and the characteristics of the program version. Notice how much useful information we gain. If there are interactions with student contexts for one student group (say, middle-class children), then we can specify that one program version should be used when mixing is possible, and recommend a different version when mixing is impossible. Where interactions are not found, we can pool the data from the two student groups, and carry out the rest of the analysis with increased power. Where interactions are found, we can either adjust for them before doing further analyses or carry out separate analyses on the interacting groups. Had we not been able to identify the interactions and allow for them, they could well have masked substantial program effects. Notice that the traditional analysis of variance models used to test for the effects of program characteristics make a tacit assumption that no student-by-student interactions exist. If they do exist, the analyses of variance lose some of their power to find both helpful and harmful program effects.

This potential problem with using analyses of variance techniques in doing program evaluations raises a fourth issue that I believe evaluators will have to address. I indicated above that a major purpose of program evaluation should be to seek out the few centers that seem to be working best. But the statistical procedures currently used for such a search generally involve the traditional analyses of variance. In this traditional analysis, when many centers are being compared, the benchmark against which center-to-center variation is measured is the average internal variation among *all* the centers. I believe that this leads to relatively weak procedures for identifying centers that are accomplishing something special. A contrived but simple example can illustrate this problem. Suppose we had studied five centers, each having three children, and the test scores of these fifteen children are those given in table 5.1. Without our making specific probability estimates, it appears that the best average, that of center 5, came

Table 5.1
Test Scores of Comparable Centers

			Center		
Child	1	2	3	4	5
1	70	65	77	75	70
2	89	88	84	85	92
3	91	98	92	95	97
Average	83	84	84	85	86

about from the same underlying causes that produced the variation among the students' scores in all the centers. But suppose instead the results were those in table 5.2. Then we would strongly suspect that center 5 was "on to something." Not only does it have a higher average score, but also the *variability* of its scores is much less than that of the other centers. If the average variability among *all* the centers was used to test whether center 5 had a significantly higher mean, we might underestimate the value of this center. There are tests for homogeneity of variance that estimate whether any centers have improbably high or low internal variance. These tests would probably identify center 5 as having an exceptionally small variance. But ideally we would like to test for the *joint* probability of a center having a high mean and a low internal variance. Such a test would enable us to identify centers that are worth replicating, to see whether their beneficial effects can be transferred to other locations.

This question of transferability of the features of successful centers leads to my final point. Much of the excitement recently generated in educational circles stems from a small number of

Table 5.2
Test Scores Showing Successful Center

			Center		
Child	1	2	3	4	5
1	70	65	77	75	96
2	89	88	84	85	98
3	91	98	92	95	98
Average	83	84	84	85	97

experimental schools that have been highly successful in achieving their goals. Examples of such schools in the late 1960s were the Parkway School in Philadelphia, and the John Adams School in Portland, Oregon. Similar excitement in the field of preschool education has been generated by the successful early work of Weikart, Karnes, and Bereiter-Engelmann. The general results of evaluations of these efforts are that they succeeded in sharply improving the affective development of the high school students and the cognitive development of the preschoolers. But a question that underlies all such early evaluations, which only time will answer, is whether the features that have made these schools successful can be transferred to other schools. I do not wish for a moment to minimize the importance of an exciting group leader or a uniquely trained specialist. But a successful research and development effort implies replicable results. Thus, an evaluation of any program must focus on finding the features that are replicable in other program centers or schools. And this introduces the crucial concept of *controllable* features into an evaluation. Examples of several characteristics that are generally controllable are the number of staff members per child, a highly structured versus an unstructured curriculum, and the hours per day of the program. An evaluator may be able to identify many features of an experimental program that he believes contribute in an important way to that program's success. But it is only the controllable features that can be recreated in other centers. Thus, if we find that having a good breakfast is important to a preschooler's educational performance, we can make sure that every child is given a good breakfast in school; this is under our control. But if we find that having a good night's sleep is important to a child's performance, unfortunately (short of taking each child out of his home at night) there is no way we can assure that each child will have a good night's sleep.

This example may seem rather trivial, but I believe its implications are important to an evaluator as he plans his study. It is expensive to study the effects of many different variables on children. It is therefore helpful to reduce the number of variables analyzed, wherever possible. If an evaluator concentrates his resources, which are usually quite scarce, on studying the effects of *controllable* variables, he can accomplish this reduction. It is useful to know how every feature of a program affects children. But it is particularly useful to know which of the many features of a program that are under our control should be developed to their optimal levels.

Conclusion

Throughout this paper I have discussed future directions; I will conclude with a historically true story. Just after the first world war, the United States Army hired a time-and-motion expert to study various phases of its military operations. When he arrived at an artillery section, he noted that a certain number of men were assigned to each artillery group, and he watched as they carried out their practice drills. After a while he noticed that there seemed to be one extra man assigned to each group. Since he couldn't understand why this was so, he traced the history of how certain numbers of men came to be assigned to do certain tasks. Finally he found the explanation for the extra man. When the artillery team had been developed, this "extra" man had been assigned to "hold the officer's horse."

While the moral of this little story is obvious, it has a serious implication for the future of educational evaluation. Evaluation is a discipline based on technical knowledge. Its practitioners therefore have a particular responsibility to rethink their procedures in light of technological advances. Further, evaluation is rarely undertaken in its own right; it is generally done in the context of a particular program that has particular goals. As a result, the evaluator's approach until now has been to ask, in light of these goals: Is the program working? In the future, we should be able to do better. If we use the tools now being developed to help us understand the effects of program features, we should be able to answer the more important questions: *Why* is the program working or not working, and how can we change its specific features to make it work better?

References

Alonso, W. "Predicting Best with Imperfect Data." *Journal of the American Institute of Planners* 12 (1968): 248-55.

Box, G. E. P. "The Effects of Errors in the Factor Levels and Experimental Design." *Bulletin of the International Statistics Institute* 38 (1961): 339-55.

Campbell, D. T., and Erlebacher, A. "How Regression Artifacts in Quasi-experimental Evaluations Can Mistakenly Make Compensatory Education Look Harmful." In *Compensatory Education: A National Debate,* The Disadvantaged Child, vol. 3, edited by J. Hellmuth. New York: Burnner/Mazel, 1970.

Campbell, D. T., and Stanley, J. "Experimental and Quasi-experimental Designs for Research on Training." In *Handbook of Research on Teaching,* edited by N. L. Gage. Chicago: Rand McNally, 1963.

Cicirelli, V. G., et al. *The Impact of Head Start: An Evaluation of the Effects of Head Start on Children's Cognitive and Affective Development.* Athens, Ohio: Westinghouse Learning Corporation and Ohio University, 1969.

Cochran, W. G. "The Planning of Observational Studies of Human Populations (with Discussion)." *Journal of the Royal Statistical Society* (London), Series A, 128 (1965): 234-65.

Cochran, W. G. "Errors of Measurement in Statistics." *Technometrics* 10 (1968): 637-66.

Coleman, J., et al. *Equality of Educational Opportunity.* Washington, D.C.: U.S. Office of Education, 1966.

Himmelblau, D. M. *Process Analysis by Statistical Methods.* New York: John Wiley, 1970.

Jencks, C., et al. "Education Vouchers." Final Report to the Office of Economic Opportunity from the Center for the Study of Public Policy. Cambridge, Mass., 1970.

Kahneman, D. "Control of Spurious Association and the Reliability of the Controlled Variable." *Psychological Bulletin* 64 (1965): 326-29.

Kirk, R. E. *Experimental Design: Procedures for the Behavioral Sciences.* Belmont, Calif.: Wadsworth, 1968.

Light, R. J., and Smith, P. V. "Choosing a Future: Strategies for Designing and Evaluating New Programs." *Harvard Educational Review* 40 (1970): 1-28.

Michelson, S. "The Existentialist Reality of Educational Production Functions." Mimeographed. Cambridge: Center for Educational Policy Research, Harvard University, 1970.

Parratt, L. G. *Probability and Experimental Errors in Science.* New York: John Wiley, 1961, pp. 110-18.

Smith, M. "Study of the Effects of Planned Variation Head Start Programs." Cambridge, Mass.: Huron Institute, 1973.

Werts, C. E., and Linn, R. L. "A General Linear Model for Studying Growth." *Psychological Bulletin* 73 (1969): 17-22.

Winer, B. J. *Statistical Principles in Experimental Design.* New York: McGraw-Hill, 1962.

Faculty Critique

by MICHAEL J. SUBKOVIAK

Let me begin by complimenting Dr. Light for a very incisive and highly readable paper. In the first part of my critique I would like to reinforce a number of Dr. Light's points that I heartily support. The second part will involve points on which we differ.

First, Dr. Light and I agree that the growing interest in evaluation is due in part to political, economic, and social forces now operating to change education from what it was in the 1960s. Federal, state, and local governments are withdrawing support from numerous educational programs. Lack of job opportunities and the declining birth rate suggest a drop in student enrollment. And the public at large will not tolerate high-risk investments in education.

In a recent paper, George Albee (1972) discusses the many changes that will occur in higher education as a result of these developments. One change seems certain. In the future, educational researchers must clearly demonstrate probable success to obtain support for new programs. A number of criteria for judging probable success come to mind. Do the anticipated effects of a new program justify its cost? Have pilot studies been performed on the same population and under the same conditions that will be encountered in actual practice? Does the proposed program have undesirable side effects? Can the success of pilot studies be attributed to Hawthorne effects? These are a few of the questions that can be asked. And as Dr. Light suggests, researchers must be prepared to answer them through careful evaluation of pilot programs.

A second aspect of Dr. Light's paper that I strongly endorse is his discussion of the impact of measurement error on conclusions drawn from a study. All too often we act as if the statistical analysis of a set of numbers is independent of the precision of those numbers. A lingering fallacy seems to be that the computer and the statistical analysis will somehow find the truth regardless of how inaccurate the data might be. As Dr. Light indicates, this could not be further from the truth. Measurement error in the data detracts from parameter estimation, results in biased covariate adjustments, jeopardizes statistical tests, and masks the effects of independent variables. The implication is obvious: We should show as much concern for the precision of our measuring instruments as we do for our statistical analyses.

A third point on which Dr. Light and I agree is that educators tend to fixate on treatment *means,* to the neglect of treatment *variances* and other informative aspects of the data. A few simple histograms or tables may reveal very interesting sidelights. For example, even if there are no differences between treatment means, a treatment with significantly smaller variance may be potentially more useful because it produces less variable and more consistent effects.

Another issue on which Dr. Light and I basically agree concerns the selection of independent variables. As he suggests, it makes little practical sense to study the effect of a good night's sleep on student performance, since amount of sleep cannot be controlled within the present school setting. However, as men of science, we should not become totally constrained by the educational structure as it exists now. Rowher (1973) has noted that significant changes are sometimes required to produce major effects. If sleep accounts for a significant proportion of the variance in student performance, then perhaps schools should substitute rest periods for study periods.

Let me now consider areas where Dr. Light's point of view diverges from mine (recognizing that it is much easier to find fault with a few points than it is to author an entire paper).

First, Dr. Light correctly notes two extremes in fitting curves to data. At one extreme the researcher fits many different curves to a single set of data. He then selects the best-fitting curve as the true description of how independent variables are related to dependent variables. This approach is unsatisfactory, since one or more best-fitting curves can occur by pure chance if enough curves are fitted to the data. At the other extreme the researcher hypothesizes a specific form of curve before collecting data. He then determines if this curve fits the data. This is the ideal approach. Dr. Light recommends a middle-of-the-road approach. He suggests fitting a "modest" number of different curves to a set of data. However, since it is difficult to determine what is meant by a "modest" amount of curve-fitting, this compromise approach may be little better than unlimited curve-fitting. Furthermore, since Dr. Light states that it is difficult to hypothesize a specific form of curve before data collection, I fear practitioners may use this as an excuse for inappropriately letting the data suggest the curves to be fit.

A second point I would like to comment on is Dr. Light's use of backward linear regression. In his example, three independent variables account for 25 percent of the variance in a dependent variable. When one independent variable is dropped from the regression equation, the other two still account for nearly 25 percent of the variance in the dependent variable. From this he seems to conclude that the dropped variable is only remotely linked to the dependent variable. This seems to me an unwarranted conclusion. The variance accounted for by the dropped variable might be redundant with the variance accounted for by the remaining variables and thus have little effect on variance when dropped. At the same time, the dropped variable might be the *single* best predictor among all the variables. Generalizing the situation to n independent variables, it may be possible to drop any one of them without doing severe damage to the total variance accounted for. However this does not necessarily imply that the dropped variable is only remotely linked to the dependent variable. It may be strongly linked.

A third point concerns the use of covariance analysis to equate experimental and control groups. In a well-controlled study, subjects are randomly assigned to different treatment groups; this tends to equate the groups on important background variables. In less-controlled studies, subjects are not randomly assigned, and covariance analysis is often used to equate the groups on background variables before comparisons are made. However covariance analysis requires that the data meet a number of rather strict assumptions, and the technique is far from robust with respect to violations of these assumptions. In fact inappropriate use of covariance analysis may either mask or exaggerate treatment differences, depending on the circumstances under which it is applied. Dr. Light does note some of the dangers of covariance analysis, but he seems to give tacit approval to its use in situations where it is likely to be inappropriate. Perhaps this is no more than a slight difference of opinion, or perhaps there is no difference at all. In any case, for some of the less-preferred designs that Dr. Light discusses, I would tend to reserve judgment rather than draw conclusions from analyses of covariance. For further discussions of these issues, there are two excellent papers by Elashoff (1969) and by Evans and Anastasio (1968).

My final remark concerns Dr. Light's discussion of large-scale evaluations that involve many treatment centers. Rather than lump successful and unsuccessful centers into an overall evaluation, he suggests that we focus our attention on a few successful centers and try to determine the features that account for their success. Seemingly valuable features might then be incorporated into other treatment centers and the process repeated until the experimental program reaches an optimal level of effectiveness. This is a worthwhile and very natural way to proceed. However, it would be both unwise and expensive to incorporate *seemingly* beneficial features into many centers before determining the true effectiveness of those features. Small, well-controlled studies of effectiveness are needed first, such as those described by Platt (1964). This point seems crucial, since Light's proposed modifications of the system are based on the effects of the most successful components. These effects may be repeatable in other centers or they may be merely chance occurrences.

References

Albee, G. W. "The Uncertain Future of American Psychology." Paper presented at the meeting of the Policy and Planning Board of the American Psychological Association, November 1, 1972.

Elashoff, J. D. "Analysis of Covariance: A Delicate Instrument." *American Educational Research Journal* 6 (1969): 383-401.

Evans, S. H., and Anastasio, E. J. "Misuse of Analysis of Covariance when Treatment Effect and Covariate Are Confounded." *Psychological Bulletin* 69 (1968): 225-34.

Platt, J. R. "Strong Inference." *Science* 146 (1964): 347-53.

Rowher, W. D. "What Could Make a Significant Difference?" Paper presented at the annual meeting of the American Education Research Association, New Orleans, February 1973.

Faculty Critique

by LAWRENCE J. HUBERT

Let me begin by complimenting Dr. Light for his paper; my comments will be an attempt to expand on some of the points he has made and to suggest tentatively several lines of future research. These comments will be somewhat quantitative in orientation.

Educators and behavioral scientists in general use the term *model* very loosely, although the concept itself has a very special meaning within a more abstract mathematical framework. By discussing this formal meaning, some of the confusion regarding the role of models in evaluation programs may be clarified. Let me begin by presenting one simple example from a field somewhat removed from the behavioral sciences, namely physics, before I discuss several possibilities closer to our hearts. I hope this illustration will provide a useful analogy.

Suppose I am investigating the distribution of shots fired at a target; the bull's-eye will be represented ideally by a single point. A pair of axes at right angles is assumed to have this target point at its origin and I can represent an actual shot by the two random coordinates (X, Y). Given this context, the following three assumptions are made:

(1) the distributions of the errors X and Y are continuous;
(2) the distribution at the specific coordinates (x, y) depends only upon the distance of this point from the origin;
(3) the errors X and Y are independent.

From these three assumptions, we can show that the error distribution in any direction must be normal (Rao, 1965).

In short, we have set up three axioms or an *axiom system* that allows us to deduce the normality of the errors. There is no physical counterpart that is actually needed to justify this abstract result, although obviously such a realization was the initial motivation for the postulates. Now, if we wish to investigate the adequacy of this axiom system in codifying reality, then we set up a *model,* which in our case would probably be a physical target along with appropriate specifications of what will be interpreted as the x and y axes, and so on. In any event, a model can be characterized as any realization of an axiom system in which the abstract terms are given appropriate operational referants and the axioms are reinterpreted as implying specific conditions on these referants (Suppes, 1970).

Although Dr. Light seems to suggest the contrary, his concept of a model is really not at this depth; and even though we can add a few interaction terms in a multiple regression framework, the evaluation structure he suggests is still at the stage of sheer curve-fitting. In other words, we are still searching for an evaluation counterpart to the psychologists' perfect learning curve, which if found would tell us precious little of what processes are actually involved. Let me strengthen this argument by an example from psychology actually involving the learning curve.

Psychologists at one time were very keen on knowing the form of a "learning function" and many assorted curves were tried. For example, if x is the response measure in question, t is time, and a, b, and c are constants, Robertson suggested the following:

$$\log [x/(a - x)] = bt - c$$

Thurstone proposed an alternative equation:

$$e_n = n/a + bn$$

where e_n stands for the cumulative errors up to trial n, and a and b are constants. Finally, another suggested learning curve can be written:

$$q_n = a(1 - b)^n$$

where a and b are constants and q_n is the probability of an error on trial n (see Estes, 1961).

The Robertson and Thurstone alternatives are essentially empirical approximations; the data seem to fit these functions, and so they are called learning curves. Unfortunately, the standard regression models used in evaluation are of a similar sort; they just seem to fit. However, the third equation also seems to represent learning data well in some instances; that is, it fits, but is based upon a set of axioms called *stimulus sampling theory* (SST) that formalizes the process of learning. In other words, our third equation corresponds to the deduced normality result in our target example, whereas the first two equations have no serious formal basis at all. A similar example could have been developed from the field of choice and decision theory.

It is interesting to point out a rather startling result obtainable from the SST formalization of learning that should give anybody wishing to fit curves cause for alarm. Specifically, we can formalize either an all-or-none or an incremental model of learning within the SST framework, but when group data are used, the mean learning curves have exactly the same form. In other words, by looking at group data, it is impossible to state whether or not learning proceeds gradually or in an all-or-none fashion.

In summary, I suggest that we begin to develop formal systems that characterize the variables in our evaluation program, deduce the necessary consequences, and see if the results fit the obtained data. If they do, support is obtained for the underlying concepts that led to our axioms; if they do not, the formalization must be revised or discarded completely. Although correlational ideas can fit into certain aspects of these endeavors, such as within the causal model framework (Blalock, 1961), I fail to see how a few added log terms, say, in a regression equation can lead to anything but an empirical treadmill for the behavioral sciences. We educators in particular will continue to be poor stepchildren of the natural sciences as long as we continue to use a single set of data both to suggest our theories and to verify them.

Ideally, the development of formal theory should precede the collection of data, but I appreciate the evaluator's dilemma of having to deal immediately with a set of rather vague ideas on how the variables of interest should be related. The statistical techniques Dr. Light discusses are of value here, but I am bothered by their cumbersome nature. Let me suggest a technique that may not be as elegant, but appears to be more straightforward, at least to me.

Suppose there are n variables of interest $(V_1, \ldots, V_n)$ and my vague theories specify that certain relations should hold between them. For instance, if $n = 4$, we can conceptualize the simple examples presented by Dr. Light, with the basic aim of seeing whether the data are consistent with the hypothesized relations among the variables. More formally, any theory can be denoted by a set of ordered pairs of variables of the form (V_i, V_j), which implies that a directed relation exists between V_i and V_j. For example, theory (1) in Dr.

Light's paper corresponds to the set $(V_1, V_3), (V_1, V_4), (V_2, V_3), (V_2, V_4)$, where the four variables have been labeled as follows:

$V_1 \equiv OSES$
$V_2 \equiv SES$
$V_3 \equiv SA$
$V_4 \equiv VAC$

As another equivalent way of conceptualizing the theory, an index of 1 can be assigned to an ordered pair if the ordered relation does not hold and a 0 can be assigned if the ordered relation does hold. Thus, our theory defines a dichotomous ranking for all $n(n-1)$ ordered pairs of variables.

The actual data are also assumed to assign a rank ordering to all $n(n-1)$ variable pairs that is defined in terms of some asymmetric measure of association. An index like Goodman and Kruskal's λ or Somer's γ are logical alternatives, but other choices are possible (see Goodman and Kruskal, 1972). What is important is some ranking of all ordered variable pairs from "closest" to "most distant" that can then be compared to the dichotomous ranking generated by the theory. In any event, the final goal is to define some measure of correspondence between theory and data by assessing the degree of association between the dichotomous ranking generated by the theory and a more complete ranking generated from the actual data.

Now, suppose we measure the correspondence between the theory ranking and the data ranking by some index such as the absolute value of Goodman and Kruskal's γ. We are still faced with the problem of assessing whether or not the value of this index suggests that the hypothesized theory is untenable. As a way of formalizing this question, I would first like to reject the null hypothesis that the links representing the theory were randomly chosen, and, after this hypothesis is rejected, to seek a practical yardstick for measuring whether the size of γ, say, is large enough for me to assert that the theory has been given empirical support.

To a certain extent the practical significance of a large γ is a matter of taste unless the researcher requires a perfect γ of 1.00 for empirical confirmation of his theory. Consequently, I will mention only briefly the problem of testing the null hypothesis of random selection of the links defining the theory.

Assuming that H_0 is true and any theory under consideration would require say, m links, there are $\binom{n(n-1)}{m}$ equally likely ways of defining a theory. For each of these ways, the γ measure can be calculated and the values accumulated in a frequency distribution to obtain an exact null distribution for γ under H_0. The distribution so obtained is "reusable" whenever a theory is hypothesized containing m links, as are the usual randomization distributions generated in nonparametric statistics. The significance level for testing H_0 is merely the proportion of the $\binom{n(n-1)}{m}$ equally likely ways of defining an m-link theory that gives γ values greater than or equal to the one actually obtained for the hypothesized theory.

The data analytic procedure discussed above seems much more straightforward than the more common multiple regression approach. Unfortunately, it requires some background in randomization tests that are usually omitted in a standard elementary statistics course, and its implementation would require more than a cursory procedural justification.

References

Blalock, H. M. *Causal Inferences in Nonexperimental Research.* Chapel Hill: University of North Carolina Press, 1961.

Estes, W. K. "Growth and Function of Mathematical Models for Learning." In *Current Trends in Psychological Theory,* edited by R. Glaser. Pittsburgh: University of Pittsburgh Press, 1961.

Goodman, L. A., and Kruskal, W. H. "Measures of Association for Cross Classifications, IV: Simplification of Asymptotic Variances." *Journal of the American Statistical Association* 67 (1972): 415-21.

Rao, C. R. *Linear Statistical Inference and Its Applications.* New York: Wiley, 1965.

Suppes, P. *Set-Theoretical Structures in Science.* Stanford, Calif.: Institute for Mathematical Studies in the Social Sciences, 1970.

Author's Reply to Faculty Critiques

I'd like to thank both of the critiquers for very clear and crisp statements of agreements and disagreements. In my paper I mentioned that I had the philosophical feeling that apparent surface contradictions can often be resolved by going into the problem a little bit further, and my general reaction is that I agree with most of what both of you said. I'll try to be specific point by point and to give examples where I can.

One of the first comments was that there's a problem in just curve-fitting. I certainly agree that curve-fitting, when trying to analyze or evaluate a program, is a very bad strategy. What I tried to indicate in the paper is that I don't really believe in curve-fitting; ideally one first has a theory and then tests it. The problem, of course, arises when one doesn't have a theory. For example, maybe one of you has a theory about why families abuse children; I don't. I say that with confident humility, because I guess most people don't. So, that is a clear case of the need for data-dredging.

There are two parts to this whole question of curve-fitting, which both critiquers mentioned, and I'd like to give another brief example of a very specific case where several models might be developed and a question would arise about which model was best. Several studies have tried to look at relationships among four key variables: a child's IQ or some other measure of intelligence; the amount or quality of education that a child receives; a child's family background; and the quality of the school or some variable like that. Let's call these independent or predictor variables. Finally, as a dependent variable, I'll take the Jencks variable, since I'm sure most of you are familiar with that: the income or job status of the child when he grows up. There is now a standard model being tried by just about everybody who is doing this work. The standard model is just multiple linear regression. Some people have tried to jazz it up a bit by putting in cross-product terms, making Y a function not only of $X_1 + X_2 + X_3$, but also of $X_2 \times X_3$, and X_2/X_1, and so on. But let me propose a couple of social theories that are competitors to the linear regression model. I hope someone will consider exploring this as a thesis topic. It seems to me this is exactly where work needs to be done.

Suppose my theory of what ultimately determines a person's income is not described adequately by multiple linear regression, but rather goes something like this: I look at the child's IQ, his education, and the socioeconomic status of the family in which he grew up, and I hypothesize that to become eligible to join certain income categories, he has to be above a certain threshold level on all three of those variables, so there is nothing linear at all about the relationships. To become a physician or a lawyer, in the last fifty years in the United States, I would guess that a person had to have (and I'm making these numbers up) a 110 IQ at a minimum, and a good education at a four-year college with pretty good grades at a minimum, and a fairly high *SES* family background at a minimum. Of course there are a lot of intercorrelations; for example, people from high *SES* families are more likely to go to a high-quality college than people from low *SES* families. Given this set of data, each of us in this room could set up an entirely different model. I would want my model to reflect a threshold approach to income determination, while someone else might prefer to use a standard linear regression.

Let me carry this one step further. It's very possible that one of you may say, "No, that's nonsense, what you just said. The way the world works is that a person's performance on his best variable is what really matters. So, you don't have to be rich or very well educated, because if you have a very high IQ you'll be okay." I'm sure there are some people here who would say that's not entirely unreasonable. I was trying to say in my paper that we should work very hard on specifying these theories, and then try to build a model. Realistically it's terribly hard to specify precise models.

About the problem of curve-fitting, I want to reiterate—I completely agree with you, and you put the point well. But I have to admit I have a problem when I look at certain kinds of data, as I'm doing right now, concerning abused children. I really don't have a theory, not a shred of a theory, and I'm just doing straight data-dredging. And I'm afraid I will end up doing dozens and dozens of tables. The only constructive thing I have to say is: let's not start interpreting results at the .05 level or the .01 level. Let's just call it curve-fitting, or data-dredging, and understand it at that; then we can use the curve-fitting to generate hypotheses for a new set of data or a more well-designed study. Maybe it will even be possible to design an experiment.

To move ahead, there were some comments or suggestions about using dichotomous ratings, rather than the Venn diagram approach I used. Goodman and Kruskall's λ measure of association was specifically suggested. Two thoughts on that. One is that I have problems with λ and similar measures of association because different families of measures focus on detecting different forms of departure from

independence. For example, without going into detail, one property
of Goodman and Kruskall's λ is that, under certain circumstances, in
a contingency table λ can be zero when, in fact, another measure,
such as chi-square, would show a substantial departure from independence. That happens when the modal row is the same for every
column or the modal column is the same for every row. I mention
that simply to point out that we have to choose a measure of association very carefully, although the suggestion to use this approach is
very interesting.

My second thought concerns the suggestion of having some dichotomous rankings, such as b_1, b_2, and b_3. This sounds like a very
attractive way of thinking about this sort of problem, in terms of
ordering or specifying a theory by saying how variables interrelate.
But you want to be sure you somehow bring in the idea of a multivariate problem, where you hold certain background variables constant. James Davis, the director of the National Opinion Research
Center in Chicago, has a very good example that he published in the
Journal of the American Statistical Association a few years ago. The
thrust of it is this: Suppose you do a simple 2 x 2 table of "age of
people" and "the amount they read." I'll simplify "age" to "young"
and "old," and "amount" to "high" and "low." It turns out that
young people read a lot more than older people. Now, if we leave it
at that, we have a little 2 X 2 table, and we can compute a λ on it.
Let's say that the data yield a positive λ. But would you want to
make some sort of policy inference from it? For example, suppose
you were a newspaper editor and you wanted to predict the reading
habits of today's young people thirty years from now, what would
you predict? I think the answer is, nothing. I hope it's nothing.
Because there are so many other variables that we have left out. So,
the question is, how do you bring them in? And I think that's hard.
In fact the point of Davis's example is that a third variable that
explained the association very well was "level of education." That is,
young people not only read more than older people but they are also
more highly educated. By bringing level of education into this as a
third variable, you can split out two tables, each one with zero
association.

You also mentioned the question of dropping a variable in my
analysis, and again your point is well taken. A variable can be defined
as important in two ways, as you pointed out. I had it in there for a

particular reason. Suppose we have a large sample of data, like the Coleman data, where for every child we have a measure of his family's socioeconomic status, the socioeconomic status of his friends, the quality of the school he attends, and finally the dependent variable, verbal achievement. The interesting question is: Is there a relationship between school quality and verbal achievement? In other words, it is no big surprise to anyone that rich kids go to fancy schools, and that rich kids have rich friends, and that rich kids do well in school. The question is, what part of the doing well in school is due to school quality, or some measure of school attributes? It seems to me that we're most interested in studying this linkage, and the backward regression is one way to do this, at least in the context of the limited model discussed in the paper.

I might just say that I had something in mind when choosing this example. It occurs to me that this is exactly what Coleman did. I've supersimplified it, but it seems to me that these are exactly the same categories of variables he collected—he collected home background, peer group background, the quality of school a child attends, and how well the child does. And he basically asked, while controlling for everything in sight, what *independent* effects does school have on verbal achievement? And he found small effects.

As a final point you suggested a set of small, well-controlled studies. I couldn't agree more. The large-scale study to identify a small number of centers that work and then find out what makes them work is not an ideal situation. The best of all worlds is to set up a series of small, well-controlled studies, when trying to understand how a program works; in other words, a genuine experiment. I believe this is such an important point that I have a paper advocating serious experimentation in the *Report of the President's Commission on Federal Statistics* (December 1971). We all know it is very hard to set up ideally designed studies, given the political and financial realities. For example, in Head Start, can we really assign children randomly to different kinds of centers if certain parents want their children to go to other centers? But the answer frequently is yes. I completely agree with you about arguing for more small, well-controlled, tightly designed studies. My own hesitancy here is to observe the unfortunate reality that our society doesn't seem to be as willing to experiment as I, and you, would like. An interesting methodological question is that if we must relax some conditions of an ideal experiment, what conditions could be relaxed at the least cost to firm inference? In other words, if we're stuck with an observational study, how can we most closely make it approximate an experiment?

Audience Discussion

Curve-Fitting and Controlled Experiments

Q: Let's take the situation when the dependent variables, like your imaginary data, don't have the theory or the models behind them. With curve-fitting, you can come up with a tight conclusion that fits beautifully here, but you try it somewhere else and it totally falls apart. What is the point of coming up with a nice, tight conclusion here when there is a good chance that it's not going to fit anywhere else?

Light: I think I understand what you're saying. You're worried about generalizability. Perhaps the answer is this: as a research philosophy or strategy, curve-fitting is a question of simple explora-tion. Curve-fitting has this specific role, despite its limitations. From an initial sample survey we can identify variables that seem to hold promise for further investigation. Promising variables can then be studied more carefully by designing small, well-controlled experi-ments. Once we're into those designed, controlled studies we start to understand things better. For example, an inference from Coleman's work is that spending an extra $200 per child in a school system, holding everything else constant, will probably not lead to soaring achievement. (I think that's a fair statement.) Fifteen years ago this was not the conventional wisdom. Coleman may be right or he may be wrong. Now we have to do some small experiments, take a variety of school districts, and focus carefully on that area.

A small, well-controlled study is the best of all worlds. But realis-tically we can look at only a few major predictor variables in an experiment, and an exploratory survey may isolate such variables as seem interesting or worth preserving. A survey is not an "end all," but it strikes me that you do learn something from a survey as a prelude to a well-designed experiment.

Q: I'd like you to be a little more careful about what Coleman discovered. What he discovered was that spending $200 per student the way they were spending it won't do it.

Light: Absolutely right.

Studies of Long-Term Effects

Q: I want to ask both you and Mr. Scriven a more general question. Some people have suggested that educators are concerned with long-range effects rather than short-range. There is the feeling that it matters relatively little whether a kid learns this particular thing or that; what we're really interested in is his attitude toward learning, the use of his brain, and so on. How do you go about sensing those long-range attitudes?

Light: Let me say something quickly about that. It has two faults. I rarely see long-term effects that are not preceded by short-term, measurable effects. This, of course, presupposes that you can measure the long-term effects if they are there. But I guess the idea that Head Start is raising IQs, when all the evaluations say it's not, is unlikely. Or, if it is working, the effects are small. It's a matter of judgment. But I am suspicious of the person who says an experiment has been going on for twenty-two years and we really don't have any results yet.

Scriven: You mean it might or it might not be working, depending on whether the knowledge held up. Reading is a practical example of real importance, and it's a particularly interesting one because reading vocabulary holds up for ten years or more. This is also true of elementary math performance. The residual problem is whether it was worth giving these skills to the children a little earlier than they otherwise would have got them. You get swamped by the natural development of these things in the ordinary bad school system. It's very different from measuring the long-term results of having taken a couple of courses in Spanish in middle school, for example. We can pretty easily test whether that knowledge is there ten years later, and we can pretty easily say where it came from.

But with Head Start and similar programs, ten years from now we're (usually) not going to find anything there that wouldn't have been there otherwise. What Head Start is supposed to do is something quite different. It's not supposed to give long-term effects in that sense; it's supposed to give the child a short-term capacity to handle what he or she otherwise would miss. So the payoff we look for with Head Start is (mainly) long-term effects in *other* things, not the two things we taught the kids. The aim was to make sure they didn't get so far behind that they couldn't take the stuff that was coming through in the early grades. So, what we do is to see if they do better than the controls with respect to the *other* things that are taught in the early grades, not the things they were taught in Head Start. It's a facilitator and not a gainer in itself. So it's an interesting case, which illustrates one of the tricky things about long-term gains. Of course, the other tricky thing is that most of the long-term gains that people are interested in are superfancy things, like integration capacity, perspective judgment, insight, and inventiveness. It's not hard to measure them, but it's hard to trace their origins.

I just got a tremendous amount of static from my colleagues at Berkeley because I introduced standards for the teaching awards that involved, roughly, pre- and post-tests and a control group—a hideously scientific kind of approach—instead of collecting letters that say, "Mr. Chips was the greatest figure in my life forty years ago when I was in college," etc. The criticisms I got often took the form, "What matters is how the students behave twenty years down the line, so it's unfair to be giving these little tests in the next quarter or the next academic year. That's not what we're aiming for. We're aiming for the big jackpot." And there I quite agree with Dr. Light: What makes a teacher think he'll get twenty-five-year results without getting intermediate results? I'm not saying that if the students do well on the intermediate scores, they're automatically going to do well on the long-term, but I am saying that unless they do well on the intermediate, the short-term scores, they're very unlikely to do well on the long-term, and anyway the teacher will never know if it was he who caused the long-term accomplishment. So, therefore, I'm giving the awards based on students doing well on the intermediate checkpoint. If you want my personal view of the matter, it's very simple. It is that the teachers are damned uncertain whether they're having any short-term effects at all; they're so uncertain that they're unwilling to look. So, they fight on the grounds that their real goals are long-term gains. This is an unkind thing to say about my colleagues, but they have pretty unkind things to say about me—for example that

I'm "mechanizing" the teaching process by suggesting that they do pre- and post-test comparisons. I do think long-term rewards are the big jackpot, but it's a jackpot in which it's very hard to trace the causal agent in many cases, and when it isn't hard to trace the causal agent, it tends to be a relatively unimportant educational goal. So we fall back on the intermediate gains, but we keep encouraging people to do long-term studies. We should always be doing those as well.

Significant Statistical Correlations of Meaningless Data

Q: I'm not in disagreement with that, except that I think both of you are still looking at the jackpot in a narrow framework, in terms of performance. I think we're interested in things that go beyond how well a person could do on a particular kind of school exercise in fifty years. We're interested in attitudes, we're interested in disposition, inclinations, and so on. That is, a person may still get a very high score on a vocabulary test in thirty years, but he may not have wanted to read a book since he left high school. How do you consider that?

Scriven: Nothing in what I've said is restricted to cognitive content gains, nor should it be (though reading books is a very poor indicator of merit). Let me make one other comment. You've made the point very well that statistical averages cover up a lot of wicked things— and, of course, you can make the same point about any kind of measure you care to mention. In this compression game, you have to throw away a lot. What model builders are doing, as I see it, is helping the evaluator with crucial conceptualizing steps. They want to give the evaluator a model that doesn't misrepresent what has happened, so that he can go on and do his bit about credentialing and say whether what happens is good or not; but *first of all* they want to be clear about what's happening. That's not a value judgment, and the value judgment business comes in for the most part a bit later, but we need the conceptualizing step first.

I have in mind a hybrid case, that may correct the tendency to think of me as too much of a philosopher in my approach. I don't like to think of myself as such, since I never took any courses in that sort of thing. In this business I'm trying to be simply a hard-headed evaluator, and that's mostly what I do.

This winter we reviewed ninety-five products produced by federal labs and centers, on a subcontract from Educational Testing Service. There were ten evaluators working on the review. After I got through a number of these products, it began to dawn on me that the evaluation reports that we were working from had one common defect. And eventually it turned out that (if I recall correctly) ninety-two of the ninety-five had this defect. Now, many of these products cost two or three million dollars to produce—they're not little casual things at all. And the teams that produce them often have a staff of scores, including a whole bunch of evaluators who submit a lot of the evaluation data with the product when it comes into the pool for evaluation. The thing that was missing was any sensitivity to the difference between statistical significance and educational significance. So, for every product, except maybe two or three, we had facts like: between the control group and the experimental group the null hypothesis was ruled out at the .001 level (or maybe at the .0000001 level); but there was no mention of raw scores. In one case, when we found out the basic facts, the situation turned out to be something like this: on an eighty-item test, the pre-test-to-post-test gain of the experimental group over the controls was three items. Now, with a group of twelve hundred kids taking this, of course the gain was significant to God-knows-what decimal! The fact is that with 150,000 subjects you could get a significance for a half-item difference on an eighty-item test. Eventually I got hold of the test, and found out which were the items that people most often got right in the post-test after failure in the pre-test. Two of them turned out to be dull, uncommon, technical uses of terms. That is, the students had learned how to use a word in a way that they'll never have to use it again, because it was used this way in the text material. So the achievement was *statistically* significant all the way down the line, but it was of zero *educational* significance. Now, that sensitivity to the difference between statistics and educational importance is something the evaluator ought to pick up pretty fast. And it's a good example of statistics really misleading the staffs of centers. It's a very crude type of error, conceptually.

Curve-Fitting and Biased Data

Q: Dr. Light, it seems to me that in reworking the child-abuse data, all you're going to come up with is characteristics of the reporting system.

Light: That's an interesting point. I think I'll be finding more than that, but I won't go into it in detail now. The reason is that there is a last step I didn't mention in my paper. It is called iterative proportional fitting. The point of it is that one can preserve, in a 2 × 2 contingency table, the interaction structure of the data and at the same time make the interaction structure quite independent of the reported marginals.

Your point is that doctors tend to report certain kinds of people more than others or certain kinds of facts more than others. I'm sure that's right, and it's a good observation. That's what the data really are like. Fortunately I'll be able to correct for that, but I won't explain how here; the analysis is given in a paper in the November 1973 *Harvard Educational Review*.

There are often different reporting biases or errors, as you say, among welfare people. To take a specific example, I looked at the state-by-state data on abused and battered children, and I found that in a northern state, I think it was Michigan, roughly 80 percent of the reported abuse cases were blacks. Now, I just don't believe that's really the case. There's probably a reporting bias, in that more poor blacks are being picked up than whites. Then I looked at some southern states, and I found many reported cases of child abuse. Guess how many were black? Very few. Now, does that mean there are no black children in the South who are abused? It probably does not. In fact, I called some judges who called some friends, and finally I found the reason for these disparities. While the southern states may have made many strides in many ways, one area in which they haven't made so many strides is in the placement of black kids in foster homes. That is still relatively segregated. They had placement facilities for whites, not for blacks, in 1967; it may be different now. In the South the reporting process is different from that in Michigan, and I would never have known it unless I had really data-dredged and curve-fitted. So, I think you may very well be right. Physicians may have biases similar to those of welfare agencies or they may have different ones. The only way we'll begin to get a handle on it is to really look carefully at how the data are most likely biased.

Just one last point about curve-fitting. It may be a good example of how post hoc explanations of curve-fitting can go in either of two ways. I keep referring to the Jencks book because it strikes me as an important work in terms of a careful analysis of an enormous amount of data. Most everyone who reads this book comes to the conclusion that it's bad for education. That's certainly the view as interpreted in the popular press. But suppose the educational system in the United States went something like this. Amount of education is put on the X axis, and income is put on the Y axis. It turns out that in the United States today, because of laws, just about everybody has a minimum of ten years of education. Certainly if we exclude the elderly people in our population this is true. Now, suppose it turns out that the regression line has a very small slope, which is what Jencks found. He found, basically, that a little bit of additional education, holding everything else constant, hardly explains, or is almost uncorrelated with, higher income. There's the threshold effect, where, if people have a certain rough minimum level of cognitive information, then education above that level really isn't an important explanatory variable. But, until you get to that level of education, it's very important.

This is one interpretation of the entire Jencks book. I'm again oversimplifying, but essentially I think that a reasonably admissible interpretation would be that the American public school system is wonderful. Because in fact what it has done is to move above this minimum an enormous number of people who would not otherwise have gotten an education. So they are on this curve where additional increments don't matter very much. If we knocked out formal education, rich people could still buy it. Now, I don't know which of these explanations is right, because we don't know what this curve really looks like. But I just throw this point out as an example of a post hoc interpretation of data that is the exact opposite of what might be called the common wisdom.

6

The Potential and Limitations of Secondary Evaluations

THOMAS D. COOK

Toward a Definition of Secondary Evaluations

Secondary Evaluations of a Primary Evaluation

The flurry of real and proposed social reforms and innovations in the 1960s was associated with an increase in systematic attempts to test whether these changes were achieving their goals, were equal to the claims being made for them, or were alleviating significant national problems. Reform and innovation took place in many areas of social life, including the legal system, welfare provisions, mental health, crime, and education. The changes in education included new preschool and school programs as well as vocational training. Ways had to be found for evaluating which of these programs were "successful," so that past and future expenditures on them could be justified. It was in response to the need for systematic feedback about program effects that evaluation research developed in the 1960s.

Seen in a broader context, the new interest in evaluation research reflected the need to determine which potential solutions actually

The author would like to thank H. M. Levin and E. J. O'Connor, Jr., for their comments on an earlier draft of this manuscript and the Russell Sage Foundation for its financial support.

solved a target problem. Such problem solving is probably as old as man, and it was certainly carried out in the social change area before the 1960s. However, few of the evaluation attempts before this time were based on systematic data. Instead, the majority relied on personal opinions, anecdotes, and testimonials from biased samples of persons who either had experienced a particular program or had a vested interest in it. Clearly, there were grounds for believing that such evaluations were not as "objective" as evaluations designed with the canons of "scientific method" in mind.

The upsurge in social change and evaluation research was associated with the growth of secondary evaluations. Most of these involved the systematic reevaluation of data reported in the primary evaluation of some new social program. In the field of education I can quickly list the major secondary evaluations, to give the reader a preliminary feel for their diversity. The Coleman Report[1] appeared and was criticized by Bowles and Levin,[2] and by Cain and Watts,[3] and the data in the report were extensively reanalyzed by a group of Harvard researchers whose results were published in a volume edited by Mosteller and Moynihan.[4] The Ohio-Westinghouse evaluation of Head Start[5] was reexamined by Campbell and Erlebacher[6] using simulated data and by Smith and Bissell[7] using some of the original data. Rosenthal and Jacobson's[8] evaluation of whether a teacher's expectancies influenced one index of intelligence was extensively reanalyzed by Elashoff and Snow.[9] In addition, the Russell Sage Foundation began a systematic program of secondary evaluations, and two of educational significance are currently underway. One is a secondary evaluation by Levin and Snow[10] of the Battelle evaluation of performance contracting,[11] and another, by some colleagues and myself,[12] is a secondary evaluation of the evaluations of "Sesame Street" by Ball and Bogatz.[13]

All the secondary evaluations above reexamined whether the conclusions drawn by the primary evaluators could be substantiated, and most of them actually reanalyzed the primary data. There have probably been many other studies with this intent; and there have definitely been secondary analyses (as opposed to secondary evaluations)[14] in which an investigator has used someone else's data to probe issues that did not interest the original investigator. As a result of such probing the secondary analysts have inadvertently corroborated or failed to corroborate some of the original analyst's conclusions.[15] Thus, though I shall restrict myself mainly to the secondary evaluations listed, I do not consider this list exhaustive. Rather, it is a list of convenience of studies that were explicitly secondary evaluations based on primary evaluations that were relevant to past, present, or future educational policy.

Secondary Evaluations of Policy-Relevant Issues Using Multiple Data Sets

Several recent papers and books bear directly on crucial issues in education. One of these is a review by Armor[16] of some evaluations of the effects of busing and school desegregation on the academic achievement of black and white children. This differs from the secondary evaluations listed previously in that multiple sets of evaluation data were considered, and this method offers a potential for replication that needs to be stringently examined.

Armor's work clearly involves a review of studies that were conceived as evaluations. Another type of research using multiple data sets requires the analysis, and sometimes the reanalysis, of both basic research and evaluation studies in such a way that a fundamental issue in education is confronted in multiple fashion by data. The works of Jencks[17] and Jensen[18] are of this nature, and the issues they examined are: Is there a lower-than-expected limit on how much we can raise IQ by environmental interventions? Do present-day schools cause achievement? Is any such achievement relevant to prestige, occupation, and income in adult life?

The Jensen, Jencks, and Armor studies are clearly secondary analyses of research reports or of the data in these reports, and all of them are clearly evaluations of whether educational resources cause particular outcomes that are desired and anticipated. But none of them focuses predominantly on the reanalysis of a particular program such as "Sesame Street" or a particular set of organizationally interdependent programs such as Head Start, and it is impossible to establish the particular primary evaluation of which they are a secondary evaluation. Moreover, the works of Jensen and Jencks do not draw heavily on research that would be labeled evaluation research by any strict definition of the term.

Nonetheless, I shall consider the Jensen, Jencks, and Armor works as secondary evaluations, for several reasons: first, they clearly deal with the valuation of major policy-relevant questions, and they involve secondary analysis; secondly, I hope to demonstrate that such works can be improved by adopting the typical secondary evaluator stance and closely assessing some of the studies that are reviewed; thirdly, the studies using multiple data sets have examined the central assumptions behind a *common class* of social change attempts (showing less concern with evaluating *specific* change attempts), and we need to know more about the problems of using secondary analyses in this way; fourthly, all secondary evaluations are improved if multiple sources of evidence can be adduced to support policy-relevant conclusions, and so we need to examine the problems that arise in pursuing this multiple replication strategy; and finally, as reports on basic and applied research grow in number, and as data banks improve, we can expect to see more secondary work of the kind represented by Jensen, Jencks, and Armor. But as the impetus for social change slackens and disillusionment grows with the ability of evaluation researchers to deliver timely, accurate, and useful knowledge, we may see fewer and fewer large-scale primary and secondary evaluations even though the need to evaluate new and old practices may not decrease. The type of secondary evaluation represented by the works of Jensen and Jencks, and even that of Armor, is less dependent on individual large-scale primary evaluations and may have superior survival value.

Evaluations to the nth Power

If there are evaluations of evaluations it should come as no surprise that there are also evaluations of evaluations of evaluations and even evaluations raised to the fourth power. Armor evaluated the effects of busing; Pettigrew, Useem, Normand, and Smith[19] responded to Armor; Armor[20] responded to Pettigrew et al.; and Wilson[21] responded to both Armor and Pettigrew! Similarly, Rosenthal and Jacobson assessed the effects of teacher expectancies on IQ; Elashoff and Snow reevaluated their data; Rosenthal and Rubin[22] evaluated the evaluation of the evaluation; and Elashoff and Snow[23] replied to their reply. More mundanely, Coleman has replied to his critics in contexts where he has[24] and has not reanalyzed his own data; Cicirelli and the team of Evans and Schiller have responded both to Campbell and Erlebacher[25] and to Smith and Bissell[26]; and provision has been made so that officials at Battelle and Educational Testing Service can respond to the secondary evaluations of the performance contracting and "Sesame Street" evaluations. Finally, whole numbers of the *Harvard Educational Review*[27] have been devoted to commentary on Jensen's and Jencks's views, while the national media have also been eager to comment upon their works.[28] I shall deal, to some extent at least, with the evaluations of evaluations of evaluations because they are essentially evaluations of secondary evaluations and as such are secondary evaluations themselves.

What makes this type of secondary evaluation potentially important is that most are written by primary evaluators in self-defense. They therefore highlight areas of disagreement between evaluators, and we might presume that these areas reflect some of the more important issues needing solution by statisticians, data analysts, and policy researchers. In addition, these replies should give us some perspective on the reactions of primary evaluators to having their work analyzed by others. Their reactions may well have important long-term consequences for the viability of secondary evaluation, especially if secondary evaluators are dependent on primary evaluators for obtaining the data for reanalysis.

Issues to Be Examined in This Paper

I have just defined secondary evaluations as (1) attempts to reassess the potential policy relevance of specific evaluation research projects through an examination of the research data, their interpretation, and their implications, and (2) attempts to use existing data from basic research or evaluations to assess the degree of empirical support for major assumptions underlying present practices or alternatives for future policy. The questions I want to explore in this paper are:

1. Why have these secondary evaluations been conducted?

2. Which implicit or explicit research models have been followed in the evaluations?

3. What are the strengths and weaknesses of each model, so that we can specify (a) the conditions under which each will be most useful, and (b) the steps that can be taken to improve each model?

4. What are some of the problems common to all secondary evaluations?

5. What practical steps can be taken to avoid these problems?

Why Conduct Secondary Evaluations?

There are more reasons for conducting secondary evaluations than are implied by the classical and very important question: Who shall police the police, guard the guardians, judge the judges, evaluate the evaluators? Some reasons have been offered in the past; other reasons may have been relevant to past evaluations but were not mentioned in published reports; and a further set of reasons does not seem to be much discussed at present but might be important for the future.

Reducing the Uncertainty about the Consequences of Important Programs

One obvious reason for conducting secondary analyses is that some primary evaluations have important policy implications, and policy makers and others want to be confident that they know what will happen if they implement certain policy alternatives. Secondary analyses have to do with building or shaking confidence and with estimating the degree of consensus that exists about the verifiability of evaluation conclusions.

It follows then that secondary analyses are most likely when an issue is important and there is some question about the extent to which the existing data actually corroborate either the conclusions of a primary evaluation or the basic assumptions underlying a social change such as busing or compensatory education. The Mosteller and Moynihan volume contains several references both to the importance of the Coleman Report's conclusions and to the possibility that those conclusions can be questioned on *methodological grounds* relating to the nature of the sample of cooperating schools, the quantity of missing data, the order in which variables entered the regression analyses, and so forth. In a similar vein, Elashoff and Snow point to instances where the teacher-expectancy effect has been used to halt intelligence testing or to shift the targeting of educational change attempts from the child or the social system to the teachers, and they then comment on the possibility that the Rosenthal-Jacobson data are uninterpretable as they appear, because of inadequate randomization, unjustifiable use of IQ norms, and an illegitimate generalization from tentative results for first and second graders to definitive results for all grades from one through six.

Specific methodological criticisms are not the only grounds for doubting a primary evaluation. The Mosteller and Moynihan volume also contains statements about the *time pressure* under which Coleman and his collaborators worked, and the context makes clear that a more leisurely inspection of the data might uncover relevant evidence that escaped the harried primary evaluators and did not show up in published research reports. Thus, even where published reports offer few grounds for suspicion, the need for speedy feedback leads to suspicion that there might be problems with the data or new questions that need to be asked and answered.

The *role relationships* between primary evaluators and program administrators give further grounds for uncertainty about the conclusions of a primary evaluation. Sometimes evaluators are dependent on the program personnel who commissioned their services and might commission new services from them in the future; at other times, evaluators called in when a program is being established develop an identification with the program. In the "Sesame Street" case, for example, Samuel Ball was associated with the show from its earliest days before he knew it was to be heavily funded and evaluated, and some persons have questioned his "independence" as an evaluator because of this.[29] Quite frankly, this has never bothered us in our secondary evaluation, but it is worthwhile pointing it out as another reason for advocating secondary evaluations. Actually, the problem of "role independence" is probably at its most acute where someone evaluates his own program or a policy-relevant issue with which he is heavily identified. For instance, Rosenthal made his professional reputation by obtaining experimenter-expectancy effects in laboratory and field settings, and the fact that he carried out the Rosenthal-Jacobson experiment is enough to make one wish for another analysis of his data or for replications of his study—efforts that he would welcome as much as anyone.[30]

Policy makers and their technical advisers may expect major flaws even when there is no obvious role conflict, no particular time pressure, and the primary evaluation report seems to be adequate. I know, for instance, of a yet unpublished secondary evaluation in which it was discovered that the independent primary evaluators had had to estimate data for a high percentage of children. The estimate had been made by assigning each child a score equal to the mean of

his experimental group. Then the primary evaluators in essence correlated treatments and outcomes; they found—not surprisingly—very
low correlations. Yet, to read the primary evaluators' report one
would have no suspicion either of the quantity of missing data or of
the way missing data were estimated. The moral is that there are
grounds for expecting possible major flaws in a primary evaluation
even when the conditions are most conducive to high quality primary
evaluations. This is a sad but, to my mind, realistic assessment of the
current state of the art in evaluation research.

Gaining a Second Perspective and the Problem of Independence

What runs through the preceding is an implicit assumption that
secondary evaluators differ from primary evaluators and add what
might be loosely called perspective. That is, they ask research questions differently, or construct indices differently, or analyze the data
differently, or have different role relationships with program personnel, or have different theoretical orientations.

Traditionally, we have expected evaluators—whether primary or
secondary—to be independent in the sense that they not be bound to
program officials by ties of business or friendship. Such independence is easy to achieve for secondary evaluators. But it does not
necessarily imply that they have open minds about the outcome of
their reevaluation. That kind of independence is difficult to achieve,
and I suspect that some of the secondary analyses I have listed were
not begun in that spirit. It is not clear, for example, that all the
persons reanalyzing the Coleman data would expect school resources
to account for more achievement variance than home factors; or that
the reevaluators of Head Start would be comfortable concluding that
the program had no demonstrable effects; or that the reevaluators of
Rosenthal and Jacobson's data conducted their work in such a way
that they could have corroborated the primary conclusions.

What is just as important is a suspicion I have that, even where a
secondary evaluation has been embarked on in the admirable, open-
minded spirit of Tukey's detective,[31] it may be completed in the less
open-minded spirit of his advocate. After all, a detective uses data to
form and test hypotheses, and it does not seem reasonable to me to
expect that he will accept a hypothesis only when *all* the relevant
data are in or that his values will play no role in hypothesis formation, testing, and acceptance. Indeed, since the evaluator probably

takes inadvertent stands *during* his work, I wonder how much the self-generation of hypotheses, self-testing of hypotheses, and commitment to his own answers bias everything that happens after a hypothesis is subjectively accepted: the questions that are asked, the answers that are obtained, the results that are or are not considered consequential, and the "first run" no-difference findings in the data that are or are not explored further. What I am suggesting is that secondary evaluations may be advocated on grounds of "independence," but they may be better justified in the long run in terms of the uniqueness of the second perspective.

This last statement will disturb readers who interpret it to mean that secondary evaluations should be undertaken by persons deliberately chosen because they have some unique perspective that is relevant to a social program—rather like asking a follower of Ivan Illich[32] to analyze data on the effectiveness of formal schooling. These readers would argue that the results of such a secondary evaluation would make it difficult to disentangle what is in the data from what the analyst's subtle or unsubtle biases may have done to the data. I am not advocating that secondary evaluations be carried out only by persons with unique perspectives about what the evaluation conclusions ought to be. This is obviously impractical when few resources are available for funding secondary evaluations.[33] Rather, persons should be funded who have as little bias as possible with respect to the conclusions and who have different perspectives from that of the primary analyst on how the data should be analyzed. However, all secondary evaluators do have biases about both conclusions and analysis style, and these need acknowledging.

In evaluations of great national significance, or in cases where interest groups have their own funds, it is important that persons with different and strong prejudices about the conclusion be allowed access to the data. To put it naively, this is because recognition of the pluralism of perspectives and interests in a political democracy should also extend to recognition that there are multiple perspectives on how to analyze data, multiple ways in which biases can inadvertently affect the relationships of data to conclusions, and few ways in which an evaluation can be conducted so that its conclusions are beyond the legitimate criticism of honest and sincere men with strong convictions about a program.

In a similar vein, it is interesting to speculate whether multiple secondary evaluations of the most important national programs may not be socially integrative. This could happen, for example, if advocates of a particular position commissioned a secondary analysis that then led them to think about the program in a way that would not have been possible without the data. In other words, if interest groups accept that the data are at all relevant to a particular policy issue, then their opinions about the issue may be modified by their own manipulations of the data in a way that they would not be modified by manipulations done by others. If data manipulation by interested parties were to have such effects—at least under certain conditions—this would be an improvement over the current state of affairs where nearly all evaluations can be attacked by interested parties or their consultants, thereby reducing the extent to which actions are influenced by data and increasing the extent to which they are instead determined by conflicts of value and interest in which the politically strongest parties win most often.

Advantages and Disadvantages of Disciplinary Myopia

There is little reason to believe that in the near future we shall see multiple secondary analyses of a single body of policy-relevant data by several analysts with different values. However, there is every indication that the values associated with training in particular academic disciplines have been an impetus to secondary evaluation and to its improvement. Jencks[34] has pointed to the frequency of attacks on the Coleman Report from economists—Bowles, Levin, Cain, Watts, Hanushek, and Kain are all in this category—and he has attributed the attack to the economist's predilection for establishing production functions that relate system inputs (typically dollars) to system outputs (typically production). Imagine a well-trained economist's surprise, then, when a sociologist like Coleman claims that system inputs (educational resources) have no demonstrable relationship to system outputs (as indexed by pupil achievement). Furthermore, since economics is a discipline in which multiple regression models are frequently used, it should come as no surprise that the report was in part attacked because of the way the predictor variables were ordered and because R^2 was used instead of beta weights.

In a similar vein, a psychologist like Rosenthal has had a distinguished career in personality and social psychology but not in educational psychology or data analysis, while Elashoff and Snow have had the latter kind of training. Thus it should come as no surprise that they looked at the Rosenthal and Jacobson data and asked questions about how the raw data were distributed, scaled, and then analyzed. These are questions that personality and social psychologists rarely consider, for all too few of them think to ask about outliers or to plot pre-test—post-test distributions of scores. Nor do they often ask about the validity of norms and norm extrapolations in the case of deviant scores. And they rarely ask whether an analysis of variance with unweighted, equally weighted, or proportionately weighted means would be appropriate, or whether the appropriate statistical test (or tests) should involve all the data, truncated data, or whatever. One good consequence of secondary evaluations is that they alert us simultaneously to the myopia of individual disciplines and to the fact that many educational problems do not respect disciplinary boundaries. Psychology, sociology, education, statistics, philosophy, biology, and genetics are all relevant to a comprehensive understanding of some problems.

Disciplinary myopia is by no means a universal evil. It is not clear that conventionally trained psychometricians or educational psychologists interested in teacher expectancies would have examined the issue as well as Rosenthal and Jacobson did—by conducting a true experiment in a naturalistic setting. Nor is it clear that the Coleman Report would have been as heavily and as usefully scrutinized if its results had not surprised capable economists by contradicting some of their frequently unquestioned assumptions. Differences in disciplinary training facilitate the adoption of multiple perspectives on an educational issue, and this reduces the risk that occurs when a single group of persons views a problem and fails to encode all of its dimensions adequately because they are set to ask only a limited range of questions or to use a limited range of analysis techniques.

The Multifaceted Training Function

A multidisciplinary perspective serves to keep us all in perpetual training, and this brings me now to consider other pedagogic functions and consequences of secondary evaluations. The Russell Sage program was in part set up to produce teaching documents that would alert practicing evaluators and those in training to some of the typical and more thorny difficulties of evaluation research as well as to some of the solutions, strategies for solution, and partial solutions that currently exist. Elashoff and Snow mentioned that they conceived of their book as a teaching aid. The Campbell and Erlebacher paper on Head Start required the deliberate simulation of data in order to point out how covariance analysis in a proxy pre-test—post-test design[35] underadjusts for the initial differences between non-equivalent groups maturing at different rates and to point out how no statistical adjustment for this problem is currently available. The points made were not new, having been made by Lord.[36] But the authors thought them worth remaking because the papers by Lord had not gained the visibility they should have.

I think it is almost beyond debate that, whether teaching is intended or not, most secondary evaluations can serve a valuable training function. This is because most secondary evaluators attempt comprehensive and data-bound critiques either of primary evaluations or of the conventional wisdom, while primary evaluators and defenders of the threatened wisdom attempt comprehensive rebuttals. All of this takes place in public debates that give the reader a chance to appreciate for himself why certain questions are asked, why certain modes of analysis are or are not used, why certain conclusions are or are not merited. Pedagogic value may also arise from the fact that no reader of secondary analyses can come away with a naive impression of the ease of conducting evaluation research or of the profession's immediate potential for providing conclusions that are beyond dispute by reasonable men—or, at least, beyond dispute by men endowed with considerable intellectual skill. Secondary evaluations help to discipline our expectations by reminding us of the current limitations of the art.

It is a fortunate irony, then, that one of the more desirable effects of an increase in the number of secondary evaluations might be a subsequent decrease in the number of secondary evaluations. That is, if secondary evaluations are successful in educating evaluators about solutions and partial solutions to the typical problems that arise in asking questions and collecting, reducing, analyzing, and interpreting data, then the quality of primary evaluations should rise, and there should be less need for secondary analyses. An important goal of secondary evaluations, therefore, is to limit their own future by educating present and future primary evaluators.

Global Assessment of the Effectiveness of Primary Evaluations

It is possible that secondary evaluations may weaken public and governmental support for primary evaluations by purportedly demonstrating the inability of primary evaluations to provide trustworthy and useful information. It would be especially unfortunate if secondary evaluations were to play such a role, for I have been impressed by the close correspondence between the findings of primary and secondary evaluators when the same questions are asked.

Take the case of the "Sesame Street" evaluations. Our analysis of the effects of encouragement to view the show resulted in conclusions that for the most part coincided with the ETS conclusions. Any *apparent* differences between what we and the ETS team found arose because we asked questions that the ETS team had not pursued in detail. First, we asked what were the effects of viewing among children who were not encouraged to view the show (encouragement entailed periodic visits by ETS field staff members to the child's home; provision of promotional materials to increase viewing; and, in some cases, post-testing of the child by staff members who knew him or her and knew his or her treatment condition). Secondly, we asked what SES group differences in cognitive gains there were from viewing the show without encouragement, and this question is clearly relevant to how "Sesame Street" might be affecting the so-called achievement gap.

In the case of teacher-expectancy effects, Rosenthal and Jacobson originally demonstrated the phenomenon strongly in only two of their six grades. The secondary analyses of Elashoff and Snow did not disprove a cautious conclusion about restricted expectancy effects. (However, as the secondary evaluators themselves pointed out, their results were not definitive, primarily because they could never adequately deal with the possible statistical regression artifact that arose because the first and second graders in the expectancy group and their controls were compared on an IQ test that is not very reliable, particularly with younger children.)

Finally, it is noteworthy that the reanalyses of the Coleman Report by the Harvard team produced, in essence, corroboration for Coleman's major conclusion about the relative importance of school resources, peer pressures, and home background in predicting academic achievement. (What is interesting is that Smith demonstrated how the index of home background was not constructed of the items that Coleman reported. Fortunately, substituting the items Coleman had planned to use for those he did use did not alter the basic conclusions, though it might have done so.)

These three examples illustrate instances where primary and secondary analysts agreed in their conclusions, when they asked the same question of the same body of data and the secondary evaluator reanalyzed these data without restricting himself to a small sample.[37] It would be all the more saddening, therefore, if this basic correspondence were overlooked in all the verbiage surrounding secondary evaluations, and if the argument of "contradictory or invalidated conclusions from secondary evaluations" was used as a weapon for discrediting primary evaluations. While it might be justified to suggest that secondary evaluations often reduce our certainty about the conclusions of primary evaluations, it would not be true to suggest that in most instances they imply different conclusions when the same questions are asked and the same data are analyzed.

We have to be careful to add two provisos to the foregoing. First, this correspondence of conclusions is of little value if the data are not capable from the outset of providing trustworthy conclusions, perhaps because of sampling biases or the like. Secondly, correspondence can occur when one of the parties is right for the wrong reasons. For example, Elashoff and Snow were careful to point out that their tentative conclusion about possible expectancy effects in first and second graders was grounded on different and, in their opinion, better analyses of the Rosenthal-Jacobson data, while Smith's conclusion about the relative amount of variation associated with peer, home, and school factors coincided with Coleman's despite a mistake in the Coleman Report about how the home background index was constructed. However, though analyses and indices may differ, the basic data in secondary evaluations do not. It is my educated guess, on the grounds of the two reevaluations cited above and our multiple reanalyses of the "Sesame Street" data, that strong effects will emerge across modes of analysis and across related indices of some construct. This is because multiple modes of analysis are called for in situations where no single mode is demonstrably correct, and the choice of modes is among those that competent persons think will approximate an answer, though no single one may be definitive. Thus, if one has multiple modes all approximating an answer in different ways, the methods are likely to be so related that strong effects will appear and reappear in analyses of the data. (This same logic holds for constructing indices, and it suggests that different indices of a single construct should typically show similar results.) One must carefully distinguish, then, between being right for the wrong reasons and being right for reasons whose degree of rightness can be questioned, although they are not wrong. The latter seems more prevalent than the former to date, though there are too few cases for confident inference.

The Accumulation of Knowledge and the Use of Multiple Data Sets

We often hear that science is a cumulative endeavor, and this truism brings me to an important reason why secondary evaluations of the Jensen-Jencks-Armor kind have been occurring recently. As more and more data accumulate in journals and technical reports, as the idea of data banks gains support, it becomes increasingly possible to examine important assumptions underlying present or future policy options through the analysis of multiple bodies of relevant data. Of course, not all the data examined are equally relevant to the central issues. Yet some scholars have obviously thought that the available data on some topics were sufficiently interpretable and replicable for them to take the stands they did. And in the coming years, as knowledge grows, we shall have more and more data available on more and more topics, and the data will sit waiting for someone to interrelate, reanalyze, and interpret them with specific questions in mind.

Evaluating multiple data sets is no easy task, and I will detail some difficulties with it in another section. Its importance, I suspect, is in part a result of inadequacies that can be found in many primary evaluations and much basic research—inadequacies related to internal, external, construct, and what might be called statistical conclusion validity.[38]

Surveys are of little use for determining whether inputs cause outputs, and their usefulness is restricted to establishing plausible null relationships and to suggesting new relationships that cannot be causally interpreted. Quasi experiments, especially in the growth situations that abound in education, are difficult to interpret, in that threats to internal validity can rarely be ruled out with a degree of certainty that would suit many persons. Finally, true experiments, in

which experimental groups are made comparable by randomization,
are difficult to set up and maintain over time. Often, they degenerate
into quasi experiments, with consequent internal validity problems.
What I am suggesting is that many primary evaluations based on
surveys, quasi experiments, or degenerated true experiments fail to
test causal propositions in a definitive manner, so they are less than
adequate as a basis for action.

Even when causal relationships can be accepted more confidently,
problems of construct validity arise. In particular, when the validity
of the presumed causal construct is questioned, the replicability of
an effect or of no effect is questioned. For instance, Ball and Bogatz
convincingly demonstrated that encouragement to view "Sesame
Street" increases viewing and causes learning. While it is important to
ask what happens if children are encouraged to view the show, it may
be more important to ask what happens to children who view the
show in their homes without any such encouragement from ETS
field staff members. After all, few children in the United States are
so encouraged. Similarly, Elashoff and Snow note the deviantly high
and low IQ scores in the Rosenthal and Jacobson first- and second-
grade data and ask about the construct validity of the findings:

Are we really dealing with the effects of self-fulfilling prophecy on the intellectual growth of imbeciles or geniuses, operating through teachers who do not
even remember the names of the individuals they have supposedly influenced so
profoundly? Or are we dealing with misunderstood test instructions? Or uncon-
trolled test administration? Or selective teacher coaching? Or teacher encouragement for guessing? Or chance? Or what?[39]

Finally, Pettigrew et al. criticize the paper by Armor on construct
validity grounds, claiming he has lumped together studies of forced
desegregation and of voluntary integration and that, if there were
more data on the latter, effects of integration on achievement would
emerge. Admittedly, the Pettigrew paper is not a response to a single
evaluation. But it nonetheless illustrates the basic point that a single
instance of a treatment, *or a set of relatively homogeneous treatments,* will rarely provide enough information to explain why a treatment had its effects and thereby to increase our chances of replicating the effects.

A relationship is externally valid if it can be replicated *across*
persons, settings, and times or if there is a specific class of persons,
settings, and times *to* which generalization is desired. Clearly, a single

evaluation typically entails testing a particular causal relationship in only one year (or other particular time span). Replication across persons and settings is more likely (1) if a random sample of persons is obtained for assignment to treatments or a random sample of settings can be chosen (both of which are rare events), or (2) if a heterogeneous collection of persons and settings is deliberately chosen (which is more typical because these conditions are more feasible). Nonetheless, critics might still ask: But would the program work at a different time, in a different place, with a different group of persons?

Finally, statistical conclusion validity refers to the use and abuse of statistics for drawing conclusions about covariation—in particular about the covariation of a presumed cause and effect. The literature on evaluation research is full of controversies about what p values mean, the use of confidence intervals versus p values, and when to use changes in R^2, changes in $\beta^2(1 - C^2)$, or β as indices of the variance associated with some independent variable in multiple regression analyses. Then, when we look not to statistical but to social or pedagogical significance, the water gets even muddier: An effect of how many standard deviations is significant? What does ω^2 mean, being as dependent as it is on the particular error term? Is an increase-in-income variance of 4 percent (β) associated with an extra year of high school as trivial as Jencks sees it or is it as meaningful as Levin claims, because Levin sees it in the context of cumulative increases for each year in high school, each year in college, and each year in graduate school? Clearly, for many persons social significance involves an inferential leap from the data, and one man's significance may therefore be another man's triviality.

This digression on validity is important, I think, because many validity problems are associated with having a single set of data, and they can be partially solved by switching from the reevaluation of a single set of data to the reevaluation of multiple sets. Let me illustrate. A set of investigations is more likely to involve instances where a particular threat to internal validity cannot be ruled out in some studies but can be ruled out in others. In addition, the construct validity of the cause is likely to be enhanced if one can review many studies and establish the attributes associated with successful instances. In a similar manner, one can check whether particular results are obtained at different times and places with different groups of respondents and with different kinds of researchers having different values. And, finally, the replication perspective gives one a chance to estimate the robustness of effects.

Combining studies that vary in quality, scope, and principal research questions is much more difficult than the foregoing paragraph implies, and I will return to it later. But combining is possible, albeit on an unsystematic basis in many instances, and it permits the acute mind to make broader and more confident generalizations than those based on secondary evaluation of a single body of data. I suspect that this is one reason why monographs like those of Jensen, Jencks, and Armor came to be written.

The Conventional Wisdom Questioned

I suspect that another reason for these monographs is simple intellectual curiosity, occasioned, first, by the apparent failure of a common class of educational innovations to achieve the dramatic gains that their advocates had promised for them and, secondly, by each author's desire to examine why this was so. The Jensen article seems to have resulted from Jensen's awareness that compensatory education had "failed," and his feeling that one reason for this might be genetically determined differences in IQ. The Jencks book seems to have resulted from the author's realization that schools did not seem to be effective in redistributing income and wealth, as had been hoped by many, and from his attempts to explain this by examining the relative importance of school and home factors in determining achievement. Finally, the Armor article seems to have been a response to the growing awareness that school desegregation and busing were not achieving dramatic cognitive gains and might even be having some adverse side effects, and because of this the author came to question the "contact hypothesis"[40] that provided the behavioral science rationale for desegregation.

Jensen, Jencks, and Armor, in their very different ways, seem to have been among the first to relate grandiose expectations to the first returns of the data, among the most intellectually vital in pursuing reasons for the apparent discrepancies between what was promised and what was delivered, and among the most speedy (or most foolhardy or most irresponsible—depending on one's perspective) in bringing what they considered to be the relevant data to the general public. In short, their work may well represent *reactions* to events rather than anticipations of them. They would have anticipated events if, at the time preschool education was being proposed and justified on the grounds of the plasticity of IQ, they had then gone to their twin studies and had engaged Hunt,[41] Bloom,[42] and others in scholarly debate. Or they would have anticipated events if, at the time federal funds were poured into education on the grounds that it would eventually be a path to redistributing income, someone like Jencks had then gone to the relevant sociological literature on schooling and income and had examined it.

Professional Enhancement

Evaluations of large-scale programs gain headlines both in social science circles and beyond. Some secondary evaluations are also highly visible, especially within the social science fraternity. Knowing this, it is possible that some secondary evaluators of programs or of assumptions behind programs conduct their work so as to capitalize on the visibility of the primary evaluation or the policy issue. What makes this point more important is that little visibility is gained by merely replicating the findings of a primary evaluator or rediscovering the conventional wisdom. Instead, visibility is more likely with results that conflict with those expected from previous work. Thus, there may be subtle pressures on the secondary evaluator to reach conclusions that stand out from those of the primary researchers, and these pressures may be related to career advancement or simply to the need to individuate oneself by being different from primary researchers. There is, after all, little career advancement or little individuation that results from replicating someone else's major findings.

We must be very careful, however, in attributing some or all of the motivation for conducting secondary evaluations to such factors. Visibility is related to the importance of an issue at a given moment, whether in the policy arena or elsewhere, and researchers are trained to expend their energies on important topics. Thus, the confounding of visibility and issue importance may mean that the major motive for conducting the research was its importance rather than its visibility. I think we owe it to secondary evaluators to examine their work at face value, irrespective of their motives for writing—and these motives are always assumed rather than proved. It is rather like the problem facing literary critics: one school looks at why the poet wrote his work and another at what his poem has to say. I have no doubt in my mind which is the more important of these schools.

Secondary Evaluation Models

The previous section dealt with a variety of reasons why secondary evaluations have been conducted or ought to be conducted. I want now to describe the implicit or explicit models that have been or could be followed, detailing the strengths and weaknesses of each, assessing what realistically can be expected of each, and outlining the conditions under which each is worth using. I present "ideal" models abstracted from previous work. A disadvantage of such ideal types is that the reader may come to believe that they are the only ones available. They are not. Mixed models are also possible in which facets of each ideal type are combined. Indeed, such mixed models are highly desirable, and the best secondary evaluations combine the features I list, in order to answer the various evaluation questions they ask.

The discussion of models is based on an analogy to an analysis of variance design involving three "factors," each with two "levels." The design is outlined in table 6.1. The first factor is whether the secondary evaluation involves the analysis of a single body of data or multiple relevant data sets. The second factor is whether the analysis does or does not involve actual manipulation of the original data so as to conduct new or different analyses. And the third factor is whether the secondary analyst's work takes place simultaneously with, or after, the primary work.

The ensuing "design" has eight cells. Comment is called for on three of the cells. First of all, the single-data-set/no-reanalysis/after-the-fact cell has entries representing two kinds of secondary evaluation. One is the simple review of an evaluation that takes place, for example, in journals in response to a published article or book or in the process of considering books or articles for publication. Another involves the simulation of data that might have been in a primary evaluation, a procedure that obviously implies data analysis, but not reanalysis of the primary data themselves.

A second cell with multiple entries is the single-data-set/reanalysis/after-the-fact cell. This cell represents most of the secondary evaluations to date, and I have classified these in two ways: evaluations of

Table 6.1
Classification of Secondary Analysis Models

		Single Data Set	Multiple Data Sets
After-the-fact secondary analysis	Without data reanalysis	Review or Simulation	Review (as in *Psychological Bulletin*)
	With data reanalysis	Evaluation of an evaluation or Evaluation of a program	Armor-Jencks-Jensen projects
Simultaneous secondary analysis	Without data reanalysis	Consultant-metaevaluator	Consultant-metaevaluator
	With data reanalysis	Secondary analysis of raw data	Simultaneous (or consecutive) secondary evaluation

evaluations, where the major question is whether the conclusions of the primary evaluation can be corroborated, and evaluations of programs, where the major question is what the effects of a particular program are. The latter implies a more general orientation than the former, with the evaluator reconsidering the basic questions of the evaluation. The two are not totally independent, of course.

A final cell to which attention must be drawn is the multiple-data-set/no-reanalysis/simultaneous cell, where the entry "consultant-metaevaluator" is the same as in the single-data-set cell to the left. Metaevaluators are persons commissioned to oversee a primary evaluation and to provide continuous feedback about it and modifications to it. An extension of this function would be to have meta-evaluators conduct their work and comment on two or more simultaneous evaluations of some nationally important program. I know of no such work in the past or proposal for it in the future, and this cell will not be dealt with in any detail in the pages that follow.

My discussion is organized around the analysis of variance analogy. It will be disproportionately concerned with after-the-fact evaluations, and this reflects a disproportionality that has operated in the past with respect to secondary evaluations. In fact, most of our experience is in this area. But this does not mean that after-the-fact secondary evaluations are the most important. Indeed, if we are to produce evaluations that are timely and whose results are accurate, at least insofar as they are validated across data analysts, then we need more simultaneous secondary evaluations. At present, the need for speedy information tends to lower the quality of the information obtained. If we are to have both quality and speed, we need more experience with simultaneous secondary evaluations.

After-the-Fact Reviews without Data Reanalysis

The first cell represents the critical review of an evaluation by persons who do not have access to the primary data and who form opinions about the primary evaluation based on (1) methodological considerations (sampling, measurement, design, and analysis); (2) examining tables and even manipulating the figures in these tables; and (3) interpreting the outcomes tabled in the report.

There are at least four contexts in which these kinds of review may be helpful to policy makers. The first is when the reviewer accepts the data and analyses at their face value and gives them a different interpretation from that of other evaluators. For example, though Pettigrew et al. do question the data on which Armor based his conclusions about busing, they also question whether the data, if valid, should be interpreted as Armor interprets them. This is because Pettigrew et al. interpret integration as successful if it increases the achievement level of blacks, irrespective of what it does to the difference in achievement between blacks and whites. This absolute criterion differs from Armor's relative criterion for attributing success to integration attempts, and the analysis by Pettigrew et al. heightens the debate by raising the issue of what constitutes successful integration. In a similar vein, Levin notes that Jencks considers trivial a 4 percent increase in income due to an extra year in high school, a 7 percent increase due to one year in college, and a 3 percent increase due to one year of graduate school. But Levin questions whether the cumulative effect of such increases is trivial at all. Finally, Kamin's[43] commentary on Jensen's article succinctly points out that 80 percent of IQ may indeed be inherited and that blacks may well score lower than whites, but that these relationships do not necessarily imply that the racial difference is due to heredity—a point with which Jensen does not disagree. Reviews with such an emphasis are particularly important because they focus on the central issue in an evaluation; they avoid discussion of complex methodological issues that policy makers cannot follow; they therefore accept—or assume an acceptance of—the data at face value. Finally, they point out implications of the data that any policy maker can understand and evaluate in terms of his own goals.

A second useful kind of review questions whether the basic data can answer the evaluation question posed. A convincing example of this can be found in social psychology. Hyman and Sheatsley[44] examined whether the basic postulates of *The Authoritarian Personality* could be accepted on the basis of the work by Adorno et al.[45] A fundamental postulate concerns whether there is a relationship between questionnaire measures of ethnocentrism and measures of psychodynamics as determined by interview. Adorno et al. had interviewers who knew the research hypotheses, knew each person's questionnaire responses, and were explicitly trained to keep the questionnaire data in mind when conducting and interpreting the semi-open-ended interviews. In effect, then, the relationship among testers, tests, and test instructions increased the chances of obtaining the expected correspondence between ethnocentrism and psychodynamics, for reasons irrelevant to the underlying theory. In education, Thorndike[46] criticized Rosenthal and Jacobson by pointing out that the teacher-expectancy effect was obtained only for first and second graders, that the IQ test used was not adequately normed for younger children who were low scorers, and that, with young children, one extra item correct could mean an increase of several IQ points. This led Thorndike to suggest that the effect might have been due to properties of the IQ measurement scale rather than to the intellectual growth of the child.

But two important points should be noted about this critique. First, it was a critique of the transformed data, and, as Thorndike acknowledged, analysis of the raw data could still be carried out to examine Rosenthal and Jacobson's issue. Secondly, it was a critique that applied only to the data from first and second graders, and no scaling artifact could reasonbly be invoked against the data from other children. This permitted Rosenthal[47] to counter Thorndike by asking how his critique of the IQ scale could account for the teacher-expectancy effects that occurred with the older children in distribution-free (but not other) analyses of the data. Thorndike's otherwise excellent review might have been improved if he had focused, not on the scaling problem, but on the totality of the evidence supposedly supporting the expectancy effect. If he had done this, he would have seen that there were two sources of evidence for the effect; that his scaling argument cast considerable doubt on the relevance of the evidence from parametric analyses of the first and second graders; but that he failed to question the relevance (or strength) of the evidence from the distribution-free analysis of third, fourth, fifth, and sixth graders. Reviews are better if they do not focus on methodological issues in a vacuum (listing the situations where the reviewer said, "Gee, that's the wrong thing to do to it!") but rather focus on the broad questions: What did the evaluator say he found? What is *all* his evidence for this conclusion? How does *all* the evidence stack up?

Some critiques of the basic data are less helpful than they appear at first glance. For instance, Bowles and Levin criticized the basic Coleman data because of the sampling bias that arose when some school districts refused to cooperate in the survey. Their point is well taken if meant as a restriction to the range of school districts over which the Coleman results could be generalized. But it is not well taken if it implies that the results for the schools sampled are necessarily invalid, because the data might very well describe per capita expenditure and achievement patterns in these schools. And it would not be well taken if it implies that the schools not sampled are necessarily different from the sampled ones in the relationship of school, peer, and home factors to achievement. They might be different, but unless the reviewer can cite high quality data to support his contention, all he can do is to raise the issue, not cast doubt on the findings of the report. Let me be clear: The reviewer might well be right, and the pattern of achievement might differ between cooperating and noncooperating schools. But he does not know this, and the best criticisms of the basic data—in my opinion—are those that purport to invalidate the relationship between the input and output variables under examination rather than those that limit the generalizability of relationships. Relationships of low generalizability are an endemic problem in all evaluations. In light of the difficulty of gaining external validity by randomly sampling from well-designated universes, we shall have to live with low or unsystematic generalizability, and little is gained by harsh criticism on this score. (However, this is no excuse for failing to recognize the limits of generalizability or for failing to achieve as heterogeneous a sample of persons, settings, and times as is possible!)

A final kind of review that is helpful is one that points out further major problems that can be examined with the available data. What makes this all the more important is that primary evaluators are frequently asked to respond to their critics, and if the critics can set up their critique so as to bring the happy constraints of data into the interchange, then the interchange should be improved. For instance, the Thorndike review could have been rephrased so as to highlight the desirability of analyzing the major Rosenthal and Jacobson table (grade X experimental condition) in terms of raw scores instead of IQ and, if the journal editors had been willing to wait a little longer, they might have been able to publish the review together with an improved analysis. In essence, the review would have been an impetus to an advancement of knowledge rather than to a mildly vituperative interchange. In the same vein, Jencks might have been moved by Levin's review to reanalyze those of his secondary sources for which real income could be ascertained (adjusted for regional variation), excluding unearned income (such as dividends and pensions), and for which data on age and extent of employment were available (thereby omitting the retired and the partially employed, such as students). In this way, Jencks would have been able to assess whether the prediction of income was improved when Levin's criticisms were taken into account. Finally, Hyman and Sheatsley rightly criticized the work on the authoritarian personality because of the plausibility of alternative interpretations that authoritarians and nonauthoritarians differed in education rather than psychodynamics. Obviously, the original authors need only to reanalyze their data in breakdowns by education level to examine this issue to some extent. Suggesting reanalyses in a review puts the debate about program effects back onto a level of data rather than prose.

I have previously remarked that reviews that concentrate on

external validity may not be helpful because external validity is rarely the central issue in the evaluations we are discussing. It is also rarely useful for policy makers to have a review that attempts to blame or praise the primary evaluation on a point-by-point basis. This is because the current state of the art does not produce evaluations that are beyond criticism; because the major issues may be lost among the more trivial; and because trivial issues can be blown out of proportion and used as an intended or unintended attack on the primary evaluator's competence, even when major issues have been well analyzed. It seems more important to me to have a point-by-point analysis of the steps leading to the major conclusions of an evaluation than to have a point-by-point analysis of the presumed strengths and inadequacies of an evaluation. The latter is, of course, very useful for teaching. But it is probably less useful for policy makers whose major interest is in one or two major conclusions from an evaluation.

Another kind of unhelpful review for policy makers is exemplified by some that Elashoff and Snow reproduce in their book. These were reviews that uncritically accepted the results of *Pygmalion in the Classroom* and expressed surprise that anyone else was surprised at the major finding (or expressed joy that the finding appeared to corroborate the reviewer's opinion) that the current problem in schools is a problem with teachers rather than with students. Given the state of the evaluation art, such uniformly glowing reviews are not likely to reflect the degree of confidence in a program that the data realistically inspire. They may also exacerbate an old problem by creating even more unrealistic expectations about what programs or single evaluations can accomplish. While credit should and must be given where it is due in reviewing primary evaluations, a review that dispenses only credit should arouse our suspicions and should alert us to look for relationships of value similarity or friendship between the reviewer and the primary evaluator.

A final kind of unhelpful review is exemplified by Snow's review[48] of *Pygmalion in the Classroom*. Snow took a very strong stand that the data did not support the primary analysts' conclusions, and he promised to reanalyze the data. He then did this. The problem here lies not in the review itself as much as in the fact that the reviewer who took a strong stand was the same person who later conducted the secondary evaluation. I suspect that the conclusions reached in some secondary evaluations may depend on any public stands about the outcome that the analyst may have taken before he began his work or during its early stages.

I have tried to suggest that the more helpful reviews focus only on central issues; pay particular attention to the basic data and their appropriateness for answering the evaluation questions; and try to point out ways in which the data can be reanalyzed. Such reviews graduate from the verdict of "Not proven in the primary evaluation" to a verdict of "Not proven as yet but can be tested in such and such a way." I am suggesting that the reviewer adopt the same critical perspective as any practicing scientist—that he try to prove false what is in the primary evaluation so that he can establish which conclusions he failed to prove false, which ones he could not test because of the quality of the data, and which ones he tested and found alternative interpretations for. Such reviews can provide useful feedback to the primary evaluator and the policy maker. They are more likely to put the subsequent discussion on a data basis and to prevent others from drawing naive conclusions from the primary evaluation.

But, when all is said and done, the review has restricted utility because of the relatively low degree to which it is constrained by the data. Thus, the reviewer is more likely to say that factor X *might* be affecting the dependent variable than he is to state that it *is* affecting the dependent variable or that it *is* affecting the dependent variable by Y amount or that it *is* affecting the dependent variable in different ways in different groups, or the like. Generating hypotheses requires knowledge, intelligence, and perseverance; testing them usually requires these same qualities plus manipulation of the data. Since the reviewer is more likely to have relevant knowledge, intelligence, and perseverance than he is to have relevant data, his reviews may well generate more hypotheses than they test. This creates the very uncertainty that policy makers want evaluations to rid them of. No other problem with reviews is as important as this.

After-the-Fact Simulations of a Primary Evaluation

Campbell and Erlebacher suspected that the Ohio-Westinghouse evaluation of Head Start contained a statistical regression artifact because of the attempt to match nonequivalent treatment and control groups on sex, race, and kindergarten attendance to make them more comparable in ability. However, there were clear signs that the control group children were somewhat more "advantaged" than the Head Start group, which led Campbell and Erlebacher to suggest that the matching underestimated possible effects of the program and that the spurious effects were not all statistically removed from post-test scores by a covariance analysis in which SES proxies were used to partial out any pre-test differences that remained after matching. To illustrate their points, they simulated pre-test and post-test data for two groups that had (1) different means at the pre-test (as would happen even after matching on third variables); (2) different means at the post-test; (3) within-group pre-test—post-test correlations of .50; and (4) no treatment effect. The post-test data were then analyzed with the pre-test as the covariate and, even though the simulation entailed no treatment effect, the analysis showed statistically significant group differences in the adjusted post-test means—the higher scoring pre-test group had a higher adjusted post-test mean. Campbell and Erlebacher concluded from this that covariance analysis fails to adjust for all the pretreatment difference between nonequivalent groups, particularly when the factorial structure of pretests and post-tests differ, and that this, plus the initial matching, rendered the results of the Head Start evaluation equivocal.

Responses to the Campbell and Erlebacher paper came from Cicirelli and from Evans and Schiller. Each paper acknowledged the correctness of the criticism of covariance analysis yet each denied its applicability to the Head Start data. Cicirelli voiced the principal objection by denying that the treatment and control groups differed by much in cognitive skills at the pre-test, thereby ensuring that any statistical regression would be slight and not enough to change the dismal overall "no difference" conclusion. Of course, no one knows just how large the pre-test ability differences were in the Head Start case, or what the pre-test—post-test correlations would have been, or what the size of any effect was, and so the issue raised by Campbell and Erlebacher creates an impasse. The parameters they used in their simulation were arbitrarily chosen for pedagogical purposes, and we have no idea how well they fit the Head Start data. If, by chance, they fit well, then a regression effect coupled with an inadequate statistical analysis might well be masking real effects of the program, because the Ohio-Westinghouse procedure definitely fails to equate nonequivalent groups. But if the parameters fit badly because the pre-test group differences were smaller than Campbell and Erlebacher estimated, then Cicirelli would probably be correct in stating that the bias due to the inadequate data analysis was small. The point is that simulations will not help us when we have no good data from which to estimate parameters.

The foregoing discussion implies that simulations can tell us what might have happened but not what did happen; that they are therefore useful for illustrating possible alternative interpretations (especially ones that are not well known); and that the degree of their usefulness depends on the extent to which parameter estimates fit reality. But there is more to simulations than this, as a paper by Light and Smith illustrates.[49]

They noted the relatively crude manner in which Jensen estimated the variance associated with the interaction of genetic and environmental factors. Jensen obtained the estimate by computing the median IQ intraclass correlation coefficient for monozygotic twins in four studies (.75), by computing the median intraclass correlation for unrelated children reared together from five studies (.24), and simply subtracting the two to give an interaction estimate of .01. This does not seem to be a stable estimate of the interaction variance, since no direct estimate was made and the indirect estimate was based on so few studies.[50] To check on the stability of the estimate, Light and Smith simulated 200 panels of five studies (each containing between 30 and 60 twins as in the studies Jensen reviewed) and then computed the standard error of the median intraclass coefficients for five different ways in which the variance due to genetics, environment, and their interaction could be partitioned. What was striking about the standard errors was their magnitude. For example, when 80 percent of the variance was due to genetics, 10 percent of the environment, and 10 percent to their interaction, the interaction standard error was .0895. This means that it is relatively likely to obtain a median r of .01 when the population median is in fact .1.

The issue then becomes: What difference does the magnitude of the interaction r make for explaining the origin of the 15-point IQ difference between blacks and whites? Light and Smith took the twelve SES categories from the 1960 United States census and assumed ten classes of genetic endowment to construct a 12×10 matrix. They then assumed that genetics accounted for 75 percent of the total IQ variance of 225 and that the environment accounted for the remainder. Since blacks are systematically overrepresented in lower SES groups it can be shown that, with blacks and whites being simulated as having identical genetic endowment, blacks as a group would have a mean IQ of 91.26 and whites 100.00. This difference would be due, of course, to environmental factors. But when 1 percent of the total IQ variance was introduced into the simulation as an interaction factor and the environmental contribution dropped to 24 percent, this resulted in a mean black IQ of 86.81 for the particular interaction pattern that Light and Smith chose. And when the interaction variance was made to equal 10 percent the black IQ dropped to 82.59.

Three points are worth noting about this. First, Light and Smith assigned identical genetic endowments to blacks and whites so that all the differences are due to the correlation of race and environment and to the interaction of race, environment, and genetics. Secondly, an estimate of the interaction as low as 1 percent can account for most of the 15-point IQ difference that separates blacks and whites in the United States today given the particular pattern of interaction weights that the authors chose. Thirdly, increasing the estimate to .10, since the Jensen estimate of .01 is so unstable, accounts for all the IQ difference without any need to invoke a simple genetic explanation.

The Light and Smith simulation differs from the Campbell and Erlebacher simulation in that the former authors were able to use the estimates given by their "protagonist" to invalidate the protagonist's conclusions in a way that cannot lead to a dispute about parameters. But, while estimates derived from data play a crucial role in disciplining the discussion in the Light and Smith paper, the authors readily acknowledge that the discipline is far from perfect. In particular, the interaction values in the authors' tables 2A and 3A are arbitrary and are subject only to the restriction that they account for 1 percent or 10 percent of the total variance, depending on the analysis. There is no discipline as to the form of the interaction, and, while it seems plausible to assume the social allocation model that Light and Smith call "malicious" (blacks are socially allocated to environments that fail to stimulate their genetic potential), it is not absolutely certain that this is so and it is certainly not certain how much this is so. Thus, the Light and Smith paper points out that the data used by Jensen can be interpreted to suit a nongenetic explanation of race differences, *or any other kind of explanation,* depending on the way one partitions the IQ variance, since the genetic, environment, and interaction variance estimates are unstable, and different consequences follow from the choice of parameter estimates.

Light and Smith cast doubt on Jensen's explanation, but they do not explain race differences in IQ. Like Campbell and Erlebacher, their work creates uncertainty about outcomes and fails to reduce uncertainty. Ironically enough, the authors admit that they could only reduce uncertainty if they could directly measure genotypes, environments, and their interactions.[51] Of course, if they could do this, they would not need to simulate at all! There is a functional sense in which simulations are like reviews: they illustrate what could have happened but not what did happen. However, they can be more helpful than reviews when they are used to estimate the plausibility of criticisms. To my mind, Light and Smith's crucial criticism of the instability of the median intraclass correlation for the interaction of genotype and environment would have been less convincing if it had been made without simulating what the standard error may have been.

After-the-Fact Evaluation of an Evaluation

The after-the-fact secondary evaluation of a primary evaluation involves asking the same questions that guided the primary data to test whether the same conclusions are reached when different analyses are carried out. In essence, one is using the primary data to evaluate the primary evaluation.

Having the data permits the secondary evaluator to check whether errors were committed in the primary evaluation and, if they were, to correct them. Smith, for example, discovered that Coleman's index of home factors was not constructed as reported. Smith then reanalyzed the data with Coleman's original index and the one he had intended to use. One can also check the distributions of raw scores, for instance, so as to ascertain if there are outliers of any importance or to see if means and variances are correlated and rescaling is required. And one can test alternative interpretations to distinguish those that are empirically viable from those that are not. An example of this comes from the analyses in which there was a reordering of the predictors that went into Coleman's regression analyses. Data serve to edit criticisms—to reduce the number of possible criticisms to those that are plausible and those that are untestable.

Secondary evaluations of primary evaluations can also involve better analyses of the data. For example, I have little doubt that Elashoff and Snow's use of raw scores was more appropriate than Rosenthal and Jacobson's use of IQ scores. I also feel that we improved on the first-year evaluation of "Sesame Street" by preserving the original design (a true experiment with children randomly assigned to being encouraged or not encouraged to view the show), breaking the data down by research site, testing whether the encouraged and nonencouraged groups differed in learning or background variables at the pre-test and whether they differed in reported viewing of the show, and then demonstrating that at the three sites where the randomly equivalent encouraged and nonencouraged groups differed in viewing they also differed in learning and that at the two sites where the encouraged and nonencouraged did not differ in viewing they did not differ in learning. This strategy of analysis avoided the problems that confronted Ball and Bogatz after they noticed that some of the nonencouraged children had watched "Sesame Street." Fearing that the control group of nonviewers had been compromised because some nonencouraged children had viewed the show, Ball and Bogatz collapsed encouraged and nonencouraged children across all sites, partitioned them into four nonequivalent viewing groups, and then—in essence—correlated viewing and raw learning gains.[52]

Typically, the analyses in secondary evaluations will be different rather than better. Take, for example, the case of a pre-test—post-test design with nonequivalent groups that may be maturing at different rates and where the evaluator has no reliable estimate of what these maturational rates are. I know of no correct way to analyze the data from such a situation,[53] and a secondary evaluator might want to try a different analysis from that used by the primary evaluator, or he might want to try several different analyses with different presumed biases in order to estimate *in very approximate fashion* a sort of confidence interval within which the effect of a program lies. When the different analyses produce comparable outcomes, a global inference about treatment effects can readily be made. The point is that the secondary evaluator will bring his own perspective on data analysis, and the question is whether different perspectives will produce comparable conclusions.

The secondary evaluator can also ask new questions. He might, for example, inquire about the *educational* significance of findings, as

opposed to their statistical significance; he might explore contingency questions that the primary evaluator did not have the commission, time, or inclination to study (e.g., does the program differentially affect boys and girls, blacks and whites, or young and old);
he might also explore the program's positive and negative side effects
by combing the available data for relevant items that will assume a
larger role in his evaluation than they did in the primary evaluation.

As a final addition to our list of advantages of this kind of secondary evaluation, we must not forget that it incorporates all the advantages of reviews and simulations: one can suggest new interpretations
of old data; one can propose new studies that need to be done; and
one can list any alternative interpretations that are not ruled out
with the data on hand.

But secondary evaluations of primary evaluations have problems;
some are generic, and others depend on the form of the secondary
evaluation. For example, Hanushek and Kain[54] took the Coleman
Report data on Negro twelfth graders in the North to establish the
relative priority of school resources, student body characteristics,
and family background in predicting achievement. This was a very
select sample of the data, and the authors reported, without citing
any data, that "other samples that we analyzed were less dramatic
but qualitatively similar." In other words, this sample was chosen
because its results were "dramatic." As it turns out, the school input
factor is associated with more variance than the peer factor in the
Hanushek and Kain analysis, irrespective of the order in which the
variables enter the analysis. This finding differs from Coleman's and
from those of all the other secondary evaluators whose work is represented in the Moynihan and Mosteller volume. We can suspect at
least two reasons for this difference: the possible sampling bias that
led to selecting black twelfth graders in the North; and the fact that
Hanushek and Kain defined school inputs in terms of Coleman's
school-resources-plus-teacher variables. The moral is that secondary
evaluations of a small sample of the total data are suspect, especially
when no compelling rationale for selection is advanced.

There are, of course, reasons for selecting subsamples for reanalysis. Smith and Bissell reasoned that it was fairer to evaluate Head
Start full-year centers than summer centers (since the former were
more likely to have an impact) and to restrict the analysis to first
graders (since they would be more likely to show effects than

children who had graduated from Head Start two or three years earlier). Smith and Bissell also claimed that the affective tests were of dubious reliability and validity and that one of the cognitive tests was invalid. Thus, they restricted their analysis to a sample of centers, children, and measures that was *most likely to reveal effects* because the program's impact was presumably strongest with these samples. Thus, they came closer to conducting what I call a "tailored" evaluation.[55] But the very fact of sample selection makes the secondary evaluators vulnerable to charges that they capitalized on sampling variation. This charge was, in fact, leveled against the authors by Cicirelli and by Evans and Schiller,[56] who demonstrated that the Smith and Bissell results were limited to the one measure and to first graders. They also demonstrated that their own primary analyses of this particular subset of the data had produced comparable outcomes, and so they claimed that Smith and Bissell did not reach different conclusions from those of the Ohio-Westinghouse study but merely presented part of the total picture of Head Start's overall effects. Secondary evaluations designed to test a program at its strongest points need to make this aim very clear, for it should serve to moderate any conclusions we draw from the data if systematic sample selection has taken place.

A major limitation of the kind of secondary evaluation under discussion is the fact that the evaluator is limited to the data collected by the primary evaluator. Should those data prove inadequate for answering questions, developing new indices, exploring side effects, or the like, there is little the secondary evaluator can do. Indeed, we could probably draw up a humorous list of threats to internal and construct validity that could be applied to discredit most evaluations and that are assessable or controlled in few studies. (The Hawthorne effect would head the list.) This restriction may not be too irksome if the secondary evaluator conceives of his task as evaluating an evaluation rather than evaluating a program. But it is nonetheless a restriction that cuts him off from examining other literature that might be germane to evaluation issues for which no adequate data exist in the primary evaluation.

A further disadvantage is that of time. Primary evaluations are set up to provide feedback that is accurate, useful, and timely. Yet most secondary evaluations take place after the primary evaluation report has been published. Since most have been done in university settings, the results of the secondary analyses became available only after several years. It is not clear that such information is useful when it appears. (However, it may be useful at some time in the future when policy alternatives like the ones evaluated may reemerge. They will, of course, be old problems and old proposed solutions, but they may be dressed in new clothes.)

Another difficulty with evaluations of evaluations concerns the individuation of secondary evaluators. Imagine conducting a careful secondary evaluation in which, after introducing one's own perspectives about questions, analysis, and interpretation, one arrives at essentially the same conclusions as the primary analyst. This is a result of importance to policy makers, but it is of no help to the secondary analyst, who thinks: "Well, I spent two years replicating someone else. That hardly helps me to stand out." Such pressure for individuation may lead secondary evaluators to contrast the differences between the primary and secondary evaluations rather than to highlight the findings that are similar. Indeed, this pressure might sometimes even lead to the recruitment of secondary evaluators who enter their work desiring to stand out from the primary work by reaching different conclusions, and I suspect that individuation may help explain why we often find a similarity between primary and secondary evaluations at the data level that is not reflected in the prose about program effects.

The pressure to do more than replicate is one of several reasons why there will tend to be antagonism between primary and secondary evaluators. But the major reason is probably that the secondary evaluator conceives of his role as evaluating the primary evaluation (to which the primary evaluator is intimately attached, of course) in as critical and as honest a way as he can. Given the current difficulties of conducting evaluation research, it is inevitable that a critical evaluator of evaluations will find much to comment on critically, and the primary evaluator is likely to take this as an attack on his competence or a reflection of unrealistic standards about what can be accomplished in a single evaluation, or whatever. In any event, relationships between primary and secondary evaluators have not been amicable in the past, with the possible exception of Coleman and some of the authors in the Moynihan and Mosteller volume (who were less harsh than earlier critics and, in the main, corroborated Coleman's conclusions).

Of course, there is no reason why relationships should be amicable. Much of the history of science is characterized by a competition between theories that is matched by a competition between theorists, and a very strong case can be made that science needs our passionate advocacy every bit as much as it needs our dispassionate distance. But the case of secondary evaluations is somewhat different, in that secondary evaluators are often dependent on primary evaluators for the release of data and, in some cases, for information that is not in the research reports (such as how testers were trained, whether they knew the hypothesis, whether any dropped out, and how this or that analysis was conducted). Persons who think they are being evaluated will be defensive, especially if they read past history in a distorted way and believe that having one's evaluation evaluated only leads to public squabbles that do one's reputation and one's ulcers (real or incipient) no good at all.

After-the-Fact Secondary Evaluation of a Program

Secondary evaluations of programs differ from secondary evaluations of primary evaluations in that the major research question is what the effects of a program are rather than how adequate the primary evaluation is for substantiating the conclusions it drew. The new question frees the secondary evaluator from the need to assess the primary evaluation and thereby the primary evaluator. Instead, he uses the data only for their help in answering the new evaluation questions he raises. As a model, therefore, it should decrease, but by no means eliminate, the potential for antagonism that is built into the primary and secondary evaluator roles.

More importantly, it should increase the probability of having the evaluator start from scratch in thinking through which evaluation questions are in fact appropriate. For instance, Ball and Bogatz asked whether children who were encouraged to watch "Sesame Street" learned from the show, as indexed primarily by cognitive tests developed by ETS to reflect the content of "Sesame Street" that were administered within about one month after the show. In our reevaluation of "Sesame Street" (rather than of the ETS evaluations), we asked the same question as the ETS team because the answer would be relevant for establishing what "Sesame Street" might accomplish if accompanied by face-to-face encouragement of the child to view the program. (Of course, parents were also indirectly encouraged to help their child by the manipulation!) Few children in the United States view the show today under the contingency of such encouragement. Most children view without the form of encouragement that the research children experienced, and in this sense it is the nonencouraged children—who were considered controls—who are the most ecologically valid treatment children. Hence, we took particular pains to ask whether nonencouraged viewers learned from viewing.

The operational question of the ETS team was derived from the overall objective of "Sesame Street," which was "stimulating the intellectual and cultural growth of preschoolers, particularly disadvantaged preschoolers."[57] This statement was interpreted by Ball and Bogatz to mean that the show would be considered successful if economically disadvantaged children learned from it. But a different interpretation of the general aim is also possible, and it relates to a national problem cited by Cooney (in the original grant proposal from which the above quotation came): the achievement gap between advantaged and disadvantaged children. The second interpretation is that "Sesame Street" should especially stimulate the growth of disadvantaged children and should thereby narrow the academic achievement gap. The exact interpretation of Cooney's statement is not clear, but whether narrowing the gap is or is not an aim of the show it has at least twice been claimed by Ball and Bogatz as a result of the show. Moreover, the gap is assumed by many persons to be a serious national problem in the preschool area. Hence, we decided to ask what effect, if any, "Sesame Street" was having on the achievement gap, partly because narrowing the gap might have been one of the original aims of the show, and largely because it certainly was a claim made for the show and certainly is a problem of relevance in preschool education.

It is not clear whether Ball and Bogatz were interested in making the gap question one of their major questions. Nor is it clear that they would have been allowed to make it a major question. After all, a good case can be made that the most useful test of what a program can do involves implementing it at its strongest rather than at its most representative. The encouragement treatment was strong and did enhance viewing, but it also had the side effect of confounding encouragement and viewing and of increasing viewing to levels above those that would have occurred without encouragement. In any event, the search for a powerful treatment may explain why the principal treatment in the ETS studies was encouragement to view "Sesame Street" rather than the viewing of "Sesame Street" by non-encouraged children. It should also be remembered that "Sesame Street" was first broadcast as an experimental program on public television. The regular audience of educational channels is dispropor-tionately biased in favor of higher SES groups—at least, among adults. Thus it might have been unrealistic to expect a public educa-tion program to reach the kind of audience that would facilitate narrowing the achievement gap, and this fact might explain why the gap question assumed a low profile in the ETS evaluations. Fortu-nately, the secondary evaluator has more freedom to pose and re-phrase questions than the primary evaluator, and we were subject to none of the restrictions that may have applied to Ball and Bogatz.

This freedom goes beyond the higher-order questions that deter-mine the character of an evaluation. It also permits data analyses according to criteria of social as opposed to statistical significance. It permits looking for generalization and negative side effects as well as examining the long-term effects of a program (which are presumably determined by whatever remains of the initial effects and the modifi-cations wrought by the child's environment apart from the program, making them measures of more than just the program effects). The secondary evaluator's freedom also extends to exploring the value implications of the data and to suggesting their policy relevance. Most primary evaluators do not consider these last two tasks to be within their role, and they are less likely than secondary evaluators to have the necessary time, or inclination, or permission to pose the relevant questions. Yet all of them are required for comprehensive program evaluation.

Evaluating a program rather than an evaluation encourages the search for relevant data from sources other than the primary evalua-tion. At the simplest level, the evaluator looks for studies conducted before or after the primary evaluation that can replicate it. More importantly, with a larger framework of questions, he will want to know, for example, whether the effects generalize to standardized tests of preschool knowledge, and to answer this he must seek out studies that used other measures. For instance, the ETS evaluators tailored their outcome measures to the content of "Sesame Street," thus precluding an analysis of what the show did on standard tests of school readiness. Fortunately, a dissertation from Fordham by

Judith Minton[58] used the Metropolitan in an evaluation of "Sesame Street," and we were able to use her data. To take another example, if an evaluator is to learn what "Sesame Street" is doing to the national gap, he needs to know the correlation between viewing and SES in the nation at large. Fortunately, we were able to obtain Nielsen and Harris television viewer survey data on this topic, and they supplemented the data from the less representative ETS and Minton samples.

But problems do arise in posing questions that were not the central focus of a primary evaluation, simply because the primary data were not collected with the secondary evaluator's questions in mind. Thus, in the case of our reevaluation of "Sesame Street," there was in the first-season evaluation a total sample of only 108 disadvantaged and nonencouraged children who viewed the show at home, and there were only 117 children in the second-season evaluation. These are not as large samples as one would like for exploring the relationship of viewing to learning among the nonencouraged children. In exploring the gap question, there were definite ceiling effects inhibiting growth among the most advantaged sample, and this was probably a result of the high priority that ETS set on creating learning measures that would answer whether disadvantaged children learned from a treatment of encouragement and viewing. There was thus a lower priority for assessing whether there was any pre-test-to-post-test growth among the higher-scoring advantaged sample, and the learning measures were less appropriate for these children. The data from other sources are not likely to be 100 percent appropriate for the secondary evaluator's needs either. For example, the viewing data from the Nielsen and Harris surveys were not broken down by geographic region and SES locator in the same analysis so that the simple relationship between SES and viewing "Sesame Street" is confounded with region. Moreover, the sample of black homes with a child from two to six is small in a national survey of a simple random sample. In fact, the number is only about fifty in the typical national survey, and no estimate of viewing by black children based on so few cases is reliable. Obviously, a stratified sample is required for more reliable estimates.

All of these problems can be examined, and allowance can be made for them to some extent, particularly if the evaluator follows a strategy of looking for multiple scores of relevant data—all of which may be imperfect, but most of which have different imperfections. Nonetheless, there is no substitute for having secondary evaluators either obtain the auxiliary data and reanalyze them for themselves (when this is possible) or commission additional studies that will provide the necessary information. Indeed, I suspect that additional data collected in light of important new questions could be used for discovering new findings, for providing focused replication of the most important relationships in the evaluation, and for testing old assumptions (e.g., about the rate at which different groups mature, so that estimates can be made of growth rates, and deviations from these expected rates can be tested). Without such additional data, secondary analyses of programs are more likely to be suggestive than definitive in answering questions for which the primary evaluation was not designed.

Indeed, there are circumstances where even a suggestive answer cannot be made. Cohen, Pettigrew, and Riley[59] set out to use the Coleman data to explore whether Negro achievement was related differently to the racial mix of the school (1) when integration had taken place and intergroup contact was positive[60] and (2) when mere desegregation had taken place and intergroup relations were no better or were worse than before. Unfortunately, the authors could not answer their question because, on the one hand, the item asking about atmosphere in the classrooms asked about the extent to which "the different races or ethnic groups . . . get along"—thereby confounding racial and ethnic factors—and, on the other hand, the correlation of school average level of interracial friendship and school percent Negro student body was .80. (The correlation was so high because of the restricted range of black-white friendships in predominantly white schools.) The authors concluded from this that they could not sensitively test how the degree of interracial friendship was related to achievement, since there was so little variability in interracial friendship at most schools. Thus, the data proved inadequate for this task, for which they were not originally collected, of course.

Despite these problems, secondary evaluations of programs are likely to be more useful than reviews of an evaluation, or simulations of it, or even evaluations of evaluations. One indirect source of usefulness, in addition to those listed earlier, is that the secondary evaluation of programs can lend visibility and context to any new questions for which the data suggest answers, and they can indicate prac-

tical ways of answering these questions more definitively. For instance, we became convinced of the importance of assessing how
"Sesame Street" graduates fared in schools. This question can be
answered relatively easily and cheaply with the ETS sample merely
by preserving the original distinction between encouraged and nonencouraged children and checking school archives at sites where the
encouraged viewed more heavily than the nonencouraged (Durham,
Phoenix, and Los Angeles). Thanks to random assignment, these
groups are comparable and can be traced through school via archives
and interviews with students, peers, teachers, and parents. In a similar vein, a quasi-experimental study is called for that concentrates on
children of different SES levels who are not encouraged to view
"Sesame Street" and who have free access to the show at home. This
will add a degree of confidence to what we now suspect about the
magnitude of effects of "Sesame Street" and about its differential
impact on group learning means. And thirdly, we need a national
survey using a random sample of homes, stratified and weighted by
race and age of child, to see how viewing is related to race and to
recognized indices of SES in the various regions of the United States
and in urban, suburban, and rural settings. Conducting a secondary
evaluation of a program permits the evaluator to make a strong,
context-based case for the next evaluation step for a particular program or whole class of programs. All of this paragraph is relevant, for
example, to evaluating "The Electric Company" or any social reform
that is made available on a universal basis but may be utilized on a
selective basis.

Like the models we previously analyzed, the secondary evaluation
of a program is likely to be dominated by the single perspective of
the principal investigator, and this will play some role in what questions are asked, how the data are analyzed, and particularly how they
are interpreted and what speculations are made about their policy
relevance. Such dominance of a single perspective is not inevitable, of
course, and attempts can be made to have secondary analyses performed by an interdisciplinary team of investigators or to have pre-
publication drafts of the secondary evaluation examined by experts
in areas representing a wide range of perspectives on the issue at
hand. Both of these strategies are to be recommended.

There are some ways in which the Mosteller and Moynihan volume
represents an important breakthrough in the secondary evaluation of

a program, though we must be careful here to define program very broadly to encompass the provision of global school resources for the purpose of raising academic achievement. Having several interested persons conduct separate analyses of the data permitted a division of labor, so that different investigators could pursue questions they considered important; in so doing, they examined most of the criticisms leveled at the Coleman Report. Jencks, for example, explored the issue of bias in the schools that entered the sample; Smith alone and Hanushek and Kain together independently examined how the ordering of predictors influenced the percentage of variance associated with school, home, and peer factors; Smith also explored the basic data down to the item level and discovered problems of index construction; Armor constructed his own indices of school and home facilities and tested how they related to achievement; and both Jencks and the team of Mosteller and Moynihan attempted to fit the survey and its results into their own perspectives on its implications for policy and for the conventional wisdom. What is more important to note is that the Harvard group was mixed with respect to disciplinary training (including sociologists, statisticians, policy scientists, and social psychologists) and these diverse evaluators could presumably cross-fertilize each other. Their previous public stands also differed to some extent on issues touched by the report. Jencks, for example, has claimed that school resources are not significant in affecting achievement or income; Armor has claimed that desegregation, as presently practiced, does not narrow the gap between blacks and whites and may have negative side effects; and Pettigrew has been associated with the position that interracial schools that are truly integrated will facilitate achievement in blacks. Bringing a variety of points of view to bear by persons who are honestly prepared to see what the data have to say will control to some extent for the idiosyncracies that inadvertently creep in when one investigator works alone—even trying to be as objective as he humanly can.

There must be ways, though, of improving on the example set by the Harvard seminar. Despite the heterogeneity of perspectives, we look in vain for the contribution of authors who have taken a strong public stance criticizing the Coleman Report or whose training and values might make them critical. If Bowles and Levin had been members of the team, this would have added strength to the point of view of the economists that Hanushek and Kain represented and would have allowed us to assess how early critics of the Report reacted after they had empirically examined the validity of the criticisms that could be tested. A second problem concerns the long delay between publication of the Coleman Report (1966) and of the Mosteller and Moynihan volume (1972). Would it be feasible to organize such seminars on evaluations of great public importance even before publication, once it is known that the results imply a change in educational policy? If the results of the performance contracting experiment had been positive instead of generally negative, this would have had important implications, and a second assessment of the data would have been called for quickly. It would certainly be advantageous, I think, to somehow forewarn a team of interested persons as soon as particular patterns of data emerge in the primary analysis, so that they could arrange to reanalyze the data as soon as possible before or after a final report is issued.

Despite these problems, the Moynihan and Mosteller volume stands out as one means of dividing labor in order to analyze a program in comprehensive fashion using a variety of different perspectives on data analysis as well as on the interpretation of the data and on the interpretation of the social problem that led to collecting the data.

After-the-Fact Program Evaluation Using Multiple Data Sets

We are all, I assume, convinced of the virtues of replication. It can edit our theories by ruling out alternative interpretations that threaten the interpretation of some studies but not others; it can extend external validity, by demonstrating relationships across multiple settings, groups, and times, or it can indicate important contingencies under which a particular relationship does or does not hold; it can refine the interpretation of constructs by indicating which instances of a treatment do and do not result in differences for a variety of outcome measures; and, finally, it can contribute to statistical conclusion validity if the statistical abuses of one study are not repeated in others and if there is some way of empirically assessing the educational significance of effects so that we can know the conditions under which large effects can be consistently obtained.

A major limitation of all the models I previously examined was that they depended on a single body of data. This is not to say that a single body excludes replication. At the simplest level, the concept of a between-subjects error term implies replication; and at a more important level, evaluations are often set up so as to replicate relationships across sex, age, site, IQ level, treatment variation, and class of outcome or process measures. But I think it fair to conclude that a single evaluation has less heterogeneity in these factors than do most bodies of relevant literature that are built on multiple research reports, and few individual evaluations have much useful heterogeneity in when or how a treatment is implemented or in the evaluator's perspective.

It is extremely difficult to review the literature on most topics. Many of the reasons for this are mundane, and I shall cover them quickly. First, there are the sampling problems associated with the fact that studies do or do not enter the literature of published and unpublished reports, and reports do or do not come to a reviewer's attention. Then, there is the problem of quality control—deciding which studies to consider and which not on the basis of their quality. There are no set criteria for quality, and the tastes of reviewers vary considerably. Even when common criteria can be established, the decisions of which studies meet the criteria are not always highly reliable, as is illustrated by the interchange between Armor and Pettigrew et al. with reference to the effects of busing (see footnotes 19 and 20).

Then there is the problem of deciding which high quality studies are of greatest relevance. Jencks et al., for example, in their discussion of the effects of school quality on occupational status[61] first refer to studies of indirect relevance and then to "two bits of direct evidence on the relationship between schooling and status," for which they cite two studies: one shows a correlation between the occupational status of Northern blacks and attendance at segregated or desegregated schools, and the other shows a correlation between the status of Catholics and attendance at public or parochial schools. Such "direct" evidence seems to me to be "indirect" for the purposes of testing causal propositions about schooling and status, because of the obvious selection differences between blacks who attended segregated and desegregated schools and between Catholics who attended public and parochial schools. What is direct evidence then?

There are also problems of estimating how many replications are sufficient for drawing reasonable conclusions. In this respect, we have already seen that Jensen used only four studies of monozygotic twins and that there may well have been a high error associated with the variance estimates he abstracted from the literature. (It is saddening to note, in passing, that premature publication based on too little evidence is probably encouraged by current reinforcement contingencies in academe.) And, as a final obvious pitfall in seeking to review multiple studies, I cannot fail to mention that those very differences among studies that give replication its potential payoff are the same differences that breed what look like conflicting results from apparently similar studies. And such conflicts of results probably contribute to the self-conscious pessimism that often arises when applied social scientists view the relevance to practice of some body of literature that they thought might be of use and have to conclude that there is so much inconsistency that they cannot use the literature for decision-making purposes.

Part of the problem of inconsistent findings has to do with the naiveté of expecting main effects of treatment instead of their interaction with subjects, settings, times, and measures. It is quite legitimate to draw up an array of studies that meets some quality and relevance criteria and then to list their outcomes in order to assess how often a particular outcome is obtained. However, this strategy rarely seems to result in cause-effect relationships that are robust over a wide range of times, settings, persons, etc., since as many null or reversed causal relationships emerge as there are replications of an expected or dominant relationship. Perhaps a more sensible strategy at this time would be to examine the list of studies for relationships that hold only under certain conditions. The problem then is to so order and describe the studies that data-related hypotheses can be advanced about the conditions under which a particular relationship holds, does not hold, or is reversed. The major problems here are that we need a large array of well-described studies before the procedure is possible.

In their review of the literature on teacher expectations, Baker and Christ[62] stated that it would have been prohibitive to reanalyze the data from all the relevant experiments, so they took the authors' conclusions at face value. This is a dangerous procedure, of course, since a critical review of some studies or a reanalysis of their data might reveal the basis for reduced confidence in the verbal conclusion of the original author. An even more difficult problem than having the wherewithal to scrutinize each study is the lack of rules of evidence for evaluating the implications of many studies. Light and Smith[63] have pointed out that many reviewers compute median values from the studies they review; others count the number of positive, null, and negative findings and "vote," on the basis of frequency, as to which relationship is most likely. In his work on the heredity-intelligence issue, Jencks was prepared to assume that the results from studies with large samples were more reliable than those from studies with smaller samples, and so he combined studies by obtaining the weighted mean variance associated with genotypes, environments, and their correlation. The median, vote, and weighted mean strategies elevate decision making above human judgment that is hardly constrained by the data, but they are nonetheless crude strategies that can be misleading even when the number of relevant studies is small. We urgently need acceptable and accepted criteria that reduce the role of personal judgment in drawing conclusions from multiple data sets.

Replication derives its advantages from repeated testings of a common cause-effect relationship when the irrelevancies associated with any one test are different across the tests. Replications that fail to make irrelevancies heterogeneous[64] are particularly dangerous because they can lead to situations where error is constant and where the relationship of the presumed cause and effect is never adequately tested. The Jencks volume seems to me to be like this, since it involves the analysis of many studies, most of which use cross-sectional designs to answer causal questions that can be answered only with careful longitudinal designs that can take adequate account of threats to internal validity (especially selection). By the same token, if one is convinced, as Pettigrew et al. are, that the effects of school desegregation can be assessed only by comparing the school performance of black desegregated children with black segregated children, then there is little point in reviewing a list of studies of desegregation that have committed the common "error" of comparing black desegregated children and white desegregated children.

The foregoing appears at first glance to be a long and forbidding list of pitfalls in the way of using multiple relevant data sets for evaluating educational reforms or assumptions. But what I would like to do next is to suggest some ways in which this important means of acquiring reliable knowledge can be improved.

First of all, I think that we need more accurate ways of describing experiments, especially the global treatment packages that are implemented under some simple label like "busing" or "encouragement to view 'Sesame Street' " or "years in school." Such experiences are not as homogeneous as the verbal labels imply: there are many ways of being bused, being encouraged, or spending years in school. Descriptions of the treatment that subjects are supposed to receive have to be complemented by descriptions of what they do receive and descriptions of the processes that follow. Observation, interviews, questionnaires, and video recordings are all useful for this purpose if they are applied to samples in a way that produces unbiased data at relatively low cost. Furthermore, I suspect we need visible guidelines that suggest to primary evaluators the dimensions for describing treatments—guidelines concerning the length of treatment exposure, frequency of exposure, social conditions of exposure, reinforcements for exposure, tester knowledge of exposure, etc. I have few illusions about the feasibility of obtaining sufficiently reliable and valid information about treatments so that we will be able to scale treatments along some common dimensions. But it is a necessary step for the future if we are not to compare apples and oranges and if we are to progress toward contingency theories of program effectiveness.

We also need work on developing criteria for assessing the quality of studies. There is already agreement that, when they can be carried through, true experiments provide less ambiguous inferences about cause than quasi experiments. Moreover, there is probably agreement that some quasi-experimental designs are stronger than others, and we could list these. There is probably also consensus that most quasi experiments without pre-tests are weak; that large-sample research is preferable to small-sample work; that longer treatment exposure is preferable to short; that blind testing is preferable to testing with awareness of treatments; that measures of high reliability and unobtrusiveness are better than measures of lower reliability and more obtrusiveness; and so forth. What these rather obvious points imply is that it should be possible to develop a framework of criteria that can be ordered for importance, applied to most studies, and used by secondary evaluators who review large bodies of literature, to establish quality control.

The support for such an idea would probably grow if it could be demonstrated that there is more obvious consistency in the results of better quality than lower quality studies. I suspect this is the case with preschool programs where more heartening results are obtained from true experiments than from quasi experiments and where the results from quasi experiments are more interpretable than those from ex post facto studies. The problem here, of course, is that the quality of the design is probably confounded with the extent of focus of the research and the carefulness of the investigator, so that any relationship between research quality and consistency of results could be alternatively interpreted. But merely to demonstrate the relationship would be an important first step.

There are distinct limits to what we can know from a research report, and I have little confidence that the studies that pass our quality control criteria on paper will also pass our criteria with respect to their basic data. For instance, Sir Cyril Burt's data on twins played a very important role in the Jensen and Jencks discussions of heritability, and this is readily understandable because of the large and heterogeneous samples used. But recent examinations by Kamin indicate that these basic data are by no means as extensive or as sound as they were thought to be. Similarly, I suspect that in many studies a cursory descriptive analysis of the distribution of scores within conditions would show basement and ceiling effects that do not appear in the standard tables of means, standard deviations, or correlations. What we need are, first, data banks into which the raw data supporting every publication or research report have to be deposited so that they can be retrieved quickly and cheaply without protracted negotiation between primary and secondary evaluators; and, secondly, flexible computer program packages that can describe data along empirical quality control dimensions so that we can quickly establish the range of questions for which a particular set of data is appropriate.

What I am suggesting is that a literature analysis is required as a first quality control step and that a speedy description of the data from studies passing that first hurdle is a necessary second step. I am thus advocating a secondary evaluation strategy using multiple data sets in which the evaluator manipulates the data of the better relevant studies to probe evaluation questions in the light of probable policy alternatives and hypotheses suggested by the literature review. Once he has the data from some high-quality studies, the secondary evaluator is in a much stronger position to assess how potential causes and effects are related and to explore the conditions modifying any such relationships than he would be without the data. Moreover, he can conduct his analyses in the full knowledge that a replication of relationships might be possible across the data sets he is reanalyzing and even across some of the studies he has rejected for quality reasons.

Let me explain this last point. Imagine that a person is evaluating whether a particular class of televised preschool programs narrows the achievement gap. He obtains the data from a subset of adequately evaluated programs where strong experimental designs were involved. Tests of the programs, however, have confounded the SES levels of the children and their regions—for example, the disadvantaged come disproportionately from the South or rural settings. This makes any correlation between SES and viewing suspect, since it may merely reflect regional preferences for programs. A stringent way of assessing whether SES and viewing are related is to correlate them within any one research site. Now, many experiments tend to have a low number of subjects for within-site correlational purposes. However, among the inadequate evaluations, in which there were, say, no valid control groups or large pre-test—post-test differences in the reliability of learning tests, there might be large samples from single sites. Such studies would not pass the first screening for quality as evaluations of a televised program, but this does not mean they would necessarily have poor measures of SES or viewing or that the correlation of the two would be meaningless for testing whether SES and viewing are related within a single geographical area.

What I am suggesting is that some bodies of data will be more useful for extensive data reanalysis than others and that the secondary evaluator should make these data his major concern, since he will not have time for the detailed examination of many data sets. This does not mean that the evidence in low-quality evaluations is of universally low quality. Quality depends on the questions being asked, and a poor evaluation for answering causal questions may have considerable descriptive information that is useful.

It is likely that reviews of the literature will become more and more common in the future and will be used to guide policy or strategies for assessing the impact of policy alternatives. The major reason for this is that the volume of partially relevant data that can be retrieved is expanding. This will avoid problems of the past where reviews have not always been of direct relevance to the issue (e.g., much of Hunt's[65] review on early childhood stimulation did not deal with humans), and it may obviate some of the problems of the present where reviews do not seem to me to recognize quality control issues at the design and data levels in bold fashion; where there is restricted concern for contingency questions; and where it is rare to see extensive reanalysis of the very best bodies of data for probing major issues. This may be because very good sets of data are rare and because it is time-consuming to conduct empirical reanalyses when one is not organizationally primed to carry out such work quickly and carefully. In the future, as data and data banks accumulate, secondary evaluations using multiple data sets will become more common, and their potential payoff is considerable. We have to begin thinking about practical ways of making this payoff accurate, useful, and timely.

Simultaneous Secondary Evaluation Using Consultant-Metaevaluators

All the preceding models of secondary evaluation had the common drawback that the work took place *after* the primary evaluation. There is an obvious utility to having the secondary evaluation take place at the same time as the primary evaluation. One way of doing this involves the use of consultant-metaevaluators whose work feeds back into the primary evaluation and is presumably used to suggest new alternatives, to note and correct potential mistakes, and to suggest and obtain additional help from the most competent sources, whom the metaevaluators know through their "invisible college" connections.

Consultants are regularly used in evaluating large-scale programs, and their functions vary as considerably as their fields of competence. What is unusual, in my experience at least, is to have consultants who are told to function as metaevaluators by the agencies contracting for the research. This concept carries the connotation that they will overview the primary evaluation and evaluate its progress. The longitudinal evaluation of the ESAA Pilot Program by System Development Corporation[66] has Scriven, Glass, and Stake cast in such a role. Its advantages may be considerable in that persons of acknowledged competence are closely linked to an evaluation and involved in its higher-order decisions. The Huron Institute is also functioning in such a role with respect to the analysis by Abt Associates of the Follow Through data.

It is interesting to note that SDC proposed these persons, and this may be one precondition for the effective use of metaevaluators. I know of a case where a social science methodologist was cast in what seemed to be a similar role by an outside agency (not the financial sponsors of the evaluation). He was at first accepted in this role by the primary evaluators, but the relationship was later discontinued for reasons that are not entirely clear. It may have been that the primary evaluators lacked trust in a metaevaluator whom they had not chosen themselves or who was not assigned to them by the sponsoring agency as a precondition for gaining the evaluation contract.

There is obviously not much information to date directly relevant to specifying the limitations and advantages of the metaevaluator role. One can foresee some difficulties, however. In the first place, the current ambiguity of the role requirements raises certain questions. Which kinds of decisions will the metaevaluators have a hand in? What will be their powers—advisory or prescriptive? What will be the basis of their authority—professional standing, personality, friendship with project directors, formal agreements with project directors, coalitions with presidents and vice-presidents over project directors' heads, formal agreements with the sponsors (rather than the implementers)? These are important issues; they have important implications concerning the "teeth" that metaevaluators will have and the quality of their relationships with project personnel. If such issues are not faced before the metaevaluators embark on their task, they may have to be settled during the work, and clarification may be much less helpful at that time. If the issues are never settled, the metaevaluators may be no more than a research advisory board whose effectiveness depends on force of personality and informal relationships with project directors and research sponsors. It should not be forgotten that metaevaluators, by virtue of the name, are like secondary evaluators of a primary evaluation. As we saw earlier, evaluations of evaluations have in the past been associated with strained relationships between secondary and primary analysts. The relationship need not be strained, of course, but it has often been so.

A precondition for success seems to be that metaevaluators know about the evaluation in much greater detail than typical research advisory boards or consultants who are used because of their narrow specialized competence. Clearly, then, metaevaluators have to set aside time and psychic energy to devote to the evaluation, and it is not always easy to liberate enough time to be on top of most aspects of an evaluation from question formation through final report. Indeed, it seems to me that a small team of top-flight metaevaluators will have a particularly difficult task unless its members succeed in making institutional arrangements to free themselves of some of the time-consuming burdens that come with widespread professional recognition in evaluation research. We need to examine how well this consultant-metaevaluator relationship works so that, if necessary, modifications can be made in the future.

Simultaneous Secondary Evaluations of the Data

Most contractors have responsibility for designing a study and for collecting, editing, analyzing, and interpreting the data. However, it is possible to imagine the situation where, for important questions, the edited data are given to more than one contractor for analysis and interpretation, and the different contractors present their results at about the same time. The advantages of this are obvious: it is relatively cheap, since the analysis of edited data is only a small part of most budgets; questions can be tackled using multiple analysis methods; there will be some heterogeneity with respect to the auxiliary questions that are asked and the inadvertant biases that color interpretation of the data; and if sponsors lose confidence in the primary analyst's skills there is someone to fall back on with a minimum loss of time. This form of secondary evaluation is closely related to the after-the-fact secondary evaluation of evaluations and of programs, and it shows most of their limitations except that there need not be a time lag between the appearance of the primary and secondary evaluations.

There is no reason why each contractor should receive the same commission, and it might in some cases be highly desirable to have one of them define his commission more broadly (asking, for example, what is the probable impact of the program nationwide, while the other focuses on its impact on the recipients in the research sample) or one contractor might concentrate more than the others on side effects or long-term effects and might use other secondary sources to help in this. Indeed, if set up properly, one of the contractors could easily concentrate on the analysis of multiple data sets during the time the other was collecting or editing data. Having multiple analysts makes it possible to examine the multiple reports for their convergence (particularly with respect to the major issue or issues behind the experimental design), their divergence (particularly when the same questions were asked), and the uniqueness of each, which results from one contractor asking questions the other did not.

There seems to be a growing realization among evaluation researchers that there is usually no single correct analysis (especially where quasi experiments are involved). This has led to an increase in the number of actual and proposed evaluations in which the data are analyzed in multiple ways, none of which is absolutely correct or incorrect. Such a strategy, when carried out by individual contractors, confers some of the advantages that would be conferred by having the same body of data analyzed by different persons with different data analysis styles. However, the current practice, while a distinct improvement over the past practice of a single best analysis, cannot confer all of the advantages of having multiple analysts do the job, since the indices that go into analyses are not likely to vary across analyses by the same person and since the early data returns may inadvertently bias the analyst toward later work that will corroborate the "findings" that are crystallizing in his mind.

A further advantage of having multiple analysts is that it might be possible to have the secondary evaluation carried out by persons at universities. As things now stand, few universities have the permanent staff of trained persons necessary for conducting large-scale evaluations. But they have staff for the more limited task of analyzing edited data, which is what university researchers often do anyway. Thus, if teaching time can be reduced in some way and if experienced programmers can be hired full-time, there is no reason why secondary evaluations of the kind we are discussing cannot be conducted beyond the pale of profit or nonprofit agencies.

To date, I know of no instances where multiple simultaneous evaluations of a single body of data have been carried out. This strategy has been proposed for Project Prime of the Bureau of Education for the Handicapped,[67] but it is not yet clear whether it will be implemented. Its advantages are real, and I hope we shall see the strategy followed in the future in those cases where an evaluation has grave enough policy implications to justify the expense.

Multiple Simultaneous or Immediately Consecutive
Replications of an Evaluation

One major purpose of secondary evaluations is to attempt to replicate findings either with the same body of data as a primary evaluator used or across multiple bodies of data. The major limitations of
such replications are that the data the secondary analyst manipulates
were not collected by him and were not tailored by him to his
objectives. Thus, he is likely to wish at some time or other that the
data were in a different form, either coming from a somewhat different design or with different measures of outcome and process. The
replication that the secondary analyst can achieve should not be
confused, therefore, with the replication that results when some part
of a design is implemented more than once and is directly tailored to
answer some question. It is the latter form of replication that is most
useful.

There are several ways in which replicated evaluation can be
achieved. One way is to have more than one contractor simultaneously design, implement, analyze, and interpret an evaluation of different instances of a program. This is particularly useful when there is
real doubt whether a program will be continued after, say, one year—
as was the case with the performance contracting experiment. Note
that I am suggesting multiple evaluations and not multiple programs.
When different policy alternatives are examined within a single evaluation (as in performance contracting), this means that each alternative must be available at least twice for evaluation by two different
contractors.

A second, and better, way is to run two or more evaluations immediately consecutively, with one contractor implementing his work
and the other beginning after the first one's data are in but before
the first final report is published. The advantage of this procedure is
that the second evaluator can learn from the inevitable mistakes of
the first and can confront any policy-related issues that have become
salient with the passage of time or because the first evaluation
flushed them out. The different negative income tax experiments[68]
incorporate some of the features of consecutive replication that have
been mentioned, as did the two evaluations of "Sesame Street" by
the ETS team, where the second was built on, and improved on, the
first.

The advantages of simultaneous and consecutive evaluations include all the advantages previously listed for other forms of secondary evaluation—accurate, useful, and timely information. They have other advantages worth noting. If two (or more) evaluations are yoked together as a single package, then neither has to carry the burden of providing all the information. If one carries this burden and is flawed in some crucial way, its information yield will be slight, and the desired information will not be made available. Moreover, if evaluations are yoked, each can have a lower profile than if it were the sole evaluation of some program. This would probably be desirable, since it might reduce the extent to which the evaluator finds himself alone, center stage, with the eyes of his employers, program personnel, research commissioners, and fellow professionals riveted on him as the source of eagerly awaited and expensively purchased information. Such a condition may not be conducive to increasing the quality of evaluations. Finally, for reasons of finance, it is likely that in some instances multiple evaluations will entail smaller samples than when all the eggs are in a single evaluation basket. This, in turn, could mean that evaluators will have greater control over how the treatments are implemented, and they will be able to respond better to the expected vicissitudes of field research. They will also be in a better position to describe the treatment and any processes mediating its effects. Smallness does not inevitably produce control and its attendant benefits, but it probably facilitates such control.

There are problems with simultaneous and consecutive evaluations, and they merit discussion. First, multiple evaluations might appear to be so prohibitively expensive that they could be justified only for the most important national programs. I doubt whether this is so, since with most multiple evaluations each one need not be as large as a single evaluation would have to be. Indeed, a decentralized series of evaluations might entail only as many respondents and sites as would be required for a single evaluation. Even when it is not advisable to make two or more smaller evaluations, there is usually no reason why one should be as large as the other, particularly if a consecutive strategy is followed. For instance, one of the evaluations might be more focused than the other and might explore the treatment's effects on a particular target group of respondents rather than on a heterogeneous collection of persons. Or the second evaluation in a series might attempt to refine the construct validity of the cause using a smaller sample than was required in the first evaluation. Or it might concentrate on only the most central issue attacked by the first evaluation, in frank recognition that a higher degree of confidence is needed for making decisions on some matters than on others.

Reducing the size of evaluations can entail special costs of a nonfinancial nature. A minor one relates to the reduced statistical power of having fewer units for analysis. What makes this consideration minor is that, in comparing sample means, the function relating sample size to statistical power is a negatively accelerated ascending one, so that a constant difference in sample size adds more power when the sample is small than when it is large. Indeed, the increment in power is often considered to be negligible when the total sample size exceeds thirty, and it is to be hoped that all primary or secondary evaluations of important issues will have considerably more than thirty observations on which error terms are based. More relevant concerns are: (1) the low statistical power of comparisons of differences in independent slopes, for this is the means by which aptitude-treatment interactions are examined, and (2) the instability of mean and variance estimates when multiple cross-classification of the data takes place, since some statistics will be based on few cases. Hence, it will be particularly dangerous to save money by reducing sample size in evaluations where within-site aptitude-treatment interactions or multiple cross-classifications are basic to important research questions.

A third problem with simultaneous and consecutive evaluations relates to their necessity in light of the fact that most primary evaluations do contain the potential for replicating relationships across research sites and samples. But, while this kind of replication is desirable, it is less independent than replication by different contractors performing evaluations at different sites. Different contractors are less likely to implement the treatment in the same manner, to have exactly the same outcome measures and measurement procedures, and so forth. More heterogeneity with respect to crucial elements of an evaluation should come from independent evaluators testing the same program than from the same contractor testing a program at different sites or times. It is important to establish limits to the heterogeneity desired of contractors, however, since there is nothing to be gained from irrelevant differences. Second contractors obviously have to ask themselves what is to be gained from the novel features of their work. More importantly, if there is a well-defined version of the treatment or a target list of well-defined learning goals, it is a waste of resources not to make an evaluation relevant to these features. By *well written* requests for proposals and vigorous monitoring of ongoing projects sponsors have to insist on specific commonalities between evaluations and to suggest specific differences where these will control for some of the irrelevancies that inevitably accompany a single evaluation.

A fourth problem arises if independent contractors reach different conclusions. No difficulties of reconciliation exist when two contractors evaluate a program and reach the same general conclusion. But when they do not, a decision has to be made about whose work will be given greater weight. Actually, an important decision point precedes this, for in most evaluations there are many lower-order conclusions about aspects of a program, and correspondences at this level are worth ferreting out and treating as strong evidence. Little can be done concerning the divergent conclusions other than to commission persons to review the evaluations to assess their methodological adequacy and to test whether the contractors might be examining different problems using the same conceptual labels. In this last case, the disagreement between the evaluations might not be true disagreement at all. We do not yet know, of course, how frequently different contractors will reach different general conclusions about the same program, and it will be worthwhile in the future charting the correspondences and differences if any simultaneous or consecutive evaluations take place.

A fifth problem has been pointed out to me:[69] the possibility that contractors may collude if they know they are evaluating the same program. The incentives for collusion include cutting costs through sharing information, "raiding" key personnel away from another contractor, and avoiding the tarnished corporate reputation that could result if different evaluations produce different conclusions and under close scrutiny one evaluation is found both absolutely and relatively inadequate. There are also opportunities for more inadvertent collusion, and this is probably more likely to occur. After all, specialists in major research organizations know most of the specialists in their fields who work for other research agencies, and at professional meetings they exchange information with each other or with third parties who pass on the information. Moreover, the same consultant may advise different organizations conducting simultaneous evaluations. I do not want to suggest that all collusion (as I have broadly defined it) is harmful. However, there is a trade-off between gaining vicarious experience by consulting others and preserving one's independence of perspective by not consulting others. Of course there are restraints against collusion of any kind. Perhaps the major one derives from the competitive nature of the evaluation research industry in the United States where, as far as large-scale evaluations are concerned, it sometimes seems as if six or seven organizations bid for and receive most of the contracts. For this reason, it is not clear whether contractors would collude, or would collude to a degree where the loss from the homogenization of perspectives is greater than the gain from vicarious acquisition of relevant information.

A final problem with simultaneous and consecutive evaluations is that their absolute quality might be lower than that of a single evaluation. Since there is less profit to be made from a smaller evaluation, the better known contractors might not bid for such contracts, or if they did bid and gain one they might assign their less experienced staff to work on it. I do not know whether these possibilities are likely, or even whether the work from less well known companies or less experienced staff members is necessarily of lower quality. But if this quality problem exists at all, I suspect that it will be reduced if there are fewer large-scale evaluations and if there are better requests for proposals, better reviews of the replies to these requests, and better monitoring of ongoing research projects.

Even if all the problems outlined above were to manifest themselves in simultaneous or consecutive evaluations, none appears insurmountable except for the problem of financial cost where multiple contingency questions have to be asked in each of the evaluations. Given the payoff of simultaneous evaluations, and the expressed dissatisfaction with many large-scale single evaluations, it may now be time to experiment with multiple evaluations even if this means that one or all are smaller than a single evaluation would be.

Some Nondesign Guidelines for Improving Secondary Evaluations

The simultaneous evaluations that we have just listed are ways of strengthening primary evaluations by building into them the concept that a program's effects will be multiply tested. This means, in effect, that "the evaluation" is composed of the different unique evaluations as a package so that no particular emphasis need be placed on any one of them. This state of affairs is highly desirable. However, we are faced at present with the reality that almost all secondary evaluations involve after-the-fact reanalyses of data either to evaluate an evaluation or to evaluate a program or to examine the evidence for some policy-related assumption. Our task, then, has to be to point to the limitations of after-the-fact analyses and to suggest concrete ways in which the major limitations of these evaluations can be overcome. The assumption underlying this is that simultaneous data analysis by more than one contractor, simultaneous replication, and consecutive replication are unfortunately less feasible than are after-the-fact reanalyses.

One major problem facing secondary evaluators is lack of access to the raw data. Some investigators feel free to pass on copies of their data to anyone who asks; others are likely to pass them on only to friends or respected professionals; others may pass them on only out of fear that not passing them on will be seen as unprofessional; others may pass them on only when high prestige organizations intervene and use their "clout"; others may pass on data they do not own, because they think that the owner (e.g., an office in the federal government) will simply take a copy and pass it on; and others may pass on data only when the secondary analyst is interested in questions that the program administrators do not consider sensitive. We know of instances where each of these factors was probably at play. What is important to note is that program officials can typically restrict or delay access to the data, if they want to. Even when they do not own the data, they can stall for time in the hope that the secondary analyst will lose interest or that the issue of the program's success or failure will become less salient. Even legal action based on the Freedom of Information Act is likely to be time-consuming, and the investigator's only hope of speedy access to publicly owned data is to have the program funding agency come right out and demand them. But this is not likely to happen, especially before a final report has been issued. It is even more difficult to get access to privately owned data. As far as I know, the secondary evaluator has little recourse except to invoke norms of an organization's public accountability for publicly available reports based on data.

The access problem could be solved if it were the policy of federal and foundation authorities to request that a copy of the complete raw data, of all research reports based on the data, and of all instruments used in measurement, be deposited in some well-known location, such as the Roper Institute at Williams College, or the Institute for Social Research at Michigan. The data would have to be deposited at the same time a final report is submitted and would then be available to all persons willing to pay the costs of tapes, research reports, photocopies of measurement instruments, and a small handling charge. This procedure would have positive consequences other than facilitating access. First, it would remove the secondary analyst from all contact with program personnel and from most contact with primary evaluators; secondly, it would make the data available for examining theoretical and practical issues to which they are relevant, even though these issues may have nothing to do with those in the primary evaluation.

Making data readily available to all who want them is easier to defend than most positions about selecting whom to fund for conducting secondary analyses of the data in question. Earlier I noted the impossibility of finding secondary evaluators whose values do not intrude into their work. I also noted the desirability of keeping these value intrusions to a minimum and laying them on the table, especially when only one or two secondary evaluations take place. The difficulty for funding agencies lies in assessing the probability of value intrusions before the fact, or in deciding that a particular value perspective is so important that its expression should be encouraged. One way of reducing, but not eliminating, the first problem is to fund interdisciplinary teams whose divergent training makes for different perspectives on methodology and on what are the most important research questions. Of course, multidisciplinary perspectives do not guarantee a heterogeneity of values on all matters of relevance to an evaluation, particularly where terminal values[70] are concerned. But they do increase the chances of heterogeneity.

It is important to increase the speed with which secondary evaluation results become available. In part, this can be accomplished by the division of labor that is possible with a multidisciplinary staff. But it can also be accomplished by having known groups of persons who can be quickly called upon, who are knowledgeable in asking the questions of evaluation research, whose experience can help them describe data quickly, and whose organizational responsibilities allow them to devote all or most of their time to the task. At present, secondary evaluation is a slow process because the relevant data are not readily available, because there is not a rich stock of secondary analysis experience available to many secondary evaluators, and because most secondary evaluations involve one or two persons who have multiple time-consuming obligations. If it is important to feed back secondary results quickly, then steps must be taken to institutionalize secondary analysis in some way, so that a simple set of data or multiple sets can be analyzed quickly and competently. (Alternatively, of course, speed and accuracy can both be gained by switching from a model of after-the-fact secondary evaluations to a model of simultaneous secondary evaluations.)

Earlier, we saw how desirable it would be if secondary evaluators not only could have access to replications or partial replications of a primary evaluation by other investigators but could also have the mandate to collect additional data should that be required. The data could be used as *direct* checks on any issues that emerge as central during the secondary evaluation and that cannot be solved using the primary evaluation data and the existing literature. I have in mind, say, achievement data from archives in order to establish the stability of pre-test time trends; the collection of data from children whose age and background are similar to those of experimental children in order to check differences in maturational rates between various groups; or perhaps even a descriptive survey to ascertain the size and composition of the audience for some social program that may be universally available but infrequently or selectively used. I do not mean that the secondary evaluators should go out and replicate a primary evaluation *in toto*. Rather, they should collect data to check on assumptions that the secondary evaluation has revealed to be crucial. It is unfortunate, however, that the need to collect auxiliary data may conflict with the need to produce fast feedback. I for one am convinced that, when a trade-off between the two is absolutely necessary, accurate data at a later date are more helpful than questionable data at an earlier date, and so I know what my priorities would be.

One of the consequences of the recent proliferation of basic and applied data may be that our technology for storing and retrieving data will expand. But we particularly need to expand our methodological capacity for summarizing data from multiple data sets in some systematic and sophisticated manner. If this does not improve, we shall find it increasingly difficult to order the new data we are acquiring in meaningful ways, and the value of expanding our knowledge will be diminished. Our organizational capabilities must also expand so that we can make accurate and speedy use of the new data for examining policy-relevant primary evaluations and for explicating and empirically analyzing the assumptions behind classes of social change treatments. At present, the technological aspect is more advanced than the methodological or organizational aspects, and I suspect that there is a real national need, first, to examine the potential of secondary evaluations of the very general kind discussed here and, secondly, to experiment with multidisciplinary teams with permanent supporting staffs who can think through and "flush out" by experience the problems associated with this work.

We will then be in a position to test how useful it is to policy makers and others to have on hand a group of persons who are experienced at examining whatever data base is available to explore policy alternatives before they are implemented on a large scale. And since this would be their job they could perhaps accomplish their work quickly and competently in any of the modes I have outlined here—as reviewers of a single evaluation, as simulators, as secondary evaluators of evaluations, as secondary evaluators of some program, as reviewers of multiple data sets with policy implications, as meta-evaluators, as data analysts who examine primary evaluation data at the same time as the primary evaluators, and even as evaluators who conduct simultaneous secondary evaluations that involve replication of some crucial aspect of a larger primary evaluation. This would provide the nation with a corps of persons who would be experienced in using the present and anticipated future accumulation of data for generating empirically tested policy alternatives without expensive replication and, in some cases, before the alternatives were even experimentally implemented.

Notes

1. J. S. Coleman et al., *Equality of Educational Opportunity* (Washington, D.C.: U.S. Office of Education, 1966).

2. S. Bowles and H. M. Levin, "The Determinants of Scholastic Achievement—an Appraisal of Some Recent Evidence," *Journal of Human Resources* 3, no. 1 (1968): 3-24.

3. G. G. Cain and H. W. Watts, "Problems in Making Policy References from the Coleman Report," *American Sociological Review* 35 (1970): 228-42.

4. F. Mosteller and D. P. Moynihan, eds., *On Equality of Educational Opportunity* (New York: Vintage Books, 1972).

5. Westinghouse Learning Corporation and Ohio University, *The Impact of Head Start: An Evaluation of the Effects of Head Start on Children's Cognitive and Affective Development* (Springfield, Va.: Clearinghouse for Federal Scientific and Technical Information, Sales Department, U.S. Department of Commerce, 1969).

6. D. T. Campbell and A. E. Erlebacher, "How Regression Artifacts in Quasi-experimental Evaluations Can Mistakenly Make Compensatory Education Look Harmful," in *Compensatory Education: A National Debate,* ed. by J. Hellmuth, The Disadvantaged Child, vol. 3 (New York: Brunner/Mazel, 1970).

7. M. S. Smith and J. S. Bissell, "Report Analysis: The Impact of Head Start," *Harvard Educational Review* 40 (1970): 51-104.

8. R. Rosenthal and L. Jacobson, *Pygmalion in the Classroom: Teacher Expectation and Pupils' Intellectual Development* (New York: Holt, Rinehart and Winston, 1968).

9. J. D. Elashoff and R. E. Snow, eds., *Pygmalion Reconsidered* (Worthington, Ohio: Charles A. Jones, 1971).

10. Neither interim nor final reports by H. M. Levin and R. E. Snow are currently available. Information about their project comes from personal reports.

11. *The Office of Economic Opportunity Experiment in Educational Performance Contracting* (Columbus, Ohio: Battelle Columbus Laboratories, 1972).

12. T. D. Cook, H. Appleton, R. Conner, A. Shaffer, G. Tamkin, and S. J. Weber, *Sesame Street Revisited: A Case Study in Evaluation Research* (New York: Russell Sage Foundation, 1974).

13. S. Ball and G. Bogatz, *The First Year of Sesame Street: An Evaluation* (Princeton, N.J.: Educational Testing Service, 1970); G. Bogatz and S. Ball, *The Second Year of Sesame Street: A Continuing Evaluation,* 2 vols. (Princeton, N.J.: Educational Testing Service, 1971).

14. Most secondary evaluations are a subclass of secondary analysis. The former concentrate on evaluating evaluations while the latter can involve reanalysis for purposes of what might loosely be called "basic research" or for purposes that have little to do with the

primary analyst's original intent. The distinction is not a hard-and-fast one, but I think it is worth making.

15. Within the last three years four dissertations in the social psychology program at Northwestern have involved the secondary analysis of multiple bodies of data relevant to educational issues. Interestingly enough, none of these has had research aims similar to those of the primary analysts but most of them have involved analyses that nonetheless corroborated some of the primary analysts' conclusions. Thus, one program within one department at one university provides multiple instances of such inadvertent replication.

16. D. J. Armor, "The Evidence on Busing," *Public Interest* 28 (1972): 90-126.

17. C. S. Jencks et al., *Inequality: A Reassessment of the Effect of Family and Schooling in America* (New York: Basic Books, 1972).

18. A. R. Jensen, "How Much Can We Boost IQ and Scholastic Achievement?" *Harvard Educational Review* 39 (1969): 1-123.

19. T. F. Pettigrew, E. L. Useem, C. Normand, and M. S. Smith, "Busing: A Review of the Evidence," *Public Interest* 30 (1973): 88-118.

20. D. J. Armor, "The Double Double Standard: A Reply," *Public Interest* 30 (1973): 119-31.

21. J. Q. Wilson, "On Pettigrew and Armor: An Afterword," *Public Interest* 30 (1973): 132-34.

22. R. Rosenthal and D. B. Rubin, "Pygmalion Reaffirmed," in *Pygmalion Reconsidered*, ed. by Elashoff and Snow.

23. J. D. Elashoff and R. E. Snow, "Pygmalion Rebutted," in *Pygmalion Reconsidered*.

24. J. S. Coleman, "The Evaluation of *Equality of Educational Opportunity*," in *On Equality of Educational Opportunity*, ed. by Mosteller and Moynihan.

25. The reply of V. Cicirelli is the chapter "The Relevance of the Regression Artifact Problem to the Westinghouse-Ohio Evaluation of Head Start: A Reply to Campbell and Erlebacher"; while the reply of J. W. Evans and J. Schiller is in the chapter "How Preoccupation with Possible Regression Artifacts Can Lead to a Faulty Strategy for the Evaluation of Social Action Programs: A Reply to Campbell and Erlebacher," both in *Compensatory Education* ed. by Hellmuth.

26. The responses to the article by Smith and Bissell are contained in the *Harvard Educational Review* (1970).

27. The issue on Jensen is entitled *Environment, Intelligence, and Heredity,* and the issue on Jencks is entitled *Perspectives on Equality.*

28. Quite apart from reviews appearing in periodicals like the *Saturday Review* there have been commentaries in sections of Sunday newspapers!

29. Ironically, a good case can readily be made that intimate knowledge of a program from its earliest days is a necessary condition for a sensitive evaluation that takes account both of what a program is meant to achieve and of what it might be achieving irrespective of its goals.

30. The issue with the Rosenthal-Jacobson study is not whether a teacher-expectancy effect can be obtained, but whether that particular experiment convincingly demonstrated a teacher-expectancy effect. Reviews of the expectancy literature both by Rosenthal and by Baker and Christ make it clear that teacher expectancies can influence pupil performance. The real issues seem to be: What mediates expectancy effects? Are these effects powerful enough to affect measures of general intelligence as well as measures of achievement (which are, of course, correlated with intelligence)?

31. J. W. Tukey, "Analyzing Data: Sanctification or Detective Work?" *American Psychologist* 24 (1969): 83-91.

32. I. Illich, *De-schooling Society* (New York: Harper and Row, 1971).

33. The difficulties of achieving "independence" have led to the recent call for advocacy evaluations in which a program is evaluated by two or more parties having different perspectives on its value. No problem arises when the advocates coincide. But a judge has to pronounce judgment in the more frequent instances where the advocates disagree. In a sense, this judge—whoever he or she may be—is a secondary evaluator chosen because he or she is more "independent" than the advocates!

34. C. S. Jencks, "The Coleman Report and the Conventional Wisdom," in *On Equality of Educational Opportunity,* ed. by Mosteller and Moynihan.

35. A proxy pre-test is one where correlates of the pre-test are used. In the Head Start case, pre-test achievement scores were not available for the Head Start or the control children. Hence, the analysts used SES measures, which presumably correlated with pre-test

achievement levels, in order to take some account of the pre-test differences in achievement between the nonequivalent Head Start and control groups. However, the procedure does not adequately account for these pre-test differences.

36. F. M. Lord, "Large-Scale Covariance Analysis when the Control Variable Is Fallible," *Journal of the American Statistical Association* 55 (1960): 307-21.

37. Another example of this point will be made later where the apparent discrepancy in conclusions about Head Start between the original Westinghouse-Ohio study and the paper by Smith and Bissell seems to be due to differences in sample selection. When these teams examined the same sample they reached similar conclusions at the data level.

38. These four kinds of validity are explicated in T. D. Cook and D. T. Campbell, "The Design of True Experiments and Quasi-experiments in Field Settings," in *Handbook of Industrial and Organizational Psychology,* ed. by M. D. Dunnette (Skokie, Ill.: Rand McNally, 1974).

39. Elashoff and Snow, *Pygmalion Reconsidered,* p. 161.

40. A recent and sophisticated analysis of the contact hypothesis and of the support for it from various disciplines in the social sciences appears in Y. Amir, "Contact Hypothesis in Ethnic Relations," *Psychological Bulletin* 71 (1969): 319-42.

41. J. McV. Hunt, *Intelligence and Experience* (New York: Ronald, 1961).

42. B. Bloom, *Stability and Change in Human Characteristics* (New York: Wiley, 1964).

43. L. J. Kamin, "Heredity, Intelligence, Politics, and Psychology" (unpublished paper, Princeton University, 1973).

44. H. H. Hyman and P. B. Sheatsley, "Some Reasons Why Information Campaigns Fail," *Public Opinion Quarterly* 11 (1947): 412-23.

45. T. W. Adorno, E. Frenkel-Brunswick, D. J. Levinson, and R. N. Sanford, *The Authoritarian Personality* (New York: Harper, 1950).

46. R. L. Thorndike, "Review of *Pygmalion in the Classroom,*" *American Educational Research Journal* 5 (1968): 708-11.

47. R. Rosenthal, "Empirical vs. Decreed Validation of Clocks and Tests," *American Educational Research Journal* 6 (1969): 689-91.

48. R. E. Snow, "Unfinished Pygmalion," *Contemporary Psychology* 14 (1969): 197-200.

49. R. J. Light and P. V. Smith, "Social Allocation Models of Intelligence," *Harvard Educational Review* 39 (1969): 484-510.

50. The estimate is also likely to be unstable because, as L. S. Kamin has pointed out, there are internal contradictions within the monozygotic twin studies that lead us to question the quality of the basic data (see footnote 43).

51. R. J. Light and P. V. Smith, "Accumulating Evidence: Procedures for Resolving Contradictions among Different Research Studies," *Harvard Educational Review* 41 (1971): 429-71.

52. The obvious point to be made here is that quasi-experimental correlational designs are not as strong as true experimental designs for drawing causal inferences.

53. For a good discussion of the difficulties involved, see L. J. Cronbach and L. Furby, "How We Should Measure 'Change'—or Should We?" *Psychological Bulletin* 74 (1970): 68-80.

54. E. A. Hanushek and J. F. Kain, "On the Value of *Equality of Educational Opportunity* as a Guide to Public Policy," in *On Equality of Educational Opportunity,* ed. by Mosteller and Moynihan.

55. T. D. Cook, "The Medical and Tailored Models of Evaluation Research," in *1972 Proceedings of the Washington Operations Research Council,* ed. by J. G. Abert and M. Kamarass (Cambridge, Mass: Ballinger, 1974).

56. V. Cicirelli, "Relevance of the Regression Artifact Problem," and J. W. Evans and J. Schiller, "Preoccupation with Regression Artifacts," both in *Compensatory Education,* ed. by Hellmuth.

57. J. G. Cooney, *Television for Preschool Children: A Proposal* (New York: Children's Television Workshop, 1968).

58. J. Minton, "The Impact of Sesame Street on Reading Readiness of Kindergarten Children" (Ph.D. diss., Fordham University, 1972).

59. D. K. Cohen, T. F. Pettigrew, and K. T. Riley, "Race and the Outcomes of Schooling," in *On Equality of Educational Opportunity,* ed. by Mosteller and Moynihan.

60. Obviously, contact between races under "negative" conditions (hostility, unequal status, etc.) is not assumed to lead to "positive" consequences of a social or intellectual nature.

61. Jencks et al. *Inequality,* p. 181.

62. J. P. Baker and J. L. Christ, "Teacher Expectancies: A Review of the Literature," in *Pygmalion Reconsidered,* ed. by Elashoff and Snow.

63. Light and Smith, "Accumulating Evidence."

64. The coinage "heterogeneity of irrelevancies" comes from D. T. Campbell.

65. Hunt, *Intelligence and Experience.*

66. The participation of Scriven, Glass, and Stake is outlined in a report entitled *Longitudinal Evaluation of the ESAA Pilot Program* (Santa Monica: System Development Corporation, 1972).

67. "Project Prime: Programmed Re-entry into Mainstream Education" (Washington, D.C.: U.S. Office of Education, Bureau of Education for the Handicapped, 1973).

68. D. N. Kershaw, "A Negative-Income-Tax Experiment," *Scientific American,* Oct. 1972, pp. 19-25.

69. The author would like to thank Peter H. Rossi for suggesting this idea.

70. A discussion of terminal and instrumental values and their definition by social scientists can be found in M. Rokeach, *Beliefs, Attitudes, and Values* (San Francisco: Jossey-Bass, 1968).

Faculty Critique

by VERNON F. HAUBRICH

Let me address eight points concerning this paper, some of which are covered in the paper and some not. But first I want to indicate that there is a problem in trying to classify responses to a piece of primary research on any sort of a grid or hierarchy. It's an extraordinarily difficult thing to classify. An individual on the street who says, "I think Jencks stinks," is giving an evaluation of Jencks's work much as the individual who says, "I'm going to cut the school budget because of Jencks," is giving an evaluation of it. And the difficulty that I had is that the paper did not seem to get into that sort of distinction. I don't want to fault the paper for what it didn't do, so let me get on to what it did do.

The first question that I would raise about secondary evaluation, as well as primary, is that anyone who wishes to evaluate these evaluations ought to pay more attention than is now being paid to the concept of "conflict head-hunting" among professors and other individuals in academic realms. I am thoroughly convinced that the whole issue of criticism—Jencks's criticism of Coleman, others' criticisms of Jencks, Jencks's criticism of other people, the different issues of the *Harvard Educational Review* that were run on Jensen—has far more to do with academic prestige and academic head-hunting than it has to do with policy making. And that touches another point: the whole issue of relating what is originally poor research to elaborated discussions of policy. It seems to me that too many professors are playing with media and news with respect to their findings. For example, we have Bowles and Levin, or even Coleman, or any of the analysts who come up with a high value in r^2, making great "finds," and news is made by explaining 30 percent of variance, when in point of fact more research ought to be done. Let me give you an opposite example: Stephens's book, *The Process of Schooling,* which I think is one of the better books of the last twenty-five years, won absolutely no attention in the media, simply because it indicated a stability in schooling that many of the news makers didn't wish to find. So, this is the first point, and Professor Cook does discuss it—in two paragraphs halfway through his paper. I think the point needs far more attention, because the question of secondary evaluation is related more to prestige, in my mind, than to any other question.

The second point is this: It seems to me that the whole notion of Jencks, Armor, and Jensen on the amount of variance that is explained in r^2 is a gigantic kind of misnomer. I think this is playing with the question of what one can explain, when in point of fact one explains very little. The paper raises this in minor points, but it should be emphasized more strongly.

Thirdly, it seems to me that questions of value belong in the paper. The issue of what is trivial and what is significant is indeed a social issue, not a research issue. When Sandy Jencks indicates that the amount of income one gets as a result of amount of schooling is insignificant, and in point of fact it amounts to between 30 and 40 percent for every four years that one spends beyond high school, it seems to me that is not an insignificant amount of income. The question of insignificance and triviality needs a strong look from a reviewer of this kind of work, and some kind of parameters need to be set about it.

The fourth point is one that I would like to emphasize over and over again. I think the major problem that has come from both the primary and the secondary researchers—Jencks, Jensen, Armor—is indeed the speed with which they have gone to press. Professor Cook calls for more speed as a help to policy makers. In my mind, this is the worst thing that could possibly happen, and I'll just give one small example of this. What you have is a work by James Coleman, published in 1966, on the basis of questionnaires sent throughout the schools to test the relationship of achievement to what is called "the massive funding of the Johnson administration." The fact of the matter was that it wasn't massive at all; it was just getting underway that year. Then you have a reanalysis of this work on the basis of what Jencks had done. He adds two or three other studies done in 1967 and 1968. Now, the children who were in school under this "massive funding" started in, let's say, 1965 in first grade or kindergarten. They hadn't even come close to graduating from elementary school, when an individual like Sandy Jencks comes up with his reanalysis in 1970, or 1971, or 1972, depending on the length of his Carnegie grant, saying, "My word, the massive funding didn't work. Look what has happened!" And he does not do it on the basis of the original research, he does it on the basis of a reanalysis of research already done on children who obviously have not benefited from this so-called massive funding. So it seems to me that the question of speed, in the reanalysis of either primary or secondary research (that is, in secondary or tertiary research), probably ought to be analyzed in terms of its fundamental harm to questions of social policies and policy makers, as well as any kind of help it may give. (I might add that policy makers rely, at this time, on social scientists who can explain 30 percent of the variance. People who rely on that level of explanation are not politically very wise or statistically sophisticated.)

This leads me to the fifth point that I think ought to be treated in the paper, and that is the evaluation of an incomplete effect. When one takes the evaluation of an incomplete effect, by Jensen, Armor, Jencks, and so forth, to policy makers who know nothing about social science research, to legislators, to congressional leaders, and to bureaus in Washington, the result is a massive disabling of the Office of Education, a massive disabling of training programs for universities and colleges, a massive disabling of programs for hospitals and medical schools, a massive disabling of education for the handicapped, a massive disabling of research in the area of cancer, and so forth, simply because the evaluation concludes that they haven't made any impact. I think the point that I'd like to make here is that there's a moral issue in social science reporting that goes far beyond academic prestige. It goes to the point of a far more cautious view of the kinds of things social scientists should say. And I find that Jensen, Jencks, and Armor do not say things in a cautious way.

Sixth point: I hoped that the paper would say something about evaluation in the context of working with children in schools. I refer at this point to a fundamental prejudice that I developed in the six-year study we conducted on desegregation here at Wisconsin. And that is, if you ship out tons of questionnaires, achievement tests, IQ tests, and the like, receive them back at Johns Hopkins, code and classify them in a particular way to gain the kinds of parameters and outcomes that one seems to find in these tests, you get stuck with two notions: first of all that these things are reliable, and secondly that they have some validity. You think you have pieces of paper that tell you something about children. In point of fact, it seems to me that one of the things that Coleman and his staff ought to have done is to visit black, white, and integrated schools in the North, South, and border states. They should have done some extensive interviews with teachers, children, principals—to try and determine what the critical variables were, before they constructed the test. Indeed, it seems to me that the actual context of evaluation must be tested against the empirical situation on the basis of personal experience so that you're not fooled by the test. I'll just give you one example: We had to throw out some tests we gave at Berkeley, because of one item in our test. Question number one said: "Policemen are our friends." That was the first thing the children had to read. Well, it was immediately apparent that the test was going to be invalid, because the children threw it on the floor and so forth. This is an extreme example, but one that leads me to say that, if Coleman had visited black schools and white schools in Jacksonville, Galveston, and Paducah, he would have noted that although the number of volumes in the library was the same, the volumes were incomplete, missing pages, in the black schools. He might have noted that the science facilities were the same in both schools, as reported by the principal, but that they were totally inadequate in terms of size for carrying out experiments in the black schools. On the basis of the questions he asked, the cleanliness of the school, which affects a whole range of attitudes on the part of the teachers, was not measured. It seems to me that if you go to a school and get a sense of what is going on there, you simply ask different kinds of questions. So a person working in secondary evaluation might want to think about making an on-site—anthropological, if you will—ethnographic visit to see what is going on in terms of the data.

The seventh point is this: The paper indicates that in the future, because of the exponential growth of data, literature review will probably have a growing importance. I have two points to make on that. Recently, I was impressed by a literature review by the Rand Corporation on the whole question of teacher effectiveness in schools. It was apparent that this review was shot through with value questions that related to cutting costs in schools. So literature review is not the issue. It seems to me that you need to aim for the question of what the literature is for and what it is not for, as well as emphasize the importance of a review in a particular area.

My eighth point is the whole question of defensiveness as an aspect of educational research. It is related to head-hunting. I'm not at all certain that academic researchers in the field of psychology, or educational psychology—the empirical realm—do not conduct research of the kind that Jencks, Jensen, and Armor conduct. I'm impressed that the few individuals working in the public schools in the area of anthropology in education do not seem to have the same mind set about the variables that they see as important or unimportant before they do this kind of research. They seem to have a much more open frame of mind, a much greater openness, about what they're looking for, and they do not insist on those pieces of paper, those tests—achievement tests, IQ tests, or whatever it is they give to children—as being valid. I'm impressed with the Gearing group at Buffalo—by the manner in which they seek out information about the classroom by being in the classroom for long periods of time and then essentially discussing what it is they've found.

Faculty Critique

by SPENCER SWINTON

Mr. Cook has made some useful distinctions in his paper, particularly in pointing out the importance of using data to edit or constrain criticisms—thus moving the discussion from merely possible to plausible sources of uncertainty—and in seeing different perspectives as sources of strength on which decision makers can capitalize.

Reading his paper led me to two thoughts—one chilling and one warming. If innovative programs, and hence primary evaluations, are to be in short supply for the next few years, we had all better master the craft of writing annotations, commentaries, and marginalia on the data of the sixties, because we are all due to become secondary and tertiary historians of the "age of belief"—when the nation had the nerve to try social experiments. My feeling is that the nerve is still there, but that more innovations will be launched on a state and local basis, making the need for techniques of pooling data increasingly important.

The warming thought comes from Mr. Cook's comments on "independence and disciplinary myopia" and Mr. Jackson's quotation of Spindler: "To be truly dispassionate in a human community would be inhuman." In letting the cat out of the bag by pointing out that evaluators, too, are only human, subject to such pressures as the need for reciprocation and individuation, the need to "stand out," he leads to what I find is the most provocative point of his comprehensive paper: a suggestion of what we might call "adversary" as opposed to "no-fault" evaluation.

His typology of secondary evaluation models concludes with very useful recommendations for simultaneous secondary evaluations of multiple data sets by several evaluators. To some extent, his Russell Sage revisit to "Sesame Street" is the first example of this on a single data set, since the suggestions were made in time to give useful feedback to Bogatz and Ball in their second-year evaluation.

Metaevaluators who represent a variety of disciplines and points of view toward data analyses can lead to improvement, but the exciting idea is to have multiple analyses of the same or multiple data sets, presumably by individuals or groups with widely divergent value orientations. It is here that the adversary arguments and cross-examinations, to convince a jury of decision makers, can lead to higher quality information in time to influence decisions. Vern Haubrich's point that speed kills notwithstanding, policy decisions are made in real time, and it is my prejudice that knowledge leads to better decisions than does ignorance. As Mr. Cook points out, more reviews unconstrained by the data can only increase uncertainty. Analyses of the same data by advocates who agree to operate within the facts of the case may lead to a reduction of uncertainty, although there are cases in which this would, and should, have the opposite effect.

Two additional benefits should appear. One is increased cooperation from innovative groups typically hostile to evaluation—such as those "imprecise humanists" mentioned by Mr. Walberg. An evaluator who can openly admit that he is on the side of the program might have more success in convincing his clients of the importance of random assignment to treatments and of measures of unintended effects than would the "prosecution," but the resulting data would then be available to all. It is ironic that some have criticized Ball for being in on "Sesame Street" from the planning stage, and therefore subject to bias, while most discussions of evaluation decry the fact that the evaluator is not called in until after basic decisions have been made. Since it is impossible to have it both ways, adversary evaluation suggests a way out of this dilemma.

The second benefit should be increased dissemination of knowledge about evaluation to program innovators and practitioners. As we tighten our belts, the fact that the old verities are in question may be seen as an opportunity. We are in this together with practitioners, and hence we are in a better position to explain such elements as random assignment, monitoring of degree of implementation, and the importance of evidence, in terms of actual decision making, not just the need to advance knowledge. This latter justification sounds hollow to groups that have been studied and studied as "problems" when they feel they know what the problems are and want help in solving them. With the evaluator in the camp of the innovator, the complaint, "What we're doing is too beautiful to measure," may give way to, "Here's what we're doing; let's work out a way to get evidence on how it works." Here at Madison, Bob Clasen had been demonstrating that it is possible to disseminate such information to practitioners in understandable and useful form.

Two points disturbed me, both dealing with convergent validity across perspectives: First there seemed to be a suggestion that, if two experiments suffer from different threats to validity, the combined results will be subject to neither threat rather than both. This flies in the face of the well-known axiom, "If anything can go wrong it will," and its corollary, "If two things can go wrong at the same time, they will." I'm sure I misunderstood Mr. Cook on this point. We certainly won't gain by pooling invalid data. The second point is a value issue. The secondary evaluator has the right to ask different questions, but this seems more appropriate at the metaevaluation stage, since too often the data and design have confounds that permit us only to tease out proxies for answers to questions that were not built in. If the charge is changed in the middle of the trial, none of the evidence may be relevant. Asking how viewing and encouragement to view can be unconfounded is a contribution, but, for example, arguing that "Sesame Street" was a failure because it did not close the gap between lower and middle class seems to be independent of any data and not really in the spirit of the constructive portions of the paper. Since viewing is confounded with encouragement in the ETS evaluation, a sensible policy implication would be to administer encouragement selectively to the target population, rather than to make the program unavailable to middle-class children.

Imagine an evaluation of a water-fluoridation program with the results in table 6.2. Let's suppose that nutrition and dental hygiene explain the class difference. The value question is: What reasonable loss function would justify hiring a dentist to drill cavities in the teeth of middle-class children, thus reducing the cavity gap, as opposed to spending the same money on education about nutrition and hygiene? Although the average class difference is still two cavities, life with three cavities may be qualitatively different from life with five.

Table 6.2
Effect of Water Fluoridation

	Mean Cavities	
	Lower Class	Middle Class
Before	5	2
After	3	0

The value position that accepts only gap reduction seems to say, "Spend public money only on services that are already near some ceiling." This strikes me as a reductio ad absurdum of norm-referenced testing, and it makes criterion-referenced evaluation even more appealing to me.

Author's Reply to Faculty Critiques

Let me start with the first point made by Professor Haubrich—that one of the real reasons for evaluations, primary and secondary, is that people are seeking glory. It was suggested that this kind of a sociological explanation of evaluation research isn't adequately stressed in my paper. I guess I have two thoughts on that. It's very hard to spend several years of one's life replicating someone else, given the reinforcement contingencies that currently control the academic community. Replications are not as highly valued as they should be, and I suspect there are pressures on secondary analysts to reach unexpected conclusions. I was in Washington the other day talking to some officials about their reactions to Jencks's work on schooling. They stated: "It's very hard to get tenure at Harvard. The best way is to write a book that is highly visible and becomes known as a path-breaking book, one that reverses the conventional wisdom. And that's just what Jencks wanted to do." These people were suggesting that Jencks's book was written for his own career ends, rather than to express what he thought. Now, Jencks is very easily criticized on a whole host of grounds. First of all he's probably a naive economist, as Levin pointed out. Secondly, Sewell, at this university, has criticized his use of path analysis as not being the most elegant and sophisticated. Well, my own predilection is to put the discussion at that substantive level, but to admit the possibility that the glory seeking is going on.

I think there's a second issue involved: We owe books and articles the right to be interpreted at face value first of all. I might read Proust's work and say, "What Proust is about, is the expression of a deviate, an oddball, a Jew who was not completely accepted by the highest society to which he went, homosexual to boot, plus the fact that he functioned best between eleven at night and six in the morning, when most people don't function too well." It's a favorite game of literary critics to talk about Proust. Why not talk about Proust's work? I think that's what is wrong. I think you have to take people at face value. You ought to criticize them at face value, too.

The next point is the issue of what is significant. Jencks talks about the relationship between years of schooling and income as being not socially significant. If you look at the data, in the way that Hank Levin has done, you can see that for one extra year of high school there's perhaps a 3 percent increase in income (if you accept the viability of multiple linear regression—the analysis that he tends to use). The first year in college there's an increase of 7 percent, and the first year in graduate school an increase of 3 percent. You can look at these individually, as Jencks did, and say 3 percent or 7 percent isn't very much. Or, you can take the Levin perspective, which is that cumulatively those three things add up to quite a bit. And I think it's only the naive people who look to the words rather than looking at the data.

As soon as you start getting into what is socially significant, our values play an even larger role than they do in all other aspects of the research process. The issue, to me, is not whether our values play any role or no role, but rather in what parts of the research endeavor do our values play a greater role versus a lesser role, and in which parts *should* they play a large or small role. After asking this, I suspect that the next important question is: what are the practical steps we can take either to minimize our own value intrusions or to revel in them and make them heterogeneous? When do we need to get a whole range of different values on the task and look at the convergence and differences across multiple value perspectives?

The next point is the speed of coming to press. That's a very, very tricky issue, and I'm in large measure in agreement with you. As you'll note in the paper, I explicitly said that I take a very different stand from Jensen, who at the beginning of his book says that partial data are better for quick decision making than tighter data that come after the fact. Now, that seems to be too black and white a picture, in the sense that any skillful administrator knows how to put off decision making for some time. There are contexts where you learn the art of procrastination—it's part of your job—and there are some situations where it is possible to procrastinate and get better data. But the basic issue still remains, do you want partially relevant data fast or better data later? My own feeling is that you should want to have your cake and eat it. That's always been my inclination. Why not have great data fast? The way to do that is to use the simultaneous secondary evaluation model that I talked about at the end of the paper and to have more than one evaluation of a program carried out at a time, each of which might be smaller than a single study. This should provide you with multiple convergence validation across experimenters, and if there are unexpected hitches at least one study will probably provide timely data. I consider that a very important task: getting around the speed issue while keeping high quality.

There's something else I wanted to say about the evaluation of incomplete effects. I have found by talking to decision makers in Washington that they are not gullible dupes who read a book like Jencks's and say, "Ah! So that's how it is." As a matter of fact, most of them check around with in-house people and people in academe and try to get convergent validity across them. It's not a question of Jencks coming in with the last word, by any means.

I *am* worried about the way evaluations are used. The commentator spoke about Jencks and Coleman being used for "massive disabling" of parts of the Office of Education. I don't know whether evaluation results are used as reasons or as justifications—whether they are used to set policy or to rationalize directions the administrator wants to take anyway. I think it's a little premature to assume, with the level of ignorance that I now see, that evaluations are used causally to change policy rather than as public relations window dressing to rationalize it. And I'm worried too about the political use of evaluations, because "no difference" findings do seem to be prevalent, at least with the larger national evaluations. I'm worried about that as an evaluation researcher, because I see in it the potential destruction of the subdiscipline called evaluation research. It has been used for political ends, to evaluate those programs that people want to get rid of. They assume that, all things being equal, the evaluation is going to be negative. I think we can all learn from this to set our expectations as evaluators lower and more realistically and to promise what we can deliver, rather than what we'd like to deliver.

Now, the next point was one to which I'm very sensitive: the point that we collect all these horrible pieces of paper, and why don't we get into the classroom? I have a great deal of sympathy with that. I think that many substantive evaluations fail to do this for reasons of

financial cost or of historical accident. Many people are more interested in outcomes than in process, and some of them don't just reify,
they deify, certain kinds of achievement pieces of paper—IQ pieces
of paper. Other people prefer to look at process variables; they claim
that we have not looked hard enough at the social processes that go
on in classrooms. Process research is obviously crucially important
for determining what goes on in schools. But my interest in this
paper was in educational interventions and the outcome variables
that are traditionally the most important ones affected by school
intervention.

Now, you talked about evaluations being shot through with people's values. The model of the independent evaluator was proposed in
the 1960s. It is, in large part, inappropriate as a model of how
evaluators go about their business. I would agree that people's values
are there and our task is to find out where they intrude most and
then to minimize their intrusion. There are a number of ways to do
that. To get rid of the narrowness due to our academic training and
discipline, you can have a multidisciplinary team of secondary evaluators or primary evaluators. You can have the first draft critiqued
by a multidisciplinary group of people, as we did with "Sesame
Street." Such people can suggest in what respects you have been
wrong or narrower than you ought to have been. But I think there's a
time when we want to lay our values on the table openly—you
should always do that anyway beforehand. One of the advantages of
multiple secondary evaluations is that you can make heterogeneous
the value perspectives of the different evaluators, with their convergence and divergence of opinion. When the values are right there on
the table, they can be minimized in one kind of evaluation, maximized in another. For instance, they are maximized in an "adversary
evaluation."

Now, in response to Mr. Swinton's points, I'm not saying that you
should just pool the studies. There may be some instances where a
selection-maturation artifact could operate and one study avoids that
problem but is inadequate by itself for ruling out effects of history.
Another study might successfully rule out a history alternative interpretation but not a selection-maturation one. So you can get the
effect in one study when selection-maturation doesn't operate, and
you can also get it in another study when history doesn't operate.
Now, the only thing that would allow you to interpret the effects

from each study as artifactual would be some higher-ordered inter-action of history and selection-maturation, which is in most condi-tions not plausible. But remember that one man's plausibility tends to be another man's mysticism. When I talk to some of my colleagues and say, "But I don't think that is plausible," I get some very strange reactions, because it is plausible to them. There are different individ-ual thresholds for the ascription of plausibility.

The second question Mr. Swinton raised I think is a $64,000 ques-tion, looking at "Sesame Street" in particular: Does it narrow, not affect, or widen the academic achievement gap that separates so-called disadvantaged and so-called advantaged children? That gets us back to a can of worms, in a sense, that Mr. Scriven mentioned: the question of goal-free evaluation. I think I look at it somewhat differ-ently from the way Mr. Scriven does. The *stated* aim of "Sesame Street" was to stimulate the intellectual and cultural growth of all children, particularly disadvantaged preschoolers. As Mr. Scriven said earlier, directives are very often window dressing. If they're not win-dow dressing, they are often hard to operationalize. But the issue is, what does the key phrase mean? Does it mean that disadvantaged preschoolers have to learn from the show for the show to be effective in terms of its objectives? If you look at it from a bold perspective, you can see that the directive is ambiguous because it might mean that the disadvantaged have to learn from the show or that the gap has to be narrowed. Now, claims have been made in the press by the ETS people and other responsible persons that "Sesame Street" is narrowing the gap. So do you look at your evaluation in terms of unambiguous claims or in terms of ambiguous goals? Because when the goals are ambiguous someone can say: "We meant our program to teach kids and not to narrow gaps. Hence, it doesn't matter too much to us if we're teaching and also widening gaps. In fact, we think it wrong that you even looked at the gap issue, because, as we meant our goals to be interpreted, affecting the gap was not one of the goals but causing absolute gains was."

You can also argue that you have to ask questions about programs that relate to national problems. The gap was defined as a national problem in the sixties, and probably still is defined that way, but to a lesser extent. A preschool program, or partial preschool program, like "Sesame Street" that is nationally available can be considered a na-tional resource. If it's a widely available national resource, it's going to be relevant to the gap in some way. It's going to widen it, narrow it, or maybe fail to affect it. Mr. Scriven's goal-free notion I interpret to mean that we do not necessarily have to evaluate according to the stated goals of the program sponsors. That doesn't mean you can't have questions guiding the research. In fact you can't do decent research unless you ask questions. The problem is, which questions do you ask? Where do you get them from? Or, in sociopolitical terms, whose questions do you ask? (That's another side of that very old problem, whose goods do you maximize?) Do you get the questions from program objectives, from claims made for programs by responsible persons, from knowing the problems to which a program is relevant, or from all these sources?

I think we have to ask: What is the national problem in preschool education? Is it the fact that all preschoolers need to know more, or that disadvantaged groups should absolutely learn more, or that the relative difference between advantaged and disadvantaged groups should be diminished? Teaching all children and teaching the disadvantaged or narrowing the gap are in part contradictory in terms of treatments. The best way of narrowing the gap or teaching the disadvantaged is to give your resources to the people who are lowest on the totem pole. Increasing the potential of all groups takes a very different strategy, in which all groups have to get the program, and it has to be tailored to the general needs of all children, rather than the specific needs of special groups, if you can so analyze them. Furthermore, I know of situations where disadvantaged children absolutely learn from a program but selectively fall behind because the advantaged gain more from it. What kind of a benefit is this? If you think the major problem is that the disadvantaged should know more, you would be happy with such a result. But if you think the major problem is the achievement gap, you would be sadder. My concern is that as a nation we don't seem to have explicated these priority problems in both preschool and regular school education. The fundamental question is: What are the fundamental questions?

7

Educational Process
Evaluation

HERBERT J. WALBERG

During the past decade or two, the study of environments has been
asserting or reasserting itself in behavioral and social science research.
The research has focused on the context of behavior, particularly on
sociopsychological processes. Originated by Darwin, it was applied to
the study of society by Herbert Spencer. Its distinctive perspectives
were incorporated into the mainstreams of sociology and psychology
by George Herbert Mead and John Dewey, and it became known as
social or symbolic interactionism in sociology and *Chicago function-
alism* in psychology during the 1920s. Since then, the psychological
study of social contexts and processes has had its advocates in Kurt
Lewin and Egon Brunswik. Bloom (1964) made a strong case for
environmental-process research in education and general psychological development. Reviewing work on growth rates and environments,
he pointed to the development of process measures as necessary for
accurate prediction and control of learning. The early work of Dave
(1963) and Wolf (1964) on home environments and of Pace and
Stern (1958) on college environments began exploring relationships
of contexts and learning. My purpose here is to review some recent
research on process measures in educational evaluation.

A forewarning: what follows is purposively an advocate's position,
not a comprehensive objective review. The evidence is selected to

illustrate effects and possibilities. The theoretical basis for the research program is presented elsewhere (Walberg, 1969, 1971), and a number of evaluations are described in a recent publication (Walberg, 1974). My themes here are three: we should examine learning, while it is taking place, especially from the learner's point of view; we should analyze the social context and processes of learning, particularly in sociopsychological perspective; and we should deemphasize standardized achievement test outcomes in evaluating educational enterprises (although these outcomes may be useful in partially validating process measures). For empirical illustration, I draw mostly from my own and my associates' research and start with the most potent educational institution—the family; then move to classroom environments to illustrate some findings on predictive validity, experimental course evaluation, subject areas, and grade level differences; and conclude with a recent process characterization of British and American "open education."

Home Environment and Mental Abilities

During the last decade, several investigations have shown that proximal measures of the child's home environment explain significantly more variance in cognitive performance than do distal measures; that is, detailed psychological assessments of parent stimulation of the child provide more concurrent validity in predicting IQ scores than social-class indexes such as parental income, education, and occupation. Extensive home interviews with parents provide assessments of environmental press that correlate about .7 with general intelligence and verbal ability scores in elementary school populations (Wolf, 1964; Dyer, 1967). Less reliable survey questionnaire measures of such things as parental aspirations for the child and number of books in the home provide less valid concurrent predictions but higher correlations than the typical .3 between social-class indexes and verbal IQ scores (Coleman et al., 1966; Plowden, 1967).

While factor analysts have long studied differential mental abilities, only in the last decade have investigators begun relating environmental characteristics to differential mental development. Cattell (1963), for example, proposed that some abilities are more malleable than others. Bock and Vandenberg (1968) showed that spatial ability is less malleable and perhaps more heritable than other abilities.

Other works discussed below (Bing, 1963; Ferguson and Maccoby, 1966; Honzik, 1967; Vernon, 1969) suggest that discrepant abilities such as high verbal and low numerical abilities are related to specific features of parental stimulation such as verbal intrusiveness. My recent study in collaboration with Kevin Marjoribanks of Oxford University (in press) assesses the relationship between a battery of environmental-process measures and differential mental abilities.

A sample of 195 eleven-year-old boys was drawn from Toronto, Canada. Approximately half were from middle-class and half from working-class homes. No indications of extreme indigence or mental abnormalities were observed in the homes, and the boys appeared to exhibit a normal range of behaviors. After a trained examiner established rapport with the boys, he administered the Primary Mental Abilities Test, which yields four IQ subscores. From a review of prior theory and empirical work (Coleman, 1966; Dave, 1963; Plowden, 1967; Vernon, 1969; Weiss, 1969; Wolf, 1964), a set of eight environmental-process areas were identified as likely to be related to intelligence measures. A two-hour interview schedule for both parents was constructed by Marjoribanks to measure the intellectual stimulation provided in the home. It included 188 six-point rating scales developed to measure the eight environmental-press areas.

Canonical correlations were computed between the eight environmental-process scores and the four measures of mental ability. Although Hotelling (1933) formulated canonical analysis four decades ago, it was not used much in substantive psychological research until recently, when computer programs became available (Bock and Haggard, 1968). Since several studies reviewed here make use of canonical analysis, a brief explanation of the technique is in order. Just as multiple correlation is a generalization of simple correlation in that it relates several predictors to a criterion, canonical correlation is a generalization of multiple correlation in that it relates several predictors to several criteria. Also, just as multiple correlation yields a set of linear weights for the predictors, to form a composite variate that is maximally correlated with the criterion, one or more pairs of canonical variates for the predictors and criteria are calculated that maximize the simple correlation between the paired composite variates from each set. Well worked out inferential tests are available to test the significance of successive canonical correlations (Bock and Haggard, 1968), and each variate may be characterized by calculating the simple correlations ("loading," as in factor analyses) between the composite variate and the original variables within its set (Darlington, Weinberg, and Walberg, in press).

Our canonical analysis of the data on the eleven-year-olds revealed that the first two canonical correlations, .781 and .462 were significant (they have probabilities of less than .001 and .005 respectively). The canonical loadings (plotted in figure 7-1), reveal that with respect to the first canonical variate, verbal and numerical abilities and, to a lesser extent, reasoning ability, are more highly associated with the environmental-process scores than is spatial ability (see table 7.1). This result supports Cattell's (1963) theory of intelligence, which asserts that the development of crystallized abilities (such as verbal, numerical, and reasoning ability) depend on environmental processes more than does the development of fluid abilities (such as spatial ability).

Table 7.1

Correlations betweeen Two Canonical Predictor Variates
and Four Mental Abilities

Environmental Predictor Variate	Mental Abilities			
	Verbal	Numerical	Reasoning	Spatial
1	.716	.702	.401	.280
2	.153	−.184	.138	.103
Multiple R	.733	.726	.425	.298

Note: All the simple and multiple correlations are significant at the .001 level except .138 (which is significant at .05) and .103 (not significant).

In their examination of the heritability of verbal, numerical, spatial, and reasoning abilities, Bock and Vandenberg (1968) also concluded that, for boys, spatial ability is not very sensitive to environmental differences. Spatial ability showed the largest component of heritable variance, and Bock and Vandenberg suggested that there is justification for including spatial ability in tests that purport to measure innate general ability, especially for boys.

The high loadings on the first canonical variate also indicate that the environmental forces are, in general, better predictors of verbal and numerical ability than social status indicators and family struc-

Figure 7-1
Canonical Loadings of Environmental
Press and Mental Abilities Measures

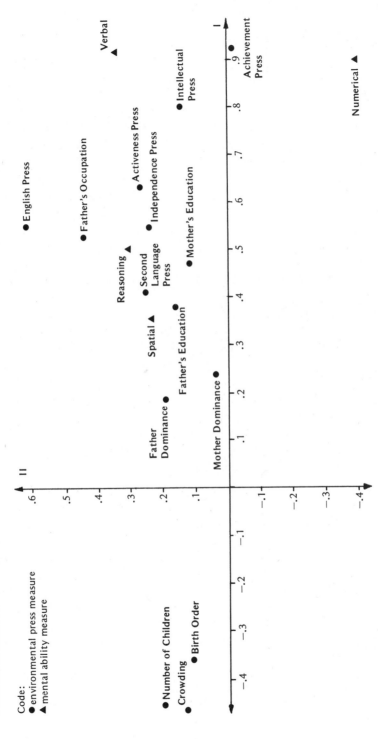

ture characteristics are. Similar results were found by Dave (1963), Wolf (1964), and Plowden (1967) in their analyses of the interrelationships among social status, environment, and cognitive performance.

After removing the variance of the first canonical variate from predictors and criteria, the loadings on the second variate reveal that the social status indicators and the environmental forces are significantly related to differentially developed abilities. It should be noted that the second variate explains less variance in mental abilities than does the first variate (see table 7.1). High ratings on press for English, father occupation, press for a second language, and, to a lesser extent, press for activeness and father dominance are associated on the second variate with high scores on verbal, reasoning, and spatial abilities, but lower scores on numerical ability. The two language-press scales reflect, in particular, a measure of parent-son interaction in activities such as reading, conversations (after school, at mealtime, and in the evenings), purposeful teaching of vocabulary, and the correction of syntactical errors in language use. The press-for-activeness scale measures parent-son involvement in both academic and nonacademic situations, while the father-dominance scale gauges the father's involvement in a son's activities.

Therefore, the second canonical variate suggests that the differential development of verbal, reasoning, and spatial abilities, as opposed to numerical ability, might be facilitated in homes characterized by high parent-son interaction. This finding is, in part, supported by Bing (1963) who found that mothers of highly verbal boys (boys who had high verbal ability scores but low numerical and spatial ability scores), in comparison to mothers of low verbal ability boys, provided more stimulation in early childhood, were more critical of poor academic achievement, provided more storybooks, and let their boys take a greater part in mealtime conversations. Bing suggested that, for boys, differential verbal ability is fostered by a close relationship with a demanding, intrusive mother. Honzik (1967) also found that a close mother-son relationship was significantly related to the development of a boy's verbal ability. For optimum verbal-ability growth, Honzik asserts that a boy at first needs a close relationship with his mother, followed by a relationship with a father or male model who not only achieves himself but is also concerned about the boy's achievement.

The findings have one substantive and two methodological implications. Substantively, by examining the canonical correlations between a set of environmental measures and cognitive abilities, the present study implies that differential environmental processes may operate selectively to develop some abilities, while leaving others relatively underdeveloped. Methodologically, Feldman (in press) observed that, while interest in the study of differential mental abilities has increased, the number of research studies has remained small. One reason for the paucity of studies has been the difficulty of defining discrepant abilities satisfactorily without confounding level and pattern of abilities. Use of canonical analysis as a technique for examining environmental correlates of differential mental abilities may overcome this difficulty. The second methodological point concerns educational evaluation more directly, and the next section is devoted to it because of its importance.

Educational Evaluation and Standardized Tests

To estimate environmental effects on psychological growth in natural settings, parallel measures on the same individuals at two points in time, and indicators of the quality of the environment during the intervening period, are most helpful (Bloom, 1964). Correlational studies of educational environments, it may be added, are more valid, accurate, and comprehensive when (1) multiple parallel measures of the students' cognitive and affective states are obtained at the two time points to gauge different varieties of educational growth; (2) multiple indicators are used to tap various a priori components of the environment and to assess their impact on different kinds of growth among different students; (3) the indicators are careful judgmental ratings by observers or the students themselves rather than "objective" counts of such things as per-pupil expenditures, class size, and the incidence of certain teacher behaviors; (4) molecular rather than molar units (that is, students or classes rather than schools or districts) are analyzed; (5) some of the parallel student measures fairly reflect the goals of the contrasted classes; and (6) simultaneous environments other than those assessed are well accounted for or have minimal effects on the educational growth in question.

It is unfortunate that very few studies of educational environments approach these standards; but it is tragic that the most ballyhooed evaluation study in the last decade, the Coleman Report (1966), aside from its other very serious methodological flaws (see Bowles and Levin, 1968), did not meet a single one and concluded that variations in school expenditures and qualities make very little difference in learning. The report and the Mosteller and Moynihan (1972) and Jencks (1972) reanalyses of it undoubtedly contributed to the confused malaise that today affects many parents, educators, and citizens concerned with public education and to the high voter rejection rates of school bond issues. To cite the report's most glaring inadequacy (and that of the reanalyses), verbal ability, which is determined in large part by heredity and home environmental processes (see the previous section of this paper), was used as the main criterion of school performance, with distal socioeconomic status rather than proximal home environment measures held constant. The other flaws of the report will not be belabored here; instead, the reader is referred to Katzman (1971) and the U.S. Office of Education report (1970) for a review of twenty-two other studies of school input-output performance. While none of them meets all the design standards of the paragraph above, they are generally better designed and meet more of the standards than the Coleman Report. Every one of these studies showed positive correlations between even crude indicators of school quality (such as expenditures per student, class size, mean years of teacher experience and education, percentage of the staff who are university, rather than teachers college, graduates, and recency of course work in graduate education) and student attainments (and ability tests), with student input characteristics held statistically constant in most cases.

Moreover, Rosenshine and Furst's (1971) review of some fifty studies of classroom instruction shows that growth in cognitive achievement appears to be promoted by clarity of presentation; use of variety in the lesson; enthusiasm, task orientation, and business-like behavior by the teacher; avoidance of strong, negative criticism; and pupil opportunities to practice criterion tasks. Other classroom studies that approach the standards mentioned earlier show that increased cognitive, affective, and behavioral learning is associated with student perceptions of high levels of cohesiveness, satisfaction, proper pacing, organization, and instructional materials, and low levels of apathy, favoritism, and friction (Walberg, 1969; Walberg, 1971; Walberg and Anderson, 1972). Moreover, different environments appear to be more conducive to learning by students of different abilities (Anderson, 1970) and personalities (Bar-Yam, 1969) and those in different courses of instruction (Walberg, 1970) (see Walberg, 1971, 1974, for an overview). These interactions suggest the possibility that components of the social environments that are optimally suited for individual students may be replicated and used to design personalized instructional environments.

Perhaps this is a good place to emphasize that some of the research reviewed in this paper concerns the development of mental abilities and educational achievement as measured by current standardized tests because there is very little comparable work published on other educational outcomes of child rearing and schooling. The available body of research provides an extremely limited basis for evaluating schools and formulating educational policies. Standardized ability and achievement tests tap (or are strongly correlated with or are often composed of) a narrow group of verbal skills (best exemplified by word recall, fluency, and recognition vocabulary) more than anything else, and, while this factor comes into play in many settings, it is far from being the sole criterion of school effectiveness, social progress, or individual worth.

Teacher grades reflect this limitation to some extent; the standardized test scores and grades kept in student records are mainly accounted for by one or two narrow verbal skill factors (Lohnes and Marshall, 1965). The more teachers use a "psychometrically sophisticated" test development and revision procedure (that is, item-to-total-score correlations for item selection), the more their achievement tests become verbal intelligence tests (Gagné, 1970). Use of such tests tends to direct instructional emphasis and energy toward a single goal and away from other worthwhile but unmeasured goals; it reinforces the historical tendency of American education since 1890 to evolve into "one best system" that may be somewhat unfair and unsuited to all in varying degrees (Tyack, 1972).

Standardized tests do not even reflect the domain of language skills completely: abstract verbal skills do not completely determine excellence in writing a poem, singing a lullaby, tutoring a child, or giving an order in the Chicago stockyards. Educational overemphasis on them can produce glibness, unconcern for concrete realities, and a narrow intellectual elitism in the young; it encourages academics in the worst senses of the term—in which pedantry and verbosity are equated with wisdom and problem solving. Since measured verbal ability is heritable and also importantly determined by home environment, educational preoccupation with it can produce a hierarchy based on genetic and social inheritance of a single factor that encourages invidious comparisons of groups and individuals. To be sure, standardized tests and grades predict how many years of conventional education a student will attain. But, once a person has attained a given number of years, these measures do not predict his or her occupational success in the fields where surveys have been conducted (for example, medicine, engineering, teaching, scientific research, and business) by the criteria of professional reputation, income, employee ratings, and on-the-job observations (Hoyt, 1965). More generally, school grades are nearly useless in predicting inventiveness, leadership, good citizenship, personal maturity, family happiness, and workmanship (Pace, 1966).

Marks can be helpful: they serve as incentives for learning and help students gauge their own strengths and progress. They should not be lightly abandoned, but they should be placed in perspective and used cautiously and wisely—or not at all. In most cases, assessments of specific skills and performances on realistic tasks reflecting the lesson content will probably be found to be more fair and useful to the teacher and student in guiding the learning process than general tests are (Ebel, 1969; Bloom, Hastings, and Madaus, 1971). Standardized achievement tests and especially aptitude tests including IQ, however, are probably doing more harm than good for the reasons mentioned and ought to be abandoned except for some research and program evaluation purposes, in my opinion. It is presumptuous, misleading, and prejudicial to call what they measure "intelligence" or "aptitude." They might be called "school mark prediction scales"; but even this term is dangerous because it assumes that marks fully capture the outcomes of schooling. Use of such scales further assumes and reinforces dangerous academic parochialism and discourages concern for individual differences with respect to other human qualities, environmental diversity, and innovation in education.

Classroom Processes and Learning Outcomes

Contrary to the above cautions about standardized cognitive tests, the next study employs them and affective outcomes to validate student perceptions of classroom processes. While satisfaction, cohesiveness, diversity, and other sociopsychological processes may be reasonable classroom ends in their own right, it is worthwhile knowing if they predict achievement, understanding, and positive attitudes toward the subject, especially if the relation is independent of initial achievement and interest in the subject and IQ. This test of incremental predictive validity is derived from psychometric tradition, but it asks if process measures can improve on conventional psychometric prediction. In other parts of this chapter, of course, an attempt is made to show the value of process measures on other grounds as well.

Fourteen scores measuring student perception of classroom processes were obtained from a national sample of 144 high school physics classes at midyear. They were canonically correlated with six cognitive, affective, and behavioral post-tests given at the end of the school year (Walberg, 1969). The analysis revealed two significant (p less than .01) canonical correlations, .69 and .49. Figure 7-2, a plot of the loadings, shows that difficulty is the best predictor of the three cognitive tests and that the noncognitive tests are best predicted by satisfaction (positively) and by friction, cliques, and apathy (negatively). Comparison of the multiple regression predictability of the learning criteria from all fourteen scores with the predictability from the two canonical predictor variates (table 7.2) shows the summary power of the analysis; for example, the fourteen-predictor univariate multiple regression model yields an R of .63 with understanding science while the first canonical variate alone yields an r of .61. Now, no claim for causality can be made from this analysis, since both the learning environment and the post-tests may have been caused by other factors, such as initial interest or achievement (or there may be causation in reverse of time—for example, classes in which students are learning a lot may be seen as difficult). Several of these rival hypotheses were discredited by entering the canonical predictor variates into regression models after psychometric predictors: the score on the corresponding pre-test given at the beginning of the school year, the IQ, the initial physics achievement, and the science interest (see table 7.2). F-tests for the increments in R^2 revealed that the process variates contribute to prediction of the post-tests after these control variables. The partial correlations and successive Rs in table 7.2 show that the additional variance accounted for is moderate (6 to 18 percent), considering the

Figure 7-2
Social Environment as a Predictor of Post-test Learning Criteria:
Canonical Loadings

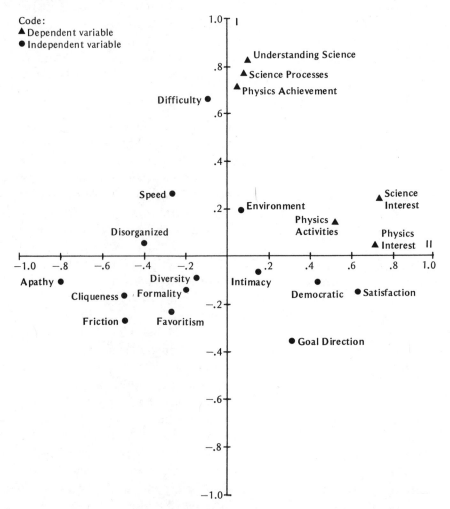

Source: H. J. Walberg, "The Social Environment as a Mediator of Classroom Learning," *Journal of Educational Psychology* 60 (1969): 443-48. Copyright 1969 by the American Psychological Association. Reprinted by permission.

Table 7.2
Simple, Partial, and Multiple Correlations between Predictors and Criteria

	Criteria											
	Cognitive								Noncognitive			
	Understanding Science		Physics Achievement		Science Processes		Science Interest		Physics Activities		Physics Interest	
Measures of Association and Predictors	Post (76)	Gain (57)	Post (77)	Gain (42)	Post (86)	Gain (68)	Post (91)	Gain (86)	Post (80)	Gain (63)	Post (86)	Gain (78)
Simple r												
Control variables												
IQ	.62*	.40*	.61*	.34*	.59*	.35*	.20	.17	.20	.17	.12	.10
Physics achievement	.53*	.25*	.63*	.01	.54*	.24*	.16	.12	.17	.02	.11	.11
Science interest	.16	.12	.18	.04	.18	.05	.45*	.00	.36*	.03	.34*	.03
Press variates												
Cognitive	.61*	.51*	.56*	.35*	.59*	.38*	.14	.11	.09	.03	.03	−.03
Noncognitive	.08	.13	.01	.08	.07	.07	.46*	.38*	.33*	.29*	.43*	.35*
Partial r												
Press variates												
Cognitive	.39*	.39*	.28*	.29*	.37*	.24*	.02	.01	−.05	−.01	−.07	−.11
Noncognitive	.05	.09	.03	.00	.04	.05	.42*	.40*	.28*	.29*	.39*	.34*
Multiple R												
Control	.66*	.41*	.71*	.43*	.65*	.35*	.48*	.17	.40*	.08	.36*	.17
Control plus press	.72†	.55†	.73†	.50†	.71†	.43†	.61†	.43†	.48†	.30†	.51†	.39†

Note: The partial correlations are between the press variates and the criteria, with control variables—IQ, initial physics achievement, and science interest—held constant. The rows of multiple correlations are for (1) the three control variables, and (2) the control variables plus the two press variates. Individual reliabilities of the criteria are in parentheses.

*Correlations significant at the .01 level.

†Significant increment in explained variance.

Source: H. J. Walberg, "The Social Environment as a Mediator of Classroom Learning," *Journal of Educational Psychology* 60 (1969): 443-48. Copyright 1969 by the American Psychological Association. Reprinted by permission.

stringency of the test, and statistically significant. Later replications with sixty-four Montreal students showed that process-outcome relations hold up in chemistry, biology, English, history, geography, and French as well as physics, even when outcomes of students in the class who have not rated the class are predicted from those who have (Walberg and Anderson, 1972), and the generality of the findings is now being investigated in Brazil, India, and other countries. It has been shown that different students learn more in classes with emphasis on different environmental processes (see Anderson and Walberg, 1974). It should also be noted that the relationship of difficulty (or intellectual challenge) to cognitive gains in physics that was observed in the study above did not replicate in other subject areas. Rather it was such socioemotional group properties as cohesiveness, satisfaction, and goal direction and the absence of disorganization, favoritism, friction, and cliques that were associated with measures of cognitive growth.

Course Evaluation and Classroom Processes

The National Science Foundation, after Sputnik, spent several hundred million dollars on course development in science and mathematics and on training programs for teachers. Very little is known about the success of these efforts, but I was fortunate enough to collaborate with Wayne Welch, now of the University of Minnesota, and others in what we hoped would be a thorough summative evaluation of one high school course, Harvard Project Physics. The design and development of the course took about seven million dollars, and we spent about half a million on four years of evaluation. It was a true experiment with a national random sample (the only one ever conducted in education as far as we know), and part of it is summarized below (Welch and Walberg, 1972; see Welch, Walberg, and Watson, 1972, for a detailed report on related formative evaluation and basic research studies).

The developers of Project Physics were originally concerned about the continuing drop in the proportion of students who take physics in high school. To attract students who are not bound for mathematical, scientific, or technical careers, and without compromising on the physics content, they attempted to develop an interest-awakening, module system of course components using a variety of media and methods for learning: a basic text, film loops, programmed instruction booklets, transparencies, laboratory apparatus, special cameras, a student handbook, and other materials. The structure of the course allows students to emphasize the aspects that interest them most, for example, rigorous mathematics, laboratory experiments, or historical readings. Perhaps the most distinctive aspect of Project Physics is its humanistic orientation—an attempt to show the place of physics in the history of ideas and its relation to technology and social development.

Elaborate and expensive procedures were used to obtain the national sample of teachers; all had to agree beforehand to teach Project Physics or their regular course depending on our random assignment. The experimental teachers were trained for six weeks at Harvard in the purposes and methods of the course; the control teachers were also brought to Harvard, cordially entertained, and impressed with their importance in the experiment, to minimize alleged Hawthorne effects.

The results of the experiment showed there were no significant differences in standardized achievement and understanding tests or physics interest and attitudes between experimental and control groups. Differences were not even reflected in tests based on the Project Physics text materials. Figure 7-3, however, shows that there were a number of differences on process variables, opinions about the course, and the image of physics.

From the experimental part of the evaluation, it appears that Project Physics reached several of the main goals established for it. Students exposed to the course performed as well as students in other courses on cognitive measures. In keeping with the humanistic, affective, and multimedia elements of the course, they perceived their classroom environments as more diverse and egalitarian and less difficult (see figure 7-3). They found their textbook more enjoyable, a historical approach more interesting, and physics less difficult. Reflecting the way the subject was to be portrayed in the course, they saw physics as more historical, philosophical, and humanitarian and less mathematical. Finally, the course did seem to have a special appeal to students in the middle-range IQ group, 112 to 119, who have increasingly tended to elect not to take physics in high school in the last decade.

The results further suggested that even with very expensive

Figure 7-3

Significant Standardized Course Contrasts and F-Ratios

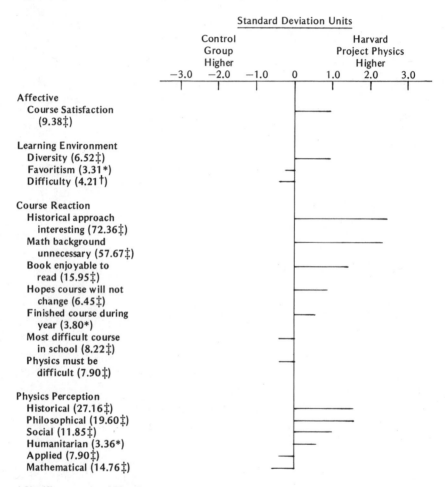

* Significant at the .05 level.

† Significant at the .01 level.

‡ Significant at the .001 level.

Source: W. W. Welch and H. J. Walberg, "A National Experiment in Curriculum Evaluation," *American Educational Research Journal* 9 (1972): 373-83.

experiments with careful definition and implementation of treatments, we are more likely to find educationally significant differences on process and related measures than on conventional achievement and attitude tests.

Subject Areas and Cognitive Press

Process measures may be used to gauge the emphasis given to various cognitive objectives during instruction even though the objectives cannot be measured well as learning outcomes. Ernest House of the University of Illinois at Urbana, Joe Steele of the University of Colorado, and I have worked together on two studies of cognitive press using the Student Activities Questionnaire, a process instrument they developed to evaluate programs for gifted children in Illinois. Their instrument can be used to obtain student perceptions of the degree of instructional emphasis given to the six levels of the Bloom (1956) taxonomy of cognitive objectives. On a four-point scale, students rate the emphasis on various cognitive activities or tasks in their class.

In one study (Walberg, Steele, and House, in press) of 121 Illinois classes, four subject areas were compared using discriminant functions with covariance control for class size, grade level, and giftedness. All three discriminant functions were highly significant (probability less than .001), and the subject areas are plotted on the discriminant dimensions in figure 7-4, along with three similar dimensions uncovered by Anderson (1971) using our sociopsychological scales (the Learning Environment Inventory described in the previous section) on 62 Montreal classes. The first function, called *convergence-divergence,* contrasts mathematics and language arts (see figure 7-4) and suggests the two well-established psychometric factors—numerical and verbal abilities. Associated with mathematics (convergence) are scales dealing with analysis and memory and the affective conditions of test and grade stress, absence of humor, and little discussion. The scales associated with the language arts (divergence) side of the dimension have to do with the cognitive objectives of interpretation, evaluation, synthesis, and translation; affective processes include student independence and participation in discussion. Figure 7-4 shows that in the first and largest discriminant functions of the Illinois and Montreal studies, mathematics is sharply distinguished from other subjects; in both studies mathematics classes were

Figure 7-4
Subjects in Discriminant Space

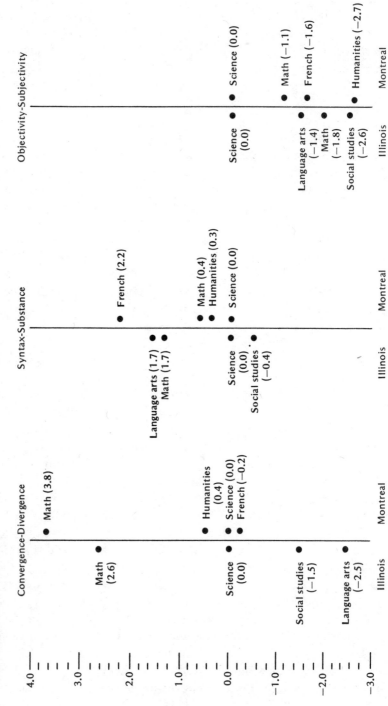

seen as unpleasant. The similarity of these findings, despite the use of different instruments, is striking.

The second discriminant function, termed *syntax-substance,* represents a contrast of language arts and mathematics with science and social studies. The function resembles Schwab's (1969) distinction of tool and application subjects in the curriculum. The scales associated with math and language arts (syntax) include the cognitive objectives of synthesis, translation, and application. Associated with science and social studies (substance) are the cognitive processes of summarizing, memorizing, and evaluating. The second function in the Montreal study is perhaps similar to this function in that the study of French is more syntactical than substantive.

The third function, labeled *objectivity-subjectivity,* contrasts science with social studies. The scales associated with science (objectivity) include independent exploration, learning and memorizing, interpreting, and synthesizing. Associated with social studies (subjectivity) are scales dealing with valuing. This function contrasts more objective acquisition and synthesis of information in science with more subjective evaluation of information in social studies. It is somewhat similar to the third Montreal function where the humanities, which are subjective, were contrasted with science.

Further mapping of cognitive processes emphasized in other subject areas might help depict the curriculum in psychological and empirical rather than logical and hypothetical terms. The coordinates found here are somewhat similar to the ones Anderson (1971) derived with an instrument tapping sociopsychological rather than cognitive classroom press. If replicated further, such orthogonal coordinates may depict the relations of the subject areas in objective, interpretable, parsimonious ways. Since cognitive processes and aspects of the social environment transcend the curriculum, instruments to measure them that focus on the press or context of instruction may enable us to relate psychological processes to subject areas in ways not ordinarily thought of by curriculum makers, teachers, and students. For example, the research raises the questions: Is mathematics inherently convergent? If not, why is it apparently conveyed convergently to the student? Should the syntactical aspects of science and social studies be given more emphasis? Should the subjective aspects of science and some objective qualities of social studies and humanities be imparted?

Grade Level and Cognitive Press

The second study (Walberg, House, and Steele, in press) using the Class Activities Questionnaire concerned the emphasis given to cognitive objectives and affective processes in grades six through twelve. A number of publications we reviewed showed that general student morale declines in the later elementary grades and in high school. We were interested in finding out how students in various grades differed in their perceptions of specific cognitive and affective classroom processes, and we hypothesized that higher-level cognitive processes such as analysis, synthesis, and evaluation would be seen as receiving more emphasis by students in higher grades.

For the same 121 Illinois classrooms, the class means on the twenty-three items were regressed on grade level (and its square, to test for nonlinearity), with giftedness, class size, and subject held constant. The thirteen criteria with significant regression weights for grade level are plotted in figures 7-5 and 7-6.

Figure 7-5, a plot of the affective criteria, shows that active class participation, independent activities, excitement, and involvement are perceived as more prominent in grades six through eight than in the higher grades, while concern about grades is perceived as more pronounced in senior high school. However, the plots are curvilinear: participation, independence, and involvement are lowest in grades nine through eleven; and concern about grades peaks at grade eleven.

Figure 7-6 shows that the lower level cognitive processes such as memorizing and knowing the best answer are seen as receiving more emphasis in the higher grades while the higher-level processes such as application, comprehension, finding consequences, and discovering solutions are seen as more prominent in the lower grades. Again, however, several plots are curvilinear; lower-level processes reach a peak and higher-level processes reach a trough in grades nine through eleven.

Contrary to the rising Thurstone curves of mental abilities during the junior high and high school years, students in the later years see more and more emphasis on lower-level, convergent tasks such as memorization. Also, they appear to engage in less independent learning and to grow increasingly alienated from their classes during the high school years. Perhaps older adolescents are simply more critical of education than younger students; but the more bureaucratic

Figure 7-5
Affective Criteria by Grade Level

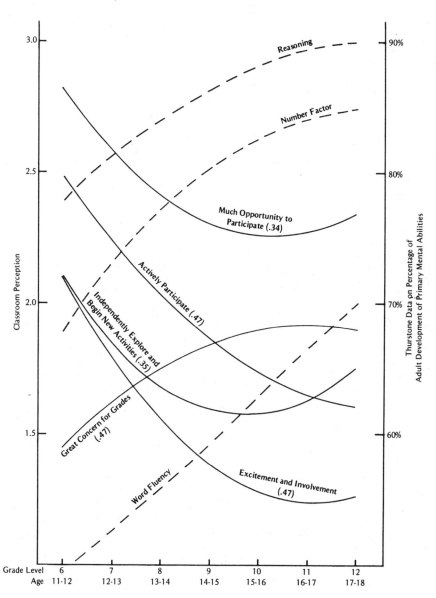

Note: Numbers in parentheses are standard errors of estimates.

Figure 7-6
Cognitive Criteria by Grade Level

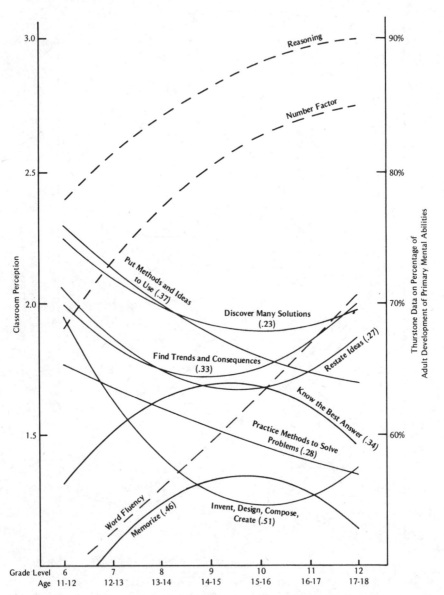

Note: Numbers in parentheses are standard errors of estimates.

qualities of high schools may also account for the trends. High schools are larger and more departmentalized than elementary schools. The elementary student may attend a school with an enrollment of several hundred pupils from his immediate neighborhood. He may have thirty of the same fellow students and the same teacher for most of the school day. The high school student may attend a school of a few thousand students drawn from an entire city; he may encounter a hundred different students and five different teachers in his classes; and he may meet a new set every semester. Instead of the more personalized formative evaluation that guided his learning in elementary school, his progress in high school is increasingly monitored with multiple-choice tests. If he wants to go to college, he is expected to prepare himself to do well on convergent standardized tests with items that require him to check the "one best answer" among those set forth by the test maker rather than formulating his own answer or, better yet, his own question.

To be sure, there are some theoretical advantages and efficiencies in large, bureaucratic schools: specialization through departmentalization, lower per-unit costs, "objective" standards, and cosmopolitanism in drawing social and ethnic groups together. Evaluations of these features suggest to me that they do not impair standardized achievement test performance. But I fear that our exploratory research on classroom processes has only begun to suggest the human costs to students (and possibly teachers): anonymity, alienation, and concentration on lower-level cognitive learning, at least from the students' point of view.

Open Education and Classroom Processes

Open education, the British Infant School, the developmental classroom, the Leicestershire Plan, the integrated day—these phrases refer to an educational movement that began in Great Britain and is growing rapidly and generating a great deal of interest among administrators, teachers, and parents in the United States. There has been very little research and evaluation on open education, aside from testimonials by exponents and reporters. Recently the Educational Development Center, an educational laboratory sponsored by the United States Office of Education, commissioned TDR (Training-Development-Research) Associates, Inc., to review the available open education literature, analyze the concept's component parts, verify the analysis with prominent open educators, and develop process instruments for classroom measurement of its properties. The research was done in collaboration with Susan Thomas, a teacher with experience in British and American open classes (Walberg and Thomas, 1972). This section presents a validation of the instruments in United States open and traditional classes and British open classes.

Before we turn to the validation, a few words on the concept and a brief summary of our recent literature review are in order. It seems better to try to present a fair representation of the concept than to advocate or attack it. Open education is difficult to characterize in the way that behavioral scientists are accustomed to doing, because it is founded on contingency and uniqueness. Each student, teacher, and event is sui generis. The feelings and behavior of the open teacher cannot be easily categorized because her guiding principle is to respond as sensitively and reflectively as possible to the unique child at the precise moment in the temporal stream and situational Gestalt of her interaction with him. Also implicit in the approach is a view of the child, especially in the primary grades, as a significant decision maker in determining the direction, scope, means, and pace of his education. Open educators hold that the teacher and the child, in complementary roles, should together fashion the child's school experience. Thus, open education differs from teacher-centered, child-centered, and programmed, textbook, or other materials-centered approaches in that it combines all three, with both the teacher and the child determining learning goals, materials, and activities.

The open education movement seems to grow out of many old truths, perhaps clichés, about children and the learning process. But open educators seem to take these ideals seriously and practically and to teach and relate to children accordingly, instead of rationalizing and convincing themselves ex post facto that existing practices are consistent with such ideals. Open education has grown out of practical experience rather than philosophical or scientific foundations. It is not a theory or system of education, but a related set of ideas and methods. Content analysis reveals that the movement resonates strongly with the educational thoughts of Rousseau in France, with those of Tolstoy in Russia, and in the United States with the methods used in the one-room prairie schoolhouse in the nineteenth century and by some Progressives during the 1920s and 1930s. Philosophically it rests on phenomenology rather than positivism, and the position of open education is antipathetic to the line of mainstream educators from Plato to the programmed instruction advocates who classify the curriculum into subjects, group learners by ability, and view knowledge as represented authoritatively by the teacher or in prescribed vicarious materials of instruction. The point of view of open educators is far more consonant with developmental, humanistic, and clinical psychology than with the branches that have been most influential in education—connectionism, behaviorism, and psychometrics.

In our study, Thomas and I scanned the major works on open education for concrete examples of eight themes. Those found were recorded verbatim under each theme. Based on the quotations, 106 specific, explicit statements were drafted that were intended to define open classroom characteristics (see Walberg and Thomas, 1972, table 1, for examples). Twenty-nine nationally prominent open educators responded to a request to agree or disagree with the statements and to criticize and suggest changes for any they found deficient. From their reactions, the original list was revised, and fifty items were selected for inclusion on an observation rating scale and parallel teacher questionnaire. The number of items for each theme reflects the attention given to the theme by the original writers, the extent of agreement by the panel of experts, and the extent to which items are observable; for example, half the items are related to provisioning, because it is so strongly emphasized by open educators and because it can be readily observed. To diminish response set in drafting the final set of scales, some items were stated negatively so that agreement would imply traditional classroom characteristics.

The sites for observations were selected on the basis of their reputation and the personal knowledge of the investigators. The sample was by no means random, but it represented urban and suburban public and private schools with administrators and teachers cooperative enough to permit intrusive observers. An effort was made to gain access to both open and traditional classes with teachers regarded as excellent by outside experts and their principals, and the sample was further restricted to classes of five- to seven-year-old children in their first three years of school.

About twenty classes each of the United States open, United States traditional, and British open types were selected. In the

United States, classrooms were observed in three major cities (Boston, Chicago, and New York), one small city (Cambridge, Massachusetts), several suburban towns, and one university town. In Britain, classes were visited in two major cities (London and Bristol), one university town (Cambridge), and two villages in Leicestershire.

The scales clearly distinguish open from traditional classes. Figure 7-7 is a plot of the standardized contrasts of United States and British open classes with United States traditional classes; these are the estimates of the raw differences in means divided by the within-cells standard deviations of the corresponding criteria (see Bock and Haggard, 1968); thus, they measure the differences between group means in units of standard deviation, and the contrasts are comparable across all criteria. It can be seen that open classes differed sharply from traditional ones on five of the eight criteria—provisioning, humaneness, diagnosis, instruction, and evaluation. Moreover, British and United States open classes were highly similar, especially on the observation criteria. British open teachers were close to United States traditional teachers on the teacher questionnaire scales in terms of seeking, and assumptions, but both open groups were similar to one another and well differentiated from the traditional group on the corresponding observation scales. Moreover, the differences between open and traditional teachers were far larger than the differences either between schools of different socioeconomic strata or between schools in United States and those in Great Britain. Thus we found consistencies between the conceptualization and anecdotal descriptions of open education on the one hand and its classroom processes as rated by teachers and observers on the other.

There are many additional valid questions to ask about the concept of open education. Perhaps we have identified some of the crucial elements of these questions. As pointed out at the outset, the concept has been the subject of very little evaluation and research, aside from testimonials by proponents. Before it is expanded from the limited number of extant experimental settings in this country, administrators, teachers, and parents quite properly should know if it leads to more learning, to higher levels of performance in reading, to greater self-esteem and self-determination, to the good life. We have developed some exploratory instruments that are indicative of presumably important aspects of open classroom processes. Seeing if these processes are related to valued educational outcomes is an

Figure 7-7
Standardized Contrasts of United States and British Open Classes with United States Traditional Classes

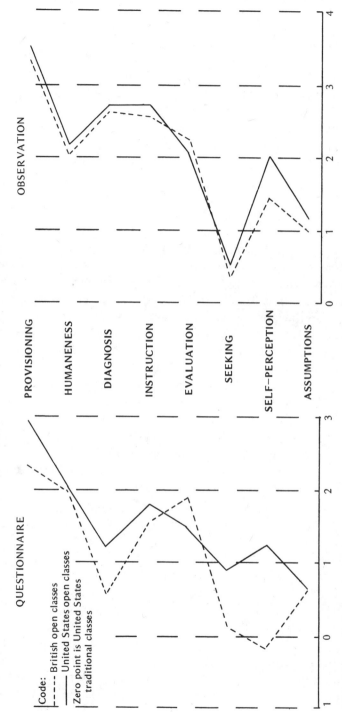

Note: The standard error of all contrasts is .31; seeking as observed is the only nonsignificant criterion.

Source: H. J. Walberg and S. C. Thomas, "Open Education: An Operational Definition and Validation in Great Britain and the United States," *American Educational Research Journal* 9 (1972): 197-208.

obvious next step for those who wish to evaluate open education. On the other hand, many of the valued outcomes cannot be measured very effectively. Even if open classrooms do not perform better on standardized convergent tests, we ought not to reject the educational concept summarily. Many sensitive observers of education would hold that its characteristic processes are ends in their own right, and I am inclined to believe that these processes lead to wholesome human relations, independent inquiry skills, and high-level cognitive outcomes even though we cannot effectively measure these ends.

Conclusion: What Next?

The reader is reminded that the purpose of this chapter was to explore and illustrate empirically a new area of educational evaluation. Those of us who have conceived, developed, and used educational process instruments welcome the interest and collaboration of other investigators in this field. We look forward to seeing how others use and refine the instruments, and we will be indebted to those who favor us with constructive criticism. As our own work moves forward in collaboration with British, Canadian, and Indian researchers, the Learning Environment Inventory has been sent on request to more than 300 investigators in Argentina, Brazil, Chile, India, Australia, New Zealand, West Germany, Holland, Sweden, England, Scotland, Ireland, Canada, and the United States. About seventy requests for the open education scales have been filled, and Steele and House have shared their instrument with a number of workers and are extending their work to other countries. Andrew Ahlgren, Paul Johnson, and David Johnson of the University of Minnesota are developing a promising instrument that assesses student perception of curriculum, instruction, and human relations in an entire school district, and they are exploring its uses for systemwide diagnosis and planned-change programs. Dean Nielsen and Diana Kirk of Stanford University have prepared a review of current classroom climate instruments. The research programs of the Illinois, Minnesota, and Stanford groups are presented in a new book on educational performance evaluation (Walberg, 1974).

Thus, formative, summative, and basic evaluative research with process instruments is growing rapidly, but additional empirical research, conceptualization, and critical scrutiny are necessary to nurture, brace, and prune this research sapling, while the larger forest of dense multiple-choice varieties has to be thinned out. Many of its species are dead and decaying and are unnecessarily obstructing the work of industrious educational elves.

Critical scrutiny of process evaluation deserves emphasis in three areas: general science, psychometrics, and evaluation. From a scientific perspective, process constructs and instruments should be comprehensive yet parsimonious; further, they should replicably indicate and predict general learning phenomena. Though conventional educational tests are criticized here, the traditional psychometric standards of reliability and validity should continue to be applied to process instruments. Finally, from an evaluation perspective, it has been shown that process evaluation is comparatively practical, convenient, and cheap, but more field work is required to find out if the instruments can be used in, or adapted to, a wider variety of educational settings. For this, they have to be reliably sensitive to valued differences in educational conditions and capable of tracing the course of educational innovations.

References

Anderson, G. J. "Effects of Classroom Social Climate on Individual Learning." *American Educational Research Journal* 7 (1970): 135-52.

Anderson, G. J. "Effects of Course Content and Teacher Sex on the Social Climate of Learning." *American Educational Research Journal* 7 (1971): 649-64.

Anderson, G. J., and Walberg, H. J. "Learning Environments." In *Evaluating Educational Performance,* edited by H. J. Walberg. Berkeley, Calif.: McCutchan, 1974.

Bar-Yam, M. "The Interaction of Student Characteristics with Instructional Strategies." Ph.D. dissertation, Harvard University, 1969.

Bing, E. "Effect of Child-rearing Practices on the Development of Differential Mental Abilities." *Child Development* 34 (1963): 631-48.

Bloom, B. S. *Stability and Change in Human Characteristics.* New York: John Wiley, 1964.

Bloom, B. S., Hastings, J. T., and Madaus, G. F. *Handbook on Formative and Summative Evaluation of Student Learning.* New York: McGraw-Hill, 1971.

Bloom, B. S., et al., eds. *Taxonomy of Educational Objectives,* Handbook 1, *The Cognitive Domain.* New York: David McKay, 1956.

Bock, R. D., and Haggard, E. A. "The Use of Multivariate Analysis in Behavioral Research." In *Handbook of Measurement and Assessment in the Behavioral Sciences,* edited by D. K. Whitla. Reading, Mass.: Addison-Wesley, 1968.

Bock, R. D., and Vandenberg, S. G. "Components of Heritable Variance in Test Scores." In *Progress in Human Behavior Genetics,* edited by S. G. Vandenberg. Baltimore: Johns Hopkins University Press, 1968.

Bowles, S., and Levin, H. M. "The Determinants of Scholastic Achievement—Some Recent Evidence." *Journal of Human Resources* 3 (1968): 3-24.

Cattell, R. B. "Theory of Fluid and Crystallized Intelligence: A Critical Experiment." *Journal of Educational Psychology* 54 (1963): 1-22.

Coleman, J. S., et al. *Equality of Educational Opportunity.* Washington, D.C.: U.S. Office of Education, 1966.

Darlington, R. B., Weinberg, S., and Walberg, H. J. "Canonical Variate Analysis and Related Techniques." *Review of Educational Research,* in press.

Dave, R. H. "The Identification and Measurement of Environmental Process Variables that Are Related to Educational Achievement." Ph.D. dissertation, University of Chicago, 1963.

Dyer, P. B. A. "Home Environment and Achievement in Trinidad." Ph.D. dissertation, University of Alberta, 1967.

Ebel, R. L. "Knowledge and Ability in Achievement Testing." In *Toward a Theory of Achievement Measurement,* edited by P. H. DeBois. Princeton, N.J.: Educational Testing Service, 1969.

Feldman, D. "Problems in the Analysis of Patterns of Abilities." *Child Development,* in press.

Ferguson, L. R., and Maccoby, E. E. "Interpersonal Correlates of Differential Abilities." *Child Development* 37 (1966): 549-71.

Gagné, R. M. "Policy Implications and Future Research." In *Do Teachers Make a Difference?* Washington, D.C.: U.S. Office of Education, 1970.

Honzik, B. "Environmental Correlates of Mental Growth: Prediction from the Family Setting at 21 Months." *Child Development* 38 (1967): 337-64.

Hotelling, H. "The Most Predictable Criterion." *Journal of Educational Psychology* 26 (1933): 139-43.

Hoyt, D. P. *The Relationship between College Grades and Adult Achievement.* Iowa City: American College Testing Program, 1965.

Jencks, C., et al. *Inequality: A Reassessment of the Effect of Family and Schooling in America.* New York: Basic Books, 1972.

Katzman, M. T. *The Political Economy of Urban Schools.* Cambridge: Harvard University Press, 1971.

Lohnes, P. R., and Marshall, T. O. "Redundancy in Student Records." *American Educational Research Journal* 2 (1965): 19-23.

Lowy, L., Blokesberg, L. M., and Walberg, H. J. *Integrative Learning and Teaching in Schools of Social Work: A Study of Organizational Development in Professional Education.* New York: Association Press, 1971.

Mosteller, F., and Moynihan, D. P., eds. *On Equality of Educational Opportunity.* New York: Random House, 1972.

Pace, C. R. "Perspectives on the Student and His College." In *The Educational Problem to 1980 and Beyond,* edited by J. L. Goodlad. Washington, D.C.: American Council on Education, 1966.

Pace, C. R., and Stern, G. G. "An Approach to the Measurement of Psychological Characteristics of College Environments." *Journal of Educational Psychology* 49 (1958): 469-77.

Plowden, B. *Children and Their Primary Schools.* London: Her Majesty's Stationery Office, 1967.

Rosenshine, B., and Furst, N. "Research on Teacher Performance Criteria." In *Research in Teacher Education: A Symposium,* edited by B. O. Smith. Englewood Cliffs, N.J.: Prentice-Hall, 1971.

Schwab, J. J. *College Curriculum and Student Protest.* Chicago: University of Chicago Press, 1969.

Tyack, D. B. "The 'One Best System': A Historical Analysis." In *Rethinking Urban Education,* edited by H. J. Walberg and A. T. Kopan. San Francisco: Jossey-Bass, 1972.

United States Office of Education. *Do Teachers Make a Difference? A Report on Recent Research on Pupil Achievement.* Washington, D.C., 1970.

Vernon, P. E. *Intelligence and Cultural Environment.* London: Methuen, 1969.

Walberg, H. J. "The Social Environment as a Mediator of Classroom Learning." *Journal of Educational Psychology* 60 (1969): 443-48.

Walberg, H. J. "A Model for Research on Instruction." *School Review* 78 (1970): 185-200.

Walberg, H. J. "Models for Optimizing and Individualizing Instruction." *Interchange* 2 (1971): 15-27.

Walberg, H. J. "Social Environment and Individual Learning: A Test of the Bloom Model." *Journal of Educational Psychology* 63 (1972): 69-73.

Walberg, H. J. "Transactional Evaluation in Professional Education." In *Studies in Transactional Evaluation,* edited by R. Rippey. Berkeley, Calif.: McCutchan, 1973.

Walberg, H. J., ed. *Evaluating Educational Performance: A Sourcebook of Methods, Instruments, and Examples.* Berkeley, Calif.: McCutchan, 1974.

Walberg, H. J., and Anderson, G. J. "Properties of the Urban Achieving Classes." *Journal of Educational Psychology* 63 (1972): 381-85.

Walberg, H. J., House, E. R., and Steele, J. M. "Grade Level, Cognition, and Affect." *Journal of Educational Psychology,* in press.

Walberg, H. J., and Marjoribanks, K. "Differential Mental Abilities and Home Environment." *Developmental Psychology,* in press.

Walberg, H. J., Steele, J. M., and House, E. R. "Subject Areas and Cognitive Press." *Journal of Educational Psychology,* in press.

Walberg, H. J., and Thomas, S. C. "Open Education: An Operational Definition and Validation in Great Britain and the United States." *American Educational Research Journal* 9 (1972): 197-208.

Weiss, R. H. "The Identification and Measurement of Home Environmental Process Variables that Are Related to Educational Achievement." Ph.D. dissertation, University of Chicago, 1969.

Welch, W. W., and Walberg, H. J. "A National Experiment in Curriculum Evaluation." *American Educational Research Journal* 9 (1972): 373-83.

Welch, W. W., Walberg, H. J., and Watson, F. G. "Experimental Course Evaluation: A Case Study of Harvard Project Physics." Manuscript, Harvard University, 1972.

Wolf, R. M. "The Identification and Measurement of Environmental Process Variables that Are Related to Intelligence." Ph.D. dissertation, University of Chicago, 1964.

Faculty Critique

by FRANK H. FARLEY

It's a pleasure for me to comment on the work of one of the most productive researchers in American education. Although such an extensive research program provides many points for discussion and comment, I will deal mainly with two notions, perhaps stimulating Professor Walberg to respond.

The paper represents an extensive, statistically well-fed presentation of some very original research, viewpoints, and possibilities for the use of educational process evaluation. It draws heavily on Professor Walberg's own research program. It musters data and observations around three important themes: (1) learning should be examined in vivo—that is, while it is taking place—and especially from the learner's point of view, (2) the social context and processes of learning should be analyzed, particularly in a sociopsychological perspective, and (3) standardized achievement test outcomes should be deemphasized in the evaluation of educational enterprises. I am in sympathy with these themes, and might add parenthetically that our own research is heavily informed by similar notions, particularly those in points (1) and (3).

The evidence and observations marshaled by Professor Walberg in support of the significance of educational process evaluation come from often quite disparate areas, with gaps and discontinuities; clearly, this marshaling of support must be aided by further recruitment at all ranks and from all able-bodied sources of data before a major army is fielded in the evaluation campaign. But the time is right! The search for new approaches to evaluation is proceeding apace. Dissatisfaction with standardized achievement testing is all about us. The concept of *process* has recently emerged at or near the top of the educational research charts. Professor Walberg's use of the notion of process in evaluation is in accord with recent emphases on process in learning research and work on individual differences. A major conclusion of the 1967 conference report on *Learning and Individual Differences* edited by Gagné was that we should be concerned with individual differences in the processes held to underlie attention, learning, and memory. Thus we might be concerned with individual differences in such putative process variables as rate of memory consolidation, rate of transfer from short- to long-term memory store, susceptibility to interference in memory, and subjective frequency estimates of prior exposure to material. Other more physiologically referenced individual differences might lie in processes of cortical arousal, in Russian concepts, of the strength, balance, and mobility of the nervous system (Farley and Severson, 1971, 1973), and so on. Mental elaboration and mental imagery may be central processes important in learning and instruction. Paivio (1971), DiVesta (1973), and others have talked about such process variables important to individual differences and learning. These processes are all held to be internal and inferred. We have conceptualized them as *process individual differences* and their measurement as *process-referenced measurement* (Farley, 1973). Some of the process individual differences just mentioned are identified through parameters of learning task performance and others through physiological measures.

All this activity in the arena of process constructs is desirable in focusing our attention on Jamesian notions of the stream of mental life—on the inference of continuity and interrelatedness in fundamental psychological phenomena. Professor Walberg's approach, in concert with basic work on learning processes and individual differences, might allow us ultimately to understand the context and conditions of mental and social development and the multivariate means of evaluating this development.

However, one or two problems bother me. One is the notion of process itself, particularly the measurement of process. This is a general problem in process-related research. In Professor Walberg's work, process measures, like the generally disliked standardized achievement tests, IQ tests, and so on, boil down to discrete test scores and tallies. Most of the measures represent samples of behavior, with assigned numerical values. Differential predictive power of the measures aside, what does the term *process* add? Could these context and sociopsychological ratings be the "new traits"? On-line, real-time continuous evaluation of, let's say, verbal behavior, which might ultimately be available to us with interactive computers, might more clearly represent an approach to process evaluation; but perhaps not. As Professor Walberg relies greatly on the construct of process, I would be interested in his comments on the convergent and discriminant validity of it in relation to his own work.

Another matter of concern to me lies in notions of cause and effect, explanation by correlation, and so on. The work reported by Professor Walberg is largely correlational. It is therefore hard to know who did what to whom. But a statement such as: "verbal ability . . . is determined in large part by . . . home environmental processes," suggests some established causal nexus. There are other similar statements in the paper. Such causal inferences are guesses based on correlation coefficients. What one might like to see derived from such nonexperimental multivariate research is an integrative model that would generate predictions about the effects of different interventions and change. Perhaps in the future Professor Walberg will be heading at least in part into the realm of experimental work on the effects of context variables, in hand of course with evaluation.

References

DiVesta, F. J. "Theory and Measures of Individual Differences in Studies of Trait by Treatment Interaction." *Educational Psychologist* 10 (1973): 67-75.

Farley, F. H. "Motivation and Individual Differences in Learning and Retention." In *Immediate and Long-term Contributions of Educational Research to Individually Guided Education*. Madison: Wisconsin Research and Development Center for Cognitive Learning, University of Wisconsin, 1973.

Farley, F. H., and Severson, H. H. "The Stability of Individual Differences in the 'Strength' and 'Sensitivity' of the Nervous System." *Educational and Psychological Measurement* 31 (1971): 453-59.

Farley, F. H., and Severson, H. H. "Individual Differences in Arousal and Strength of the Nervous System?" *Psychophysiology* 10 (1973): 205.

Gagné, R. M., ed. *Learning and Individual Differences*. Columbus, Ohio: Charles E. Merrill, 1967.

Paivio, A. *Imagery and Verbal Processes*. New York: Holt, Rinehart and Winston, 1971.

Author's Reply to Faculty Critique

Let me give several responses. I would like to emphasize the importance of Professor Farley's central concerns. I would welcome people entering the area of process research, and, as I mentioned, a great number of people *are* using instruments that we've developed. I heartily agree with what Mr. Farley just said about experiments. I hope that people who use these instruments use them in experiments rather than in correlational studies. As a general response to Mr. Farley's commentary I would reiterate that this was an advocate's paper. If I were to play the role of the objective evaluator of the paper, I would have brought out the points that Mr. Farley made myself. They are ones that have bothered me, particularly the two critical points he mentioned.

The Jamesian notion of "stream of mental life" suggests one of the difficulties I've had in conceptualizing processes. Maybe philosophers can give some help here. I'm not sure whether processes—that is, perception, satisfaction, cohesiveness, intimacy, the democratic qualities of a group—are means or ends. We have treated them in both ways in much of our research. They do have predictive validity in the sense that, if a group seems to be cohesive and satisfied, the students look forward to coming to it, they don't form cliques, there is not a lot of disorganization, and their goals seem to be well formed and clear in their minds. We then find that this pattern is associated with gains in cognitive performance and positive attitudes toward the subject. So we can justify these environmental processes on the basis of standardized outcomes, such as cognitive learning. Some have suggested to me that these processes or student perceptions ought to be viewed as ends in their own right, that we ought to try to optimize the social circumstances, the group's perception. I think there's a value in doing that—an extended form of validity that one could perhaps derive from the Jamesian notion of stream of mental life. There's a marked contrast between the judgment of a student who is exposed continuously to the treatment and can make very sensitive, human valuations about the quality of the educational experience for him, and the characterization of his educational experience by a standardized test or even the characterization of his environment by the predominant technique of the last twenty years—counting the teacher's acts every few seconds. The real causal variables determining the learning norms and so on may not be the lesson or what the teacher does so much as the nature of the classroom group. So, these process measures are difficult for me to conceptualize, too, as you can see from my last few comments. Are they means or are they ends? Should we in fact use them as goals, if a program can produce a more democratic or more satisfying classroom environment? Here I guess I agree with one of Jencks's points: that *one* of the criteria for the quality of schooling is the extent to which it is satisfying to students who go there. We certainly look at many other institutions of our culture in that way—movies, for example.

Mr. Farley also made an excellent point about the source of variance in the scores on the Learning Environment Inventory. Are they a function of the social environment (the group, that is) or a function of personality? I'm not sure how to analyze this. When you have a student rate the qualities of his classroom group, I believe to some extent it should be considered a personality trait, as Mr. Farley was suggesting. But there's also probably some objective notion. This has to do with the difference between obtaining means of classroom groups on these perceptions and looking at the individual characteristics. What seems to flow from getting a rating of the environment is an amalgamation of the organism and the stimulus. In psychology, historically we've said there's the stimulus and there's the organism. In talking about perceptions, we say that any score on such a variable is a joint function of both of those things. I think that both these factors enter into the determination of the scores.

With respect to inferring causality from correlations, I am in entire agreement with Mr. Farley on the need for experiments; the first time the Learning Environment Inventory was used was in a large, national experiment. While many of our studies since then have been correlational, we would encourage others to begin experiments. There are several going on now in our own shop in which interventions have been made, and I know of other people around the country who are using process constructs to try to characterize treatments applied on the basis of random assignments.

Audience Discussion

Definition of Process Variables

Q: What are process variables? It seems to me, as a beginning step, that that is a misleading term. Climate variables, or something like that, would be more appropriate. I don't know anything about these that makes me think of process.

Walberg: Well, there are a couple of problems here. One is that we've admittedly and unhappily used different words to characterize them; we haven't always called them process variables. Sometimes we call them environment variables, and sometimes we call them climate variables. In much evaluation work we've had a series of pre-tests and a series of outcomes (in general, standardized achievement tests and others of that nature); the process constructs are measured in between the two, and we obtain them during the *process* of learning, so as to emphasize that it's an ongoing thing. It's not a terminal product; we're not viewing it as an end or a goal, but rather as a means. On the other hand, if we value cohesiveness, satisfaction, and intimacy in their own right, then maybe we should look at them more as ends.

Another way of thinking about the distinction is by considering three phases: input, process, and outcome. We have a kind of black box in evaluation: treatment and an outcome. What we're trying to emphasize in doing process research is characterization of the ongoing process rather than simply what it indicates at the end. Clearly our research has evolved over seven years; it wasn't programmed at the beginning. We still have much to learn, especially about the best terms to use in characterizing learning settings, processes, and outcomes.

Q: But the ongoing process can clearly be an outcome of the treatment.

Walberg: Yes.

Dimensions of Process Variables

Q: I am interested in the classroom process, but I don't think I would ask the sorts of questions you ask of children, to find out what the process is. If children feel uncomfortable or happy, I wouldn't say that that's what is going on in the schools. I have a hunch you think you're getting a whole dimension that you're not really touching by using that word *process.*

Walberg: With respect to the comprehensiveness of the scales, the initial instrument was designed from the largest study that had ever been done of adult groups. It was done by Hemple and Westy at Ohio State, in the 1950s, and they attempted to develop all the possible ways one might evaluate a group. Ours was specifically designed from that point of view, but to be applied to a group of children in classrooms. So we tried to make it both comprehensive and relevant to what was going on in classrooms. But if you're suggesting in your comment that the students have a limited perspective, I certainly agree with you. In addition to using the students' perceptions, we often use an observer who comes in that day and makes the same sort of ratings. Or, in our studies of open education, we had the teacher do the rating. I think to get a comprehensive look you need as many perspectives as possible. But at the same time (I'm in sympathy with Mr. Karier's position here) I think, as evaluators and educators in general, we have a tendency to overlook the student, and the student has a terribly important role. After all, he's the recipient of instruction, and he is a good judge of what the instruction is worth at that moment. We at least ought to get his opinion on it, although his opinion may be somewhat limited.

Q: Professor Walberg, do you run into problems with some of your questionnaires? One of your graphs shows various attributes going up and down. You mentioned a twenty-seven-item questionnaire, I think, that you people at Illinois handled. Aren't you constructing an objective rating scale and not taking into account different verbal abilities of the subjects at different age levels? Would you consider using some completely open-ended measure?

Walberg: We've considered it, and we've done some work on it. In evaluating Project Physics, we used a number of open-ended questions; for example: "How does physics affect everyday life?" and "What is light?" Those aren't technically good essay questions, but they're extremely open-ended. The student could respond to them in an affective or a cognitive way. Our purpose was to try somehow to get an objective look at the differences between various courses. And so we used computer procedures that could count the number of times a given word was used. We could measure the technical vocabulary in physics or the number of times that words with positive affect, like "nice," "good," and "fun," were used. So, we *have* looked at open-ended things. We have generally tried to take, or make, a scale for the particular project that we're working on.

In some ways we look at the learning environment measures as we would look at the semantic differential, but in a far more modest way. The semantic differential should not be looked at as an instrument, but rather as a methodology of research. With a particular curriculum project—on social studies, or English, or physics, or open education—the evaluator ought to tailor the instrument to the purpose of the evaluation. I think Mr. Cook made this point earlier about the "Sesame Street" evaluation. You ought to tailor the instrument so that it's sensitive to what you're trying to look at, whether it's age, or curriculum, or whatever variable interests you. When people ask to use the Learning Environment Inventory, we give them permission, but we encourage them to modify it, rather than taking the one we happened to make the first time as a kind of universal test. It could be shortened, lengthened, used essentially as an adaptable methodology rather than as a fixed instrument like the Stanford-Binet test.

Q: You presented a graph showing observations in all the open classrooms that are parallel to questionnaires. Was the observation a rating scale?

Walberg: In that study we used several sources of information. One was a literature review describing what open education was. We tried to look at orthodox, British open education, rather than the American version, which seems to have about five different subschools now, like open architecture, the open corridor, or any of the other types. We examined the original writings and then tried to see whether they conformed with the teacher's view of herself. Thirdly, we had an observer make ratings in the actual classrooms. In those cases, the instrument that was developed had very concrete and specific items, describing teacher behavior in the classroom, and parallel ratings were made by the observer and by the teacher. Then these were correlated to get an index of agreement or, one might say, interrater reliability.

Philosophy and Process Evaluation

Q: Let me ask an analytic question of both Mr. Cook and Mr. Walberg. One of the points you both made is that many studies find no significant differences in education. And one of the points Mr. Walberg put nicely is that perhaps *philosophers* should look at some of the problems we're having: we need some help. What might be the implications of the argument, for instance, that by basing your research on the work of Gagné and others you inevitably will get no significant differences, because of some very difficult analytic problems. Perhaps the notion of reinforcement, for instance, is circular and really explains much less about human behavior than we give it credit for. Another example might be this: we analytically, though artificially, distinguish cognitive from affective functioning; yet we know very well, both phenomenologically and realistically, that they are not separate. If you look at any work in the history of science, you find that scientific research has never proceeded in that way. What would be the implications on our common sense talk then, in terms of research and schooling, if we found that the basic perspectives we are employing are less than useful?

Cook: To answer that I'll have to go into my life history a little. I was for two years a graduate student in sociology at a German university. Sociology in German universities is a highly politicized discipline. And the question people kept asking was, "What is the use of that? What are we doing it for?" I left Berlin to do graduate work in the United States in the South. And here I experienced profound culture shock, because the important questions were not "ends" questions, but "means" questions, instrumental questions: "How do we do this?" Everybody worked very hard learning how to do a thing; nobody asked, "Why are we doing it?" That was a real culture shock for me. It took me a long time to get over it, and I'm still finding my way back. I resonate to the idea of opening up our closed shop to philosophers who will force us to ask that question more than we do. There are other good questions they might raise, particularly in language realms. Over the last twenty years psychology as a discipline has lost its roots. Its roots go back to philosophy. Some of the men who have made great contributions to the field in fact have independent identities as philosophers—they think of themselves that way.

Walberg: Your question is a very difficult one. I think the thrust of it is, "Why don't psychologists listen to philosophers and others, particularly with regard to education?" I'm in full agreement with its importance. I've noticed, as a psychologist and a member of the AERA, that we never get a philosopher's paper or a historian's paper in the journal. We tend to talk to other psychologists, rather than even biologists and sociologists. We have a great deal of trouble communicating even with the sister disciplines that are presumably closest to ours. I think that there are dangers in applying the basic sciences and their influences to education. It may be that to be effective, educational research has to "become its own man," so to speak, but critically combine disparate disciplines. It has to develop a unique, autonomous system of inquiry, epistemology, and analysis, so that when a naive economist (as Mr. Jencks was characterized by someone earlier) says that schools are failing because they are not promoting equality of income, educators don't immediately tend to think, "Well, that's just awful. We've been doing a terrible job." After all, education does involve more than psychology; curriculum obviously involves many substantive disciplines. I think that we need to look at educational research problems in a far more holistic way. The unfortunate thing is that the way scholarship has evolved, we've all become more specialized; educational psychologists speak to an audience of educational psychologists and rarely think deeply about philosophical questions. I would think that philosophers, historians, and others could be very helpful. Conferences such as this one, bringing people from different points of view together, should be encouraged.

8

Ideology and Evaluation

in quest of meritocracy

CLARENCE J. KARIER

It is my understanding that *evaluation* is a complex process of assigning value to phenomena, while *ideology* represents the set of values and attitudes that make up the composite picture of social and individual philosophy by which men in a given culture profess to live. In this context, evaluation inevitably occurs within some kind of value orientation that is part of an ideological framework. This does not mean that men will always be true to their ideological commitments; nor does it imply that all these commitments are necessarily reasoned and understood. Indeed, often they are so thoroughly assumed, they remain unexamined. What I propose is that evaluation inevitably implies certain values and that these values are crucial in understanding the ways in which men organize their social existence.

Social institutions reflect what men have come to value in any particular culture. For example, we might examine the political,

In writing this paper I have profited from both the research and the dialogue of a number of people at the University of Illinois. I am particularly indebted to Russell Marks, Stephen Yulish, Lauren Weisberg, Paul Violas, Leo Kazaniwskj, Peter Sola, Marion Metzow, Erik Kristiansen, Brisbane Rouzan, and Michael Becker. The research reported here was supported in part by the Spencer Foundation and in part by the College of Education at the University of Illinois, Urbana-Champaign.

economic, religious, or educational institutions of a culture to seek clues to what is valued in that culture. In this regard, a study of the educational institutions can be most fruitful. I suspect that this is true because people usually will not tolerate for very long the imposition of "wrong" values on the education of their children. This is especially true in American education because this country's social philosophy is deeply rooted in the work of eighteenth- and nineteenth-century Enlightenment thinkers, who saw the creation of educational institutions as crucial to national progress and fulfillment.

The purpose of this paper is first to analyze and describe the Enlightenment ideology that became part of the operating educational philosophy of the United States in the twentieth century; secondly, to show how these ideas found expression as part of an ideal meritocratic system and as part of the real system; thirdly, to analyze how the educational reward system became ideologically structured to control and channel people; fourthly, to show that the heated nature-nurture debate has historically functioned to obscure the reasons for basic shifts in social policy; and finally, to suggest that in our quest for meritocracy we have often confused our ideal with the real despite repeated confrontations with evidence that our basic social philosophy may serve more to destroy than to enhance the dignity of man in the twentieth century.

The Enlightenment ideology that Condorcet, Diderot, Jefferson, and Madison espoused included education as the key to national progress and the perfectibility of man. Progressive developments in scientific knowledge, they thought, would break the chains of ignorance and superstition that enslave and ensnare men to support evil social systems. The rational man would thus stand free and tall. Since evil was caused by ignorance, and education could banish ignorance, mass compulsory education of an enlightened humanity could be expected to banish evil, while it set men free. Jefferson preached his "crusade against ignorance" to overcome every form of social evil, improving human nature and the social order progressively. The ideology of the Enlightenment, thus, carried with it a strong argument for universal schooling.

While some assumed that those who knew the good would be more apt to do the good, others settled for the notion that a knowledgeable humanity might function by an ethic of enlightened self-interest. In either case, talent and virtue were intimately related. Jefferson

believed in a natural aristocracy of the two. A really good educational system, he believed, would be a meritocratic system that rewarded
both. Proposing a rigorous evaluation procedure, he would "rake
from the rubbish annually" in order to ensure that only the best
would go on to higher education at public expense.[1]

The good society, for most sons of the Enlightenment, was the
meritocratic ideal where men took up their positions in life not
because of special privilege resulting from wealth, caste, status, or
power but because of natural talent and virtue. The various inequalities that resulted from caste, class, and privilege had to be overcome
in order to allow the true natural talents of men to emerge.

All men, however, were not viewed as equal in talent. As Antoine
Nicolas de Condorcet put it: "We, therefore, need to show that these
sorts of real inequality [wealth, status, and education] must constantly diminish without however disappearing altogether; for they
are the result of natural and necessary causes which it would be
foolish to wish to eradicate."[2] Few held the notion that "all men are
created equal" in any absolute sense, except in the eyes of God or
the law. The revolution of the rights of men was to be directed
against those ancient artificial barriers that prevented the full development of mankind. The millenium, some believed, was not far off.
As Saint-Simon put it in 1814, "The golden age is not behind us, but
in front of us. It is the perfection of social order. Our fathers have
not seen it; our children will arrive there one day, and it is for us to
clear the way for them."[3] Less than a century later, Edward Bellamy
in *Looking Backward* (1887) echoed similar sentiments as he spoke
for many liberal progressive reformers: "The Golden Age lies before
us and not behind us, and is not far away. Our children will surely
see it, and we, too, who are already men and women, if we deserve it
by our faith and by our works."[4]

The Enlightenment dream became the American dream. Those
who were worthy by their "faith" and their "works" might participate in ushering in the new meritocratic social order. Through their
efforts to perfect social scientific knowledge and to apply that
knowledge to our social institutions, educational reformers would
participate in the fashioning of that utopian ideal. If advances in the
physical sciences meant an increase in the power of men to control
and predict physical phenomena, then any comparable progress in
our knowledge of human behavior might, when applied, usher in an

equal advance in our control and prediction of human behavior. Helvetius, the philosopher of Enlightenment environments, put it well when he suggested that "to guide the motions of the human puppet it is necessary to know the wires by which he is moved."[5]

With a similar perspective in mind, Auguste Comte, in *Positive Philosophy,* predicted that in the scientific society of tomorrow, a universal system of positive education would teach men to know and do their duty in such a way as to diminish, if not eliminate, conflict between individuals. The masses were to be educated to know and want the good; they were to develop those proper social attitudes so necessary to their ability to fit into the social-occupational structure of the evolving educational state. Thus, the Enlightenment dream included more than the mere identification and development of natural talent. It also entailed shaping social attitudes so that the individual might more easily fit into the organic whole of society. This perspective was, perhaps, best reflected by Edward Ross, who suggested that to educate is "to collect little plastic lumps of human dough from private households and shape them on the social kneadingboard."[6]

A considerable number of new social scientists who applied their intellectual efforts to help organize the educational state in the United States in the twentieth century were ideological sons of the Enlightenment. In general, they thought of science as the process of classifying and ordering phenomena along the lines August Comte had laid down in *Positive Philosophy.* In applying this philosophy, they usually saw themselves as cultivating both a science and a profession of education in the overall national interest. Deeply involved in the problems of industrialization, immigration, and urbanization in the opening decades of the century, these men helped shape the compulsory educational state.

The idea of using compulsory schooling to solve social problems was not, of course, new. Horace Mann's argument for the common school as a "balance wheel of the social machinery" reflected an earlier thrust. Now, however, at the dawn of the twentieth century, with waves of immigrants from southeastern Europe flooding the centers of American culture,[7] with industrial and urban needs for standardized consumers as well as producers,[8] came the acute need to create an educational system that would classify, standardize, socialize, and Americanize youths on a massive scale. This was to be done in the interest of national progress.

To many Americans who listened to the debates over evolution in the closing decades of the nineteenth century, the Enlightenment idea of progress and the theory of Darwinian evolution seemed to blend logically into each other. Herbert Spencer helped when he said: "To be a good animal is the first requisite to success in life and to be a nation of good animals is the first condition of national prosperity."[9] The idea of evolution, cast in the American model of progress, made sense to those who were nurtured on the belief that this land and its people had a "manifest destiny" that included not only such weighty responsibilities as assuming the "white man's burden" but also the more awesome messianic challenge of "making the world safe for democracy." National pride mixed easily with Anglo-Saxon racism under the rubric of cultural evolution. American racism rested on the assumed superiority of that special racial mix fortuitously drawn from northern and western Europe. Those who saw themselves as members of the superior race usually looked with fear and uncertainty on the new immigrants. If evolution was to continue along the Enlightenment lines of perfecting man—indeed, if the progress of the nation was to continue—then the problem of dysgenics would have to be overcome. Race degeneration was the shadow that stalked and, at times, mocked the troubled racial superiority image of the American.

Darwin pointed to the problem when he said: "The weak members of civilized societies propagate their kind. No one who has attended to the breeding of domestic animals will doubt that this must be highly injurious to the race of man."[10] Americans also knew that "good" breeding counted, and that the future progress of their nation depended, in part, on creating laws and institutions that would, in effect, prevent the degenerates of the culture from reproducing. Both eugenics and euthenics were propelled by the Enlightenment quest for the perfectibility of man and society in the context of a social and intellectual climate dominated by Darwinian evolution. Enlightened America led the world in the field of eugenic sterilization laws.[11] In the thoughts and actions of many early educational reformers, such as Lewis M. Terman and David Starr Jordan, as well as later reformers, such as Arthur Jensen and William Shockley, one can sense a continuing fear of race pollution as well as a belief in race superiority. America at the turn of the century was so thoroughly a racist nation that the following eulogy by the editors of the *New York Times* supposedly honoring Frederick Douglass could go unchallenged:

Amid the universal commendation of Frederick Douglass as a colored man, who, against the greatest difficulties and in the most unfavorable circumstances, achieved well-deserved distinction, it might not be unreasonable perhaps, to intimate that his white blood may have had something to do with the remarkable energy he displayed and the superior intelligence he manifested. Indeed, it might not be altogether unreasonable to ask whether with more white blood, he would have been an even better and greater man than he was, and whether the fact that he had any black blood at all may not have cost the world a genius, and be, in consequence, a cause for lamentation instead of a source of lyrical enthusiasm over African possibilities.[12]

The superiority of the Anglo-Saxon Nordic race over the Alpine, Mediterranean, and Negroid races continued to appear in the literature of social and educational reformers of the first three decades of the century. Many American educational psychologists were no less racist than their nation. Not yet a generation away from black slavery and Indian genocide, the Anglo-Saxon American faced the massive immigration from southern and eastern Europe with fear and dread. Over and over, these fears found expression in the arguments for intelligence testing, tracking in schools, eugenics laws, Americanization programs, guidance movements, and finally immigration restriction. Leadership for most of these movements came from the ranks of the liberal progressives who saw themselves as committed to the intelligent, orderly reform of society.

Many educators, such as David Starr Jordan (chancellor at Stanford), A. Lawrence Lowell (president of Harvard), Leon C. Marshall (dean at the University of Chicago), John R. Commons and Edward A. Ross (professors at the University of Wisconsin), served on the national committee of the Immigration Restriction League and actively lobbied for discriminatory immigration restrictions against southern and eastern Europeans. Other educators with similar views, such as Lewis M. Terman, H. H. Goddard, Frank Freeman, Edward L. Thorndike and C. C. Brigham lent their efforts to rationalize and standardize the educational system efficiently along the lines of what they viewed as the emerging social order. That social order was hierarchical and stratified.

Meritocracy: The Dream and the Reality

The hierarchical social class system was maintained then, as it is today, not so much by the sheer force of power and violence, but by the ideological beliefs of people within the system. There is, perhaps, no stronger social class stabilizer, if not tranquilizer, within a hierarchically ordered system than the belief, on the part of the lower class members, that their place in life was not arbitrarily determined by privilege, status, wealth, and power, but rather is a consequence of merit, fairly derived. This idea is fundamental to the maintenance of the meritocratic educational state in twentieth-century America, which is basically class structured.[13] If enough men believe that the system is based on merit and that all who participate have an equal opportunity to demonstrate their merit, and thus determine their social and economic position, then the system may, indeed, be judged fair.

Real equal opportunity is, of course, difficult to approximate and may ultimately be impossible to achieve in a hierarchically ordered social system. The idea of equal opportunity has served as a credibility valve, if not a safety valve, that maintains the social class system under the mantle of meritocracy. To believe that such a system is fair, one must assume equal opportunity or something plausibly approximating that condition. In a society like ours with a hierarchical social-economic structure, where the rich have superior health and educational care and the poor have inferior health and educational care, one realizes rather quickly that equal opportunity is not only difficult to approximate but ultimately impossible to achieve without a social revolution. Such a realization fundamentally throws into question the fairness of the system. Many of the arguments for equal opportunity in the twentieth century appeared to be rhetorical devices to appease the oppressed and thereby protect the established social system. Indeed, the more heated debates involving equal opportunity usually occurred at just those times when the credibility of the meritocracy was being challenged.

Although the educational state in the twentieth century became the mirror image of the hierarchical social order, there were some in the nineteenth century who held out hope for a more egalitarian system. Recognizing the consequences of inequality of wealth, Robert Dale Owen advocated state boarding schools:

Respect ought to be paid, and will always be paid, to virtue and to talent; but it ought not to be paid to riches, or withheld from poverty. Yet if the children from these state schools are to go every evening, the one to his wealthy parent's soft carpeted drawing room, and the other to his poor father's or widowed mother's comfortless cabin, will they return the next day as friends and equals? He knows little of human nature who thinks they will.[14]

Owen knew that before one could develop equal educational opportunity, one had to lessen the impact of inequalities of wealth and privilege on the lives of the young. Ignoring this crucial point, some forty years later, Lester Frank Ward, the father of the "American concept of the planned society,"[15] argued that the evils of social class hierarchy could be overcome by developing a universal state system of publicly supported day schools. As he put it, the state "may . . . compel the most unwilling, even where his unwillingness grows out of principle or religious scruple, to go into the army and invade a foreign country. Why then may it not compel him also to send his children to the public school or to go himself?"[16] Ward insisted that "the interests of society are paramount."[17] In the cause of progress and the cultivation of a true meritocracy, he further insisted that the ignorant must not be allowed to remain in their ignorance, but must be coerced if necessary to become enlightened. In his view, "the task of education is a positive task. It must be forced upon an unwilling people. No laissez-faire policy will do. To wait for the ignorant to demand it before giving it to them is like waiting till you have learned to swim before venturing into the water."[18]

While Ward believed the old social class hierarchy might disappear in his new meritocracy, one senses that a new hierarchy based on native talent would emerge. Progressive increase in knowledge on the part of all classes was dependent, he believed, on a kind of knowledge not readily grasped by all people.

And this substantial knowledge which alone is capable of promoting great progressive schemes and working vast social ameliorations is of the kind which does not come by experience, by spontaneous effort, by impulse, ambition, and avarice, it is of the kind which comes only by study, by calm reflection, by assiduous labor. It is of the kind which the young and the ignorant would never choose, which the wild natural spirit of man never loves. It is the kind which must be enforced by regulations, established by law, maintained by custom. Those who know its value must compel its acceptance by those who do not. Wisdom, not years is the true maturity. The wise of the state are the parents of the ignorant. As the parent compels the attendance of his unwilling son at school, so the consolidated wisdom of the state must obligate the benighted citizen to do what is for the interest of the state and of morality, as well in matters of education as in matters of civil rights.[19]

In Ward's true meritocracy, there would still be the struggle between the wise and the ignorant with the resulting need for compulsion. It would still be necessary, as Rousseau put it in the *Social Contract,* to "force men to be free," or, as Ward put it, to "force men to be educated." This, again, was the faith of the Enlightenment. Since evil was a product of ignorance and schooling was the instrument by which ignorance might be eliminated, the state had the right, indeed the duty, to protect itself and its citizens from evil by instituting compulsory public schooling. Compulsory schooling, compulsory military training, and compulsory public health care emerged on the basis of similar arguments.

Ward's blueprint for the coming educational state in the United States carried with it not only the justification for compulsory schooling and the functional role of the knowledgeable expert, but also the utopian vision that all social institutions might be used to cultivate and extend the "native power" of all members of the community. The day would come, he believed, when "the reign of hierarchy will be at an end, and that of equality will be inaugurated."[20] When that day dawned, Ward argued, "the false arbitrary value now set upon individuals will disappear and their true intrinsic value will take its place." Men and women alike will be judged and find their place in life on the basis of true intrinsic value.

The true value of a new born infant lies, not in the social position of its parents or ancestors. It is not even measured by what it actually will do during its life. It lies in what it might do under the proper circumstances; in its naked capacity for acquiring the ability to do when subjected to conditions favorable for the development of that native power. This is the true standard for the determination of real worth of a human being.[21]

When he turned from his ideal society to the real society of 1871-73, Ward asked:

What are we lauding? What are we rewarding? What are we condemning and punishing? I will tell you. We are lauding circumstance. We are rewarding wealth. We are condemning the unfortunate victims of social imperfection. We are punishing wretched beings for being what we have made them.[22]

The way out of this malaise was to construct a kind of educational state where natural merit could be rewarded. Such a system, Ward believed, would recognize "the average natural equality of all men, not only in rights but in capabilities, and propose to insure to each the opportunity of placing himself in the highest sphere for which nature has qualified him to move."[23] Although Ward believed in what he called the "average natural equality" of all men, he did not believe in absolute equality of capabilities. He argued, however, that the differences among men were not as great as most suspected. While he further insisted that his ideal social system would do away with all artificial hierarchies based on caste, title, race, sex, wealth, power, and the like, his meritocracy would still have a natural hierarchy based on true talent. As he put it:

> On the ruins of our present false and fictitious hierarchy will be built a system of true and natural hierarchy in which each will be satisfied to occupy the place to which nature assigned him and none will be able by any means of deception, false appearances, wealth or power, to receive the advantages of a higher place.[24]

The educational state in the United States should, he argued, be a meritocratic state where the child's true worth would be seen in terms of what he might become if only "circumstances permitted." While Ward made a strong case for a utopian future, he made an equally strong case for using the educational power of the state for direct social control. Predating the efficiency and social control language of Cubberly, Terman, and Thorndike by some three decades, Ward argued in the 1870s that "every child born into the world should be looked upon by society as so much raw material to be manufactured. Its quality is to be tested. It is the business of society as an intelligent economist to make the most of it."[25]

Ward had delineated what was to become the hope and the ideal of much of the reform-minded educational philosophy in the twentieth century. The school was to be the vehicle through which nature's raw material would be processed and men and women would find their true stations in life. Ward's meritocracy would not only sift and winnow what nature had wrought but also "manufacture" a better man. Perceptively, Ward saw that if universal schooling was to sort for natural talent and at the same time "manufacture" better people, the first step would be to develop a universal testing and evaluation system. As he put it, "The process of universal education is that of first assaying the whole and rejecting only so much as shall, after thorough testing, prove worthless."[26] The testing and evaluation program was the crucial vehicle through which the educational state could be organized, shaped, and directed.

Crucial, also, was the utopian vision of an open meritocratic society where all would receive their just rewards on the basis of their true natural talent. Again and again we find this utopian assumption reflected in the testing literature of the twentieth century. Few, however, held Ward's ideal image of the good society. More were willing to accept the social system as they saw it. For most, the good society was the existing hierarchical and socially stratified system. Repeatedly, the evaluators tested and measured the consequences of social conditioning and social repression, and insisted they had accurately measured natural talent and virtue. So Richard Herrnstein, writing one hundred years after Ward, argued in his essay "I.Q." that "experts in the field" had concluded that genetic factors accounted for 80 percent of IQ, while environment controlled 20 percent. The more society equalizes environment, he then concluded, "the closer will human society approach a virtual caste system."[27] Rather than rallying against such a result, he suggested we should be preparing ourselves to accept it.

Greater wealth, health, freedom, fairness, and educational opportunity are not going to give us the equalitarian society of our philosophical heritage. It will instead give us a society sharply graduated, with ever greater innate separation between the top and the bottom, and ever more uniformity within families as far as inherited abilities are concerned. Naturally we find this vista appalling, for we have been raised to think of social equality as our goal. The vista reminds us of the world we had hoped to leave behind—aristocracies, privileged classes, unfair advantages and disadvantages of birth. But it is different, for the privileged classes of the past were probably not much superior biologically to the downtrodden, which is why revolutions had a fair chance of success. By removing arbitrary barriers between classes, society has encouraged the creation of biological barriers. When people can freely take their natural level in society, the upper classes will, virtually by definition, have greater capacity than the lower.[28]

From Herrnstein's Harvard Yard perspective, apparently, "society had removed the arbitrary barriers between classes," and natural talent was now presumably freely surfacing, thus accounting for the social class system that presently existed. The educational state in this country had been developing toward Herrnstein's conception of meritocracy for half a century.[29] As he put it: "The data on I.Q. and social-class differences show that we have been living with an inherited stratification of our society for some time."[30] Unlike Ward's ideal meritocracy, which rejected the "caste, class, race, wealth and power bias" of his world, Herrnstein's ideal meritocracy clearly mirrored as well as justified the existing social class system. A century after Ward called for the development of the compulsory educational state to overcome arbitrary social class privilege, Herrnstein was asserting that we were now arriving at a real meritocratic state. By conveniently ignoring the factors of privilege, wealth, power, status, and race, through which his society functioned, Herrnstein could equate his ideal meritocracy with the real meritocracy. Under such circumstances, he could conclude that unfortunately our quest for merit had led not to a lessening of social hierarchy, but toward a greater hierarchy.

For the children of the privileged, the American dream was a success; while for the children of the repressed, it had become a nightmare of futility and hopelessness. Ward's utopian dream had vanished. In its place had emerged a class system heavily based on wealth, status, and privilege, and now justified by an educational system that professed to reward the meritorious through a "scientific," "professional," "objectively determined" testing system. Herrnstein's conclusions about the meritocracy of the present and future were drawn from the experience of over half a century of testing within the educational state. That Herrnstein came out essentially where the testing movement began was not, however, surprising. He, like Binet, Terman, Goddard, Thorndike, Yerkes, and others before him, had tested the results of the socialization process and ascribed the findings to natural talents. The creation of the educational state was, in the end, not a way out of Ward's soulful plea that "we are punishing wretched beings for being what we have made them."

Rationalizing the System: Testing, Predicting, Sorting, and Tracking

From the very start, tests were seen by those who created them as modeled on the then-existing social order. Alfred Binet and T. H. Simon asserted:

An individual is normal when he is able to conduct himself in life without need of the guardianship of another, and is able to perform work sufficiently remunerative to supply his personal needs, and finally when his intelligence does not exclude him from the social rank of his parents. As a result of this, an attorney's son who is reduced by his intelligence to the condition of a menial employee is a moron; likewise the son of a master mason, who remains a servant at thirty years is a moron; likewise a peasant, normal in ordinary surroundings of the fields, may be considered a moron in the city.[31]

Most testers, including Binet, Terman, Thorndike, Jensen, and Herrnstein, recognized that social class differences not only would influence an individual's performance on a test, but also were the foundation of the tests themselves. These men usually accepted the social class system as a given, and then proceeded to argue that social class differences added validity to their observations. Thus, Francis Galton in *Hereditary Genius* pointed out that the physical superiority of the English leaders confirmed, in his thinking, the heritability of genius by suggesting that the gifted leaders were "massive, vigorous, capable-looking animals." On the other hand, Ward maintained that "it would be more nearly true to say that they are superior because they are where they are."[32] Receiving the blessings of a privileged environment, genius could be expected to be physically superior. Galton, Binet, and Thorndike, however, read the physical superiority of the social elites as proof of genetic superiority. At this crucial point, each not only accepted but also in his own way tacitly justified the existing social order. One can sense this in the statement by Binet and Simon that

our personal investigations, as well as those of many others, have demonstrated that children of the poorer classes are shorter, weigh less, have smaller heads and slighter muscular force, than a child of the upper class; they less often reach the high school; they are more often behind in their studies. Here is a collection of inferiorities which are slight, because they are only appreciated when large numbers are considered, but they are undeniable. Some probably are acquired and result from unavoidable and accessory circumstances; others are congenital.[33]

Binet's, Terman's, Thorndike's, Jensen's, and Herrnstein's observations of the social order repeatedly confirmed, in their minds, the validity of their tests. The rich were obviously brighter than the poor, just as they were physically superior to the poor. Ideologically in tune with their social order, the successful tester in America created tests that reflected that social order and the values implicit in that order.

Most testers were fully conscious of this connection and often saw themselves as guardians of the class system. The important thing, however, was the maintenance and development of what H. H. Goddard viewed as an "aristocracy in democracy." In such a social system, the natural aristocracy would rule through the leadership of the people. In *Human Efficiency and Levels of Intelligence,* Goddard argued:

The disturbing fear is that the masses—the seventy million or even the eighty-six million—will take matters into their own hands. The fact is, matters are already in their hands and have been since the adoption of the Constitution. But it is equally true that the eighty-six million are in the hands of the fourteen million or the four million. Provided always that the four million apply their very superior intelligence to the practical problem of social welfare and efficiency.[34]

Goddard, like Herrnstein fifty-one years later, assumed a positive correlation between social class and native intelligence. He further expressed both the need for the intelligent to rule the ignorant masses and the need to educate the masses so that they would accept intelligent leadership. Part of that acceptance would depend on the organization and use of tests in the schools themselves. The test questions were written and rewritten by professional educators who held definite attitudes toward the rich, the poor, the well-washed middle class, and the ill-kept immigrant child. The scores that the tests yielded would predict not only academic success in a school that reflected these values but also social success in the society that reflected those class values. The child, then, needed guidance toward his proper role in society. As Terman put it:

At every step in the child's progress the school should take account of his vocational possibilities. Preliminary investigations indicate that an I.Q. below 70 rarely permits anything better than unskilled labor; that the range from 70 to 80 is pre-eminently that of semi-skilled labor, from 80 to 100 that of the skilled or ordinary clerical labor, from 100 to 110 or 115 that of the semi-professional pursuits; and that above all these are the grades of intelligence which permit one to enter the professions or the larger fields of business. Intelligence tests can tell us whether a child's native brightness corresponds more nearly to the median of (1) the professional classes, (2) those in the semi-professional pursuits, (3) ordinary skilled workers, (4) semi-skilled workers, or (5) unskilled laborers. This information will be of great value in planning the education of a particular child and also in planning the differentiated curriculum here recommended.[35]

The test, originally based on skills appropriate for varying occupational classes and eventually standardized on the basis of class, could now be used for designing a curriculum appropriate for that class and for guiding and channeling the child toward the occupation for which his assumed "native brightness" fit him. The schools would now assay his raw material and put him through a manufacturing process that would teach him to accept social inequalities. As Frank N. Freeman, from the University of Chicago, argued: "It is the business of the school to help the child to acquire such an attitude toward the inequalities of life, whether in accomplishment or in reward, that he may adjust himself to its conditions with the least possible friction."[36] The individual "must not think of education as a personal privilege." Its function was to fit him into a community. It was erroneous to assume "that education is a gift by the state to the individual for the benefit of the individual. The only valid conception of public education is that it is for the purpose of fitting the individual to take his place in the life of the community."[37]

It was the arguments of men like Terman, Freeman, and Thorndike that helped bring the ability-tracking curricular model into the public school. Children were to be homogeneously grouped according to native ability and then educated appropriately.

Included in Freeman's argument, however, was a social class disclaimer. If the tracking system were based on wealth or birth or some other external circumstances, he argued, it would be undemocratic. On the other hand, if it is based "upon the inherent capacity of the individual, it is just and in conformity to the demands of public welfare."[38] As long as Freeman could believe that the tests really measured intrinsic capacity and not social privilege, his utopian meritocratic view of the system could be maintained. This belief in the tests was important for educators who could not acknowledge the social consequences of their activities in testing and tracking in the schools.

Terman, like Freeman, had come to believe so thoroughly in the idea that IQ was a measure of innate ability that he could not see anything questionable in his own study of gifted children, which found that "more than 50 percent of our group have sprung from the top 4 percent or 5 percent of the vocational hierarchy. The professional and semi-professional classes together account for more than 80 percent. The unskilled labor classes furnish but a paltry 1 percent or 2 percent."[39] If one believes, as Terman and Herrnstein seemed to believe, that the social class system has sorted out the best, then these findings are acceptable. Terman argued that it was far more important to cultivate society's intellectual elites than to become too concerned with the dullards. He advocated a three-track system supplemented by a special track for the gifted and a special track for the intellectually disadvantaged, all of which, interestingly enough, corresponded to the five classes of occupations into which he envisioned children being channeled.[40]

IQ, Dysgenics, and Racism

Although Ward was interested in the elimination of artificial burdens, such as caste and race, that would obstruct the free development of natural talent in his meritocratic state, he did not believe in
the equality of the races. He was convinced, as many of his liberal
followers were, that the black race might be superior in feelings and
sentiment but was inferior in cognitive abilities to the white race. In
Pure Sociology, Ward suggested that the black man who raped a
white woman did so not only out of lust but also out of an almost
unconscious desire "to raise his race to a little higher level." Combining a bit of male chauvinism with his racism, Ward asserted that it
was more permissible for a male of a superior race to have sexual
relations with a female of an inferior race than it was for a male of an
inferior race to have sexual relations with a female of a superior race,
because in the first instance it would be a matter of "leveling up"
while in the latter case it would be a matter of "leveling down."[41]

While Ward tended to blend all Europeans into the intellectually
favored race, as opposed to blacks, yellows, and reds, Terman was
more discriminating. Just as he believed in the genetic superiority of
the professional classes, so he believed in the racial superiority of the
northern and western Europeans and Jews over Negroes and southern
Europeans. He, like other liberals—David Starr Jordan, Edward Ross,
and later William Shockley—was vitally concerned with the differential birth rate and the danger of genetic pollution "that threatens the
very existence of civilization."[42] Terman saw two factors creating the
danger:

(1) The racial stocks most prolific of gifted children are those from northern and
western Europe, and the Jewish. The least prolific are the Mediterranean races,
the Mexicans and the Negroes. (2) The fecundity of the family stocks from
which our gifted children come appears to be definitely on the wane. This is an
example of the differential birth rate which is rapidly becoming evident in all
civilized countries. It has been figured that if the present differential birth rate
continues, 1,000 Harvard graduates will at the end of 200 years have but 50
descendants, while in the same period 1,000 South Italians will have multiplied
to 100,000.[43]

Under these circumstances, Terman advocated immigration restriction, various eugenic and sterilization measures, and massive testing
of children so that the gifted could be identified and specially educated.

In "Were We Born That Way?" Terman argued in 1922, as Herrnstein was later to assert in 1971, that the social class occupational system was based on IQ.[44] The arguments used by both are instructive. First, the test questions were created on the basis of behaviors generally appropriate to certain occupations, which were hierarchically arranged according to the social class system. The tests were thus initially developed and standardized on the basis of occupation and social class. Both Terman and Herrnstein then found that the median IQ of unskilled workers was lower than the median IQ of skilled workers. And finally, they concluded that a person's IQ affects his occupation and social standing. The circularity of the argument is completed in such a way that the belief system necessary to perpetuate the notion of an educational meritocratic state is maintained. If one takes the argument the other way, and suggests that the complicated socialization process involved in social class determines IQ, then questions of equity as well as of social justice immediately come to mind. Neither Terman nor Herrnstein confronted this problem.

The racist bias of Terman's thought runs through his "scientific" testing.[45] Similarly, his contempt for the lower classes pervades his science. Terman viewed the bottom 20 percent of the IQ and social class scale as a liability to a democratic society. Like many other liberals,[46] he saw his professional role as that of an expert guiding the irrational, ignorant masses to make the most of their limited abilities. His opinion of the lower class was this:

On questions of larger social and national policy they vote blindly or as directed by political bosses. They are democracy's ballast, not always useless but always a potential liability. How to make the most of their limited abilities, both for their own welfare and that of society; how to lead them without making them helpless victims of oppression; are perennial questions in any democracy.[47]

Terman and H. H. Goddard were both concerned with "aristocracy in democracy." The "scientific" tests that they helped to create and the "professional" testing movement that they led repeatedly confirmed and reinforced their racist and elitist beliefs, in large part because they were created out of those beliefs. Goddard, Terman, Yerkes, Brigham, and Thorndike—all eminent leaders in the testing movement—were overt racists.[48] Terman believed that the American black was vastly inferior to the white man and that the mulatto had enough white blood to increase his intelligence to a "mid-position between pure negro and pure white."[49]

C. C. Brigham, in *A Study of American Intelligence,*[50] also concluded that the Nordic race, from which our older American stock was drawn, was superior. The immigrant who represented the Alpine and Mediterranean races was inferior to the Nordic race, but far superior to the Negro. The Negro represented the very bottom of the genetic pool.[51] The fear of polluting that pool with inferior blood, through racial mixture, plagued the racial superiority image of Brigham and others throughout the century. "We must face a possibility of racial admixture here that is infinitely worse than that faced by any European country today, for we are incorporating the negro into our racial stock, while all of Europe is comparatively free from this taint."[52]

Toward Breeding a Better Race

Just as Brigham feared the taint of inferior blood on the American nation, so did Lewis M. Terman, Ellwood Cubberly, and Edward Ross. These distinguished Stanford professors all would agree with their former president, David Starr Jordan, who argued:

The original framework of our nation has been weakened and blurred by racial dilution. The loose adulation of the Nordic races now current, however exaggerated, is based on a primal and vital fact. In history and temper ours is a Nordic nation. Its freedom was won and its integrity maintained by Nordic methods and those races or members of races who have not valued freedom and order are politically and socially a burden on our progress.[53]

The superiority of the Nordic stock, throughout American history, had been clearly demonstrated. "Can we share freedom safely with peoples who do not want it and whose highest aim is merely to vegetate?" Jordan asked.[54] His answer was an emphatic no! The gates of Ellis Island and San Francisco had to be closed to inferior people.

Immigration restriction, though helpful as a temporary device, was not a final solution, however, and extermination of a race was not possible. Ultimately, the final solution rested in selective breeding. Jordan asserted:

We would not smother nor exterminate races or nations to save food, but we cannot yet feed them all, and the time has come to consider improving the breed by selection. To this end, much serious thought of serious people must be given while in no sense can the present statute of 1924 [immigration restriction] be regarded as final and conclusive.[55]

Forty-seven years later, a Nobel Prize laureate, William Shockley, also from Stanford University, stepped to the speakers' rostrum at the American Psychological Association and pointed once again to the problem of racial pollution. He, too, rejected Hitler's solution for dysgenics and proposed instead that a voluntary sterilization bonus plan be made available to all welfare recipients. The plan he proposed would permit the state to pay a welfare recipient $1,000 for every point of his or her IQ score below 100, if he or she voluntarily submitted to a government sterilization operation. Thus, Shockley argued, both our dysgenic problem and our welfare problem would be solved within a generation.[56]

Shockley's solution was not far removed from those espoused earlier by David Starr Jordan and Edward L. Thorndike. In Thorndike's last major work, *Human Nature and the Social Order* (1940), he wrote:

By selective breeding supported by a suitable environment we can have a world in which all men will equal the top ten percent of present men. One sure service of the able and the good is to beget and rear offspring. One sure service (almost the only one) which the inferior and vicious can perform is to prevent their genes from survival.[57]

To Thorndike, the genetically inferior were the poor. They were also the vicious. The assumption that the more talented are more virtuous as well as more wealthy is one that lies at the base of much school practice in the educational state. In many ways, Thorndike made explicit what others had merely assumed. Well within the Enlightenment ideology that assumed a strong correlation between talent and virtue, Thorndike argued that "to him that hath a superior intellect is given also on the average a superior character."[58] His empirical "scientific" study of human behavior led him to conclude that "the abler persons in the world in the long run are the more clean, decent, just, and kind."[59] He also asserted that it has paid the masses to be ruled by intelligent leaders, because such men are by and large of superior justice and goodwill.[60]

Thorndike was, perhaps, the most influential shaper of the meritocratic educational state in the early twentieth century. For almost half a century, he held sway at Columbia University, teaching thousands of teachers and administrators, publishing 50 books and 450 monographs and articles. His massive three-volume *Educational Psychology* (1913) set the tone of that discipline for almost two decades. From his pen flowed a prodigious number of educational maxims, psychological laws, textbooks and scales of achievement for elementary, secondary, and college courses in various fields, dictionaries for elementary and secondary schools, and teacher's manuals. He not only told the teachers what to teach and how to teach it, but also told them how to evaluate their work. Because he wrote so many of the texts and the tests used in elementary and secondary schools, his impact on American educational practice was both immediate and extended.

Thorndike believed in the genetic superiority of the white race over the black race, just as he firmly believed that the good society was ultimately a society ruled by talented, morally righteous, and wealthy people. He found wealth, character, and intelligence positively correlated. Like Ward, he was a son of the Enlightenment who believed that the progress of humanity was achieved through the manipulation and reform of men by social institutions. Thorndike, however, carried the idea of social melioration and the perfectibility of mankind to one of its possible conclusions, eugenics.

Ward's belief in the future development of a scientific society where men would collectively control the course of their future destiny led him, too, to espouse eugenics. In 1891 he wrote:

> It is the right and the duty of an energetic and virile race of men to seize upon every great principle that can be made subservient to its true advancement, and undeterred by any false ideas of its sanctity or inviolability, fearlessly to apply it. Natural selection is the chief agent in the transformation of species and the evolution of life. Artificial selection has given man the most that he possesses of value in the organic products of the earth. May not men and women be selected as well as sheep and horses? From the great stirp of humanity with all its multiplied ancestral plasms—some very poor, some mediocre, some merely indifferent, a goodly number ranging from middling to fair, only a comparative few very good, with an occasional crystal of the first water—from all this, why may we not learn to select on some broad and comprehensive plan with a view to a general building up and rounding out of the race of human beings? At least we should by a rigid selection stamp out of the future all the wholly unworthy elements. Public sentiment should be created in this direction, and when the day comes that society shall be as profoundly shocked at the crime of perpetuating the least taint of hereditary disease, insanity, or other serious defect, as it now is at the comparatively harmless crime of incest, the way to practical and successful stirpiculture will have already been found.[61]

Over the next two decades, however, Ward shifted his position on eugenics. By 1906, before the American Sociological Society, he was arguing against the idea of improving society by breeding theories. Shortly before his death (1913), he made the distinction between what he considered positive and negative eugenics. Positive eugenics was the social process by which the superior are encouraged to reproduce, while negative eugenics was the social process that prevented mental and physical defectives from reproducing their defects.[62] Ward had no quarrel with negative eugenics, but he objected to positive eugenics as national policy on a number of grounds. While he agreed with the ultimate end of the eugenicists—the perfectibility of the race—he differed with their method. He objected that positive eugenics inevitably put someone in a master position over the normal man. Man, he believed, was master over the animal world and over his own defectives; therefore, eugenics was permissible in those areas. But, he argued, "normal people are their own master." At this point, he eulogized nature and argued in a modified Spencerian way that it should be allowed to take its course. Besides, he asserted, men had "brains enough"; what they now needed was knowledge.

Edward L. Thorndike, on the other hand, believed with Francis Galton that the great progress of civilization had been made through the investigations and discoveries of geniuses. His ideological perspective of the good society was, like Herrnstein's, essentially hierarchical and socially stratified. While Ward insisted that the society in which he and Thorndike lived was governed more by privilege of wealth and status than by native talent, Thorndike argued that the wealth, privilege, and status that existed were consequences of the innate talents and abilities of the upper-class members.

A Differentiated Curriculum

Reacting negatively to Ward's repeated insistence that we had not yet tapped the intellectual resources of all people, Thorndike attacked Ward's thought as "intellectual communism." He challenged his opponent to turn to a more realistic, practical view of the curriculum and the educational process. Ward, he said, ought to try to teach various six-year-olds the same thing in the same way and see the results.[63] Arguing the practical case for individual differences, Thorndike proposed a differentiated curriculum based on tested abilities. In the name of education for individual differences, the child was to be given a curriculum appropriate to his presumed abilities. This, in turn, locked him into the social class from which he came. The ideological perspective of the professional educator about the social order had a direct bearing on the content, methods, and design of the curriculum in the educational state. One of the great myths of the twentieth century has been the belief that a differentiated curriculum based on assumed individual abilities and needs would result in increased choice on the part of the individual. From the very beginning of the century, the differentiated curriculum has served to channel, control, and limit the choices of individuals.

A major difference between nineteenth- and twentieth-century educational practices lies in the differentiated curriculum of this century. It was the differentiated curriculum, created by educational professionals, that objectified the student's abilities and channeled him toward an occupation.[64] Repeatedly, Thorndike, Terman, Freeman, and others justified the differentiated curriculum on the grounds of (1) making the system more efficient, and (2) protecting the child from failure. It was black and immigrant children who were being protected from failure. Freedom to be successful, of course, necessitates running the risk of failure. B. F. Skinner was quite correct when he suggested that the kind of psychology that has dominated the American curriculum leads one "beyond freedom and dignity." The current efficiency craze in American education—involving behavioral modification techniques, systems analysis, performance-based instruction, accountability, and the like—in many ways is but an extension of the earlier efficiency movement[65] and involves the same problems of objectification, manipulation, choice, and freedom.

Thorndike knew that the educational state he had helped create was serving definite class interests. He found these interests acceptable because, in his thinking, they represented the best. He seemed never to lose sight of his ideological model of the good society and directed most of his efforts toward it. In *Your City,* he developed what he called a "goodness" or G scale for objectively determining the value of the 310 largest cities of the United States. Among the criteria he listed were:

1. Percentage of persons eighteen to twenty attending schools.
2. Average wage of workers in factories.
3. Frequency of home ownership (per capita number of homes owned).
4. Per capita support of the Y.M.C.A.

5. Per capita number of automobiles.
6. Per capita circulation of *Better Homes and Gardens, Good Housekeeping,* and the *National Geographic.*[66]

Thorndike's model of the good society reflected the values of middle America, which was bent on moving to the better homes and gardens of the suburbs after World War II. No doubt his success as an educational leader rested heavily on the fact that his personal values coincided so closely with those of the well-washed middle class that dominated the educational state.

The "Nature" of Women and Their Role in the Educational State

Unlike Ward, who made an impassioned plea for equality between the sexes, Thorndike believed that because men were more variable than women one might find more genius among the male than the female of the species.[67] He admitted that, in general, women might be as intelligent as men and could usually profit from similar kinds of education, but he asserted that the variability factor accounted for the disproportionate number of males to be found in graduate work. Women, he believed, were instinctively different from men, and those differences should be taken into account in their guidance and tracking through the educational state toward their occupational destiny. In *Educational Psychology, Briefer Course,*[68] he explained:

Two instincts are worthy of special attention. The most striking differences in instinctive equipment consists in the strength of the fighting instinct in the male and of the nursing instinct in the female. No one will doubt that men are more possessed by the instinct to fight, to be the winner in games and serious contests, than are women; nor that women are more possessed than men by the instinct to nurse, to care for and fuss over others, to relieve, comfort and console. And probably no serious student of human nature will doubt that these are matters of original nature. The out-and-out physical fighting for the sake of combat is preeminently a male instinct and the resentment at mastery, the zeal to surpass and the general joy at activity in mental as well as physical matters seem to be closely correlated with it. It has been common to talk of women's "dependence." This is, I am sure, only an awkward name for less resentment at mastery. The actual nursing of the young seems likewise to involve equally unreasoning tenderness to pet, coddle, and "do for" others. . . . The fighting instinct is in fact the cause of a very large amount of the world's intellectual endeavor. The financier does not think merely for money nor the scientist for truth nor the theologian to save souls. Their intellectual efforts are aimed in great measure to outdo the other man, to subdue nature, to conquer assent. The maternal instinct in its turn is the chief source of woman's superiorities in the moral life. The virtues in which she excels are not so much due to either any general moral superiority or any set of special moral talents as to her original impulses to relieve, comfort and console.[69]

Since the social demands on women were to serve and the intrinsic nature of women was to "pet, coddle, and 'do for' others," while the intrinsic nature of man was to compete and overpower, it logically followed, for Thorndike, that men and women ought to receive a partially differentiated curriculum—one that channeled women into occupations appropriate to their nature, such as nursing, teaching, and medicine, while men were channeled into the more competitive world of statesmanship, philosophy, and scientific research.[70] The social and occupational roles of men and women of virtually every group were thus rationalized within the educational state in behavioral terms.

Just as the social inferiority of immigrants and blacks was reflected in the curriculum content, so, too, was the inferior status of women. Much children's literature still reflects a social-psychological profile of women as inferior to men. The sexist characteristics of current children's literature are premised on assumptions similar to those that Thorndike and others held about both the place that a woman ought to hold in society and her true nature. Again, the group is first classified as having certain characteristics, then treated as if its members have those characteristics, and ultimately tested to prove that they do indeed have those characteristics. Given Thorndike's perceived role for women, it makes sense to look at children's literature to see how these roles are taught. In a recent study of 2,760 children's stories in 134 books, the following ratios were determined:

Boy-centered stories to girl-centered stories	5:2
Adult male main characters to adult female main characters	3:1
Male biographies to female biographies	6:1
Male animal stories to female animal stories	2:1
Male folk or fantasy stories to female folk or fantasy stories	4:1[71]

The qualities of ingenuity, creativity, bravery, perseverance, achievement, adventurousness, curiosity, sportsmanship, generativity, autonomy, and self-respect are model behaviors reflected in the children's literature. The odds *against* a female being projected in one of these positive roles are four to one.[72]

The Aristocracy of Expertise

While the same educational process seemed to be applied to all children, the children of the privileged classes enjoyed one kind of education, appropriate for their place in life, while the children of the repressed received another kind, appropriate for their lesser position in life. The profile of the repressed had behind it not only the force of empirical evidence but also the sanction of the "scientific professional" expert who would correct the pseudo-thinking of what Thorndike called the half-educated man.

The world suffered, Thorndike believed, from too many half-educated men. Such men deluded themselves into thinking that they could and should be able to understand their world. The solution was to be found in cultivating a reliance on the professional expert: "The cure is twofold, consisting of the displacement of pseudo-thinking by real expertness on the one hand or by intelligent refusal to think on the other."[73] If the common man would only learn to refuse to think and to accept the advice of the professional expert, a more well-ordered meritocratic society could emerge. Perhaps the fact that Thorndike's conception of the lower-class poor, southern European immigrants, blacks, and women went relatively unchallenged bore testimony to the public's "intelligent refusal to think," and thus its acceptance of the authority of this professional expert. On the other hand, it seems more likely that Thorndike's stereotyped profiles of repressed people came so close to the conventional views held by the rising middle class that most of his assumptions in these profiles seemed self-evident and therefore went unquestioned. Not until middle-class ideology began to shift, and some no longer believed in the inherent inferiority of women, blacks, or immigrants, did both the profile and the practice begin to be questioned.

Because of his hierarchical view of the good society and the place of genius in that society, Thorndike repeatedly called for more reliance on the knowledgeable expert for policy formation within the educational state. Forty years before think tanks Thorndike was arguing:

Wherever there is the expert—the man or woman who has mastered the facts and principles on which the best present practice in a certain field is based, and who can adapt this best present practice to special circumstances ingeniously—should we not, in fact, let him do our thinking for us in that field?[74]

A functional part of the rationalization of the student in the educational state depended on the development of a kind of expert professionalism, clothed in the rhetoric of science, serving what these experts considered to be the community.

Immigration Restriction and Americanization

On July 11, 1911, Colonel Theodore Roosevelt wrote to Professor Edward Ross, complimenting his old friend on an article on the "yellow peril" that Ross had written following a recent trip to China. Roosevelt, like other progressives, was concerned with dysgenics and the maintenance of the genetic superiority of the Anglo-Saxon strain in the United States. A few weeks later, Ross responded to Roosevelt's letter, pointing out just why he went to China:

I have been anticipating that in a few years an effort will be made to take down the barriers against oriental immigration as part of a policy of pushing our trade with the orient. So I busily collected material with the idea of preparing an unanswerable argument against Chinese immigration that should be free from the least taint of race prejudice.[75]

Self-consciously aware of what he was doing, Ross, like so many other progressives, was deeply involved in shaping national policy on immigration restriction. Discriminatory restriction was necessary against Chinese as well as southern Europeans, not only because of race and economics, but also because of the difficulty of socializing and Americanizing these groups. Ross argued that he favored "a percentage basis for restricting immigration because it will apply the sharpest restriction to just those strains of the later immigration which offer the greatest difficulties of Americanization."[76]

Passage of the Immigration Act of 1924, which made permanent the earlier discriminatory immigration restrictions against Orientals and southern Europeans, symbolized a victory for many liberal progressives concerned with the racial and social stability of the American community. Ross actively lobbied Congress and the executive office, as so many other progressives had for the past two decades, to close the gates. The job, however, was only half done; the other half was to socialize and Americanize the immigrant and his children properly so that they might be made safe for American democracy. Gregory Mason, describing what the Rochester, New York, public schools were doing for the foreign-born and their children, warned:

"Hyphenated citizenship is as dangerous to a republic as a cancer to the human body. Education is the knife to use in cutting out the hyphen, and the public schools of Rochester are a laboratory in which it has been proved that the operation can be done."[77]

Throughout the first half of the century, schools were organized to educate the immigrants away from their un-American traditions and to educate the children of immigrants away from the ways of their un-American parents. The new conditions in America necessitated state intervention. As Marion Brown, principal of City Normal School, New Orleans, put it, "their parents are no longer to be depended upon for safe guidance; hence our American schools must prepare these children for the new conditions."[78] The children were to be shaped to fit the Anglo-Saxon standard. With that standard went a sense of nationalistic fervor and destiny. Brown spoke for many educators, who saw themselves shaping the immigrant's children for the exigencies of an emerging *Pax Americana,* when she said:

As Rome brought order, peace, and personal freedom to the various nationalities in her borders, so today must the teacher endeavor for each of the ethical microcosms that we call American children; bring them to the Anglo-Saxon standard, train them to self-control that means freedom, the love of country that foreshadows the brotherhood of man, the developing personality that can take only justice and right as its standard, a consummation possible only through knowledge of the mazes of inherited tendencies, by sympathy with the soul struggling in shackles of ancestral bondage.[79]

The educational state in America was thus organized to channel millions of youth into what the channelers believed was their social destiny. The shapers and molders of this assumed meritocratic system reflected the collective values of an emerging middle class that had been nurtured largely on liberal Enlightenment social philosophy. Racism, sexism, and elitism were as much a part of the thinking of the framers of the system of mass schooling as were their beliefs in professionalism, scientific testing, progress, social meliorism, eugenics, and meritocracy.

The Nature-Nurture Debate: Toward a False Consciousness

If one believes that the good society is the meritocratic society, if one becomes accustomed to ignoring certain kinds of social injustice and repression, and if one further assumes equal opportunity, then it becomes relatively easy to view the existing reward system in the educational state as a meritocratic system. A person who becomes sensitive to the inequities of this system, but who still quests for meritocracy, usually turns his efforts toward the near-impossible task of equalizing opportunity in an unequal system. This has often been the stance of the fighting liberal or radical struggling to get some repressed group its share in the system.

If, however, one goes beyond the problem of selecting the right kind of educational rake with which to "rake from the rubbish annually," if one questions the kind of social system that not only produces "rubbish" but also leads one to conceive of human beings as "rubbish," a whole set of disturbing social issues emerges. The side of Enlightenment philosophy that viewed man as a product of his social conditioning and called for the application of new knowledge in the interest of the perfectibility of man and his social institutions carried with it a very distinct objectification and depersonalization. From the very start, this served to destroy the dignity of human beings. Man was not the end, but rather a means for other men's purposes. Human beings *could* thus be viewed as "rubbish." Ignoring this perhaps fatal flaw, later social thinkers would concern themselves with the kind of social system that they perceived produced that "rubbish." One such was Lester Frank Ward, making the anguished plea: "We are condemning the unfortunate victims of social imperfection. We are punishing wretched beings for being what we have made them." Other sons of the Enlightenment, such as Thorndike, Jensen, and Herrnstein, considered the rubbish to be less a consequence of social conditioning than of nature. Thus they saw genetic manipulation as the answer. While these men might disagree over the causes and over the exact extent to which the social rubbish might be eliminated, most of them agreed on the desirability of eliminating that rubbish in the interest of the progress of humanity toward a more meritocratic order.

The nature-nurture paradigm leads one to think in opposites. However, it is important to recognize that most men who participated in that dialogue in the twentieth century held common assumptions about the good society. It is also important to recognize that the nature position does not necessarily imply a conservative social philosophy, nor does the nurture position inevitably coincide with a liberal social philosophy. Some of the leading hereditarians, such as Terman and Jensen, have considered themselves liberals. The myth that the hereditarian position is conservative is perpetuated by the false assumption that such a person cannot take social action to correct the defects of nature. In fact, he can, as so many progressive liberal reformers in the past have done, join the eugenics movement, call for the sterilization of the genetically defective, organize social institutions so as to encourage selective breeding by caste or class, stand guard over the genetic pool through such social legislation as immigration restrictions, and call for more effective education in the name of making the most of what we have.

Those who believe that nurturing has the predominant effect, as did Lester Frank Ward, might cover the nature side by supporting sterilization of the genetically defective, and then argue for the same educational reforms in the interest of both efficiency and equality of opportunity. The idea that hereditarians are conservative and environmentalists liberal thus tends to mislead and interfere with an adequate assessment of the function of educational rhetoric in the twentieth century.

Although the study of the influence of genetics and environment on human behavior is a legitimate study in itself, the findings from these areas of inquiry do not incline one to support a radical or a socially conservative view of the organization of society. Nevertheless, evidence from these areas has been repeatedly used as if it necessarily supported one kind of social policy or another.

The nature-nurture argument surfaced in every decade of the twentieth century. At times, the issue seemed to smolder; at other apparently more critical times, it was a source of heated public debate. The argument thus engaged the conscious attention of thousands of educators and laymen throughout the century. If, indeed, this paradigm was so misleading, then why did it appear so crucial to so many people? In seeking an answer, it might be helpful to look at the broader social context surrounding the debate and ask the critical question Russell Marks asks: "What social difference does it make if one believes that I.Q. is 60 percent genetic and 40 percent environmentally determined or if one believes, like Jensen, it to be 80 percent genetic and 20 percent environmentally determined?"[80]

Close scrutiny of the social context of this continuing debate leads to a suspicion that the surface justifications for a given course of action that were raised in the discussion often obscured more potent unstated reasons for that action. For example, while the heredi-tarians stressed the genetic defects of southern Europeans to justify discriminatory immigration restriction (in 1924), their argument obscured the interests of other powerful groups in closing the gates for decidedly economic and social reasons. It was in the economic interest of large industrialists and bankers to close the gates. They now needed to manage the existing labor supply rather than have access to an unlimited supply of cheap labor, which could produce social instability in the urban manufacturing centers.[81]

Intense public interest in this question has usually come to sym-bolize a significant shift in social policy. In this regard, the Terman-Lippmann debates in 1922[82] are instructive. In answer to Terman's hereditarian arguments for discriminatory immigration restriction, Lippmann did not attack the notion of meritocracy or the notion that people are intellectually different because of inheritance, but rather attacked the inadequacy of the tests themselves. He concluded his remarks with a strong plea for accurate, performance-based test-ing as a useful vehicle in classifying people along the lines of demon-strated merit:

> Instead, therefore of trying to find a test which will with equal success discover artillery officers, Methodist ministers, and branch managers for the rubber busi-ness, the psychologists would far better work out special and specific examina-tions for artillery officers, divinity school candidates and branch managers in the rubber business.[83]

While both Terman and Lippmann considered themselves liberals, they presented distinctly different rationales for the same merito-cratic social ideal. Terman insisted that IQ and inheritance were the determining factors in placing people in the meritocracy. Lippmann, like so many current liberal educational reformers, begged the na-ture-nurture question by arguing for performance-based testing. He nicely represented those nature-nurture liberals who found their way out of the argument in the 1930s and 1940s by asserting that IQ tests were merely good achievement tests—they were predictors of possible success in school, if not in society, and should be used accordingly. Lippmann was in line with Allison Davis and many others in those decades who took the next step and used an effi-ciency argument. They called for more effective tests to make more efficient use of human resources (which by this time included blacks) for the nation's industries.[84] The country's broader social policy with respect to the races was shifting. Increasingly, segregation was pictured as economically wasteful and contrary to good, efficient business practices; all people needed to be integrated into the work force for efficiency's sake.[85]

Both Lippmann and the present-day efficiency advocates of performance-based testing, each in his own way, are part of the Enlightenment ideology that propounded an objective classification of occupational performances in the name of efficiently run machines.[86] The liberals who turned to performance-based testing, then as now, begged the causal question of why the difference in performance and raised no serious challenge to the differential reward system itself. Thus, the system remains effectively intact, well protected from critical scrutiny.

A similar phenomenon, accompanied by a major shift in social policy, seems to have occurred during the more recent nature-nurture debates following the publication of Arthur Jensen's thesis in the *Harvard Educational Review*. Not only have many liberals since taken the performance-testing way out, but once again the overall argument seems to have effectively obscured a change in the direction of basic social policy: a withdrawal of white liberal support for black liberation movements.

Arthur Jensen's assertion that intelligence is approximately 80 percent heritable was not born of immaculate conception. Drawing on the experience of fifty years of race- and class-biased testing, Jensen found that blacks in America were 15 IQ points below whites, although he noted that, in his experience in administering IQ tests to children of impoverished backgrounds, a small bit of "play therapy" usually boosted the IQ score of the youngster from 8 to 10 points. He found the IQ differences in the races significant. In retrospect, it seems incredible that he so easily discounted the cultural bias of the tests and the conditions under which they were administered. What appears more incredible, however, is the ease with which his findings were accepted by so many "professional" educators. In Russell Marks's words, what social difference does 80 percent heritability make?

Jensen's article, "How Much Can We Boost I.Q.?" was cast in the social context of initial disappointment with many of the Great Society's social and educational reform programs. These programs failed,

Jensen argued, because they were trying to do the impossible—that is, raise IQ, which is 80 percent genetically determined. To many educators, who failed, for a variety of reasons, to make an educational difference in the lives of ghetto children, Jensen's explanation was attractive. The heredity argument not only explained their failure, but also, more importantly, justified it. An explanation for Jensen's almost instant popularity among many liberal educators might also be found in the change of attitude that had occurred among many earlier supporters of the civil rights movement. For those who believed the movement had gone too far too fast in fanning the economic and social aspirations of the repressed, Jensen's argument took on significance. Frightened by the conflict and violence in the burning of cities in the mid-sixties, the organization and development of militant black groups, and the Ocean Hill/Brownsville experiment, many liberals wanted the movement to cool off, and they ceased to give vigorous support to educational programs that effectively raised the aspirations of repressed minorities. Arthur Jensen's article signaled the beginning of the end of much liberal support for the black liberation movement in the educational state.

The fact that intelligence may be 50 percent heritable or 80 percent heritable does not, in and of itself, lead one logically to come out for one kind of social action or another. Placed in the context in which Jensen used his argument, and the context of broader social movements of the period, however, the nature-nurture arguments took on profound social importance. To Jensen, most intervention programs, such as Head Start, had failed because they were trying to change the cognitive ability of the child through a process of a heavy emphasis on cognitive learning. Since he concluded that the black ghetto child was cognitively inferior due to hereditary factors, programs designed to improve their cognitive ability were thus also doomed to failure.

In true liberal spirit, Jensen then asserted that, if we studied the learning behavior of black children more carefully, we would find that they excelled at associative learning tasks. Sympathetic to the Bereiter-Engelman approach, Jensen called for a differentiated curriculum and methodology to capitalize on the presumed talents of the preschool ghetto child. He here argued, as Terman, Thorndike, and other predecessors had, that once we know what the child's abilities are, we must design a curriculum to meet his presumed needs most effectively. The child, once again, is to be protected from failure. In the name of individual differences, the black ghetto child is to be classified and tracked virtually from birth to adulthood, given associative learning tasks that will prepare him to enter the job market on the lower social economic levels. Jensen first made a very strong case that the occupational hierarchy is related to IQ and that formal schooling cultivates the cognitive trait or G factor, which he found so necessary for entrance into higher occupations; then he concluded that the G factor is heritable and that blacks are short of this inheritance; and finally he called for special education for ghetto children so as to cultivate their rote associative learning skill, which will be necessary if they are to become happy workers on the lower level of the job market.

While Jensen suggested that job requirements might be reviewed to allow persons of lower intelligence to occupy positions of somewhat higher social status, he did not fundamentally question or challenge the hierarchical, stratified system or the presumed meritocratic principle on which it rests. Confronted with the social consequences of a repressive society, Jensen, like so many educational reformers before him, took the traditional way out. Face to face with the children of the oppressed and with the devastating psychological and social consequences of that repression, these reformers attribute learning problems to genetic defects and then proceed to "protect the child from failure" by channeling him through a differentiated curriculum that marks him for his place in life.

Thus, the nature-nurture paradigm often appeared in the twentieth century as a kind of false consciousness among educators and laymen alike. It was false first because the argument seemed to explain and justify certain actions while it often obscured the more potent reasons behind them. Secondly, it inclined people to group themselves in polar opposites when, in actuality, they agreed on basic assumptions more than they disagreed. And thirdly, it was false because, contrary to conventional wisdom, hereditarians were not necessarily conservative and environmentalists not always liberal. Thus, Andrew Hacker missed an important point when he said: "The contretemps started a few years ago by Professor Arthur Jensen is a case in point. Nothing came of it because in this field at least, each researcher's ideology determines his approach to the data."[87] Each researcher's ideology does determine his approach to the data, and perhaps nothing did "come of" the argument, but the important point was that something certainly came "with" it. Compensatory programs were drastically reduced as liberals withdrew their support of black liberation movements. Jensen's work was profoundly significant, not, perhaps, as a single, direct, causal factor, but as part of a syndrome of factors. The significance is to be found not in the persuasiveness of the evidence, but in the social reasons why people were persuaded.

A similar analysis can be made of Christopher Jencks's most recent work, *Inequality.*[88] Jencks and his colleagues shaped their study toward predetermined ends, not only by the evidence that they selected and left out,[89] but also by the way in which they handled the data and drew their conclusions.[90] The major thesis that they set out to prove was that inequalities in the United States are not caused by inequalities in schooling, but ultimately result from luck and merit. Merit is cast in terms of job competency or performance. For Jencks, the schools are not vehicles of either social mobility or social repression. This, indeed, was the end of that Enlightenment faith in schooling. The meritocracy, however, still remained well grounded. Jencks's faith in Horatio Alger stories of achieving mobility appeared unshaken. The study's conclusion was the kind of explanation most sons and daughters of the privileged classes like to hear. It is comforting to believe that one "made it" not because of the superior wealth, privilege, and status of one's parents, but rather because of one's own efforts. Jencks's work is attractive to many liberal policy makers for other reasons as well. Insofar as his ideas are seriously accepted by the corporate liberal establishment in this country, we can expect the withdrawal of support for formal education from liberal foundations and governmental agencies. The social implication of Jencks's thesis is not likely to be the equalization of wealth (which, in the end, he proposes) but rather the decline in general support for schools. Here, again, the persuasiveness of the evidence is not as significant as the reasons why people are persuaded. Thus, it seems that our recent nature-nurture dialogue symbolizes a major shift in social policy. Godfrey Hodgson noted in a recent article that

liberal education policies of the last few generations . . . and the intellectual assumptions on which they were built, are in bad trouble. They have lost support in the ranks of the social scientists who provided America, from Roosevelt to Johnson, with a major part of its operating ideology.[91]

While it is clear that many liberal educational policies of yesterday are in trouble, present-day social scientists may still be providing the necessary "operating ideology"; the direction has merely changed.

Conclusions

If evaluation is that complex process of assigning values to phenomena, and ideology represents the set of values and attitudes that make up our social philosophy, then our sketch of the quest for meritocracy in the American educational experience over the last century tells us a good deal about ourselves, both then and now. Included in that sketch were the fears, hatreds, oppression, and racism of a competitive world, as well as a utopian hope and dream for a better future. How was it possible, one might ask, to turn that Enlightenment dream so quickly into what has become, for many, a repressive nightmare? Many of the problems we face are continuing historical problems. They involve questions, not so much of how to assign values in any operational way, but rather of the nature of the American ideological dream and the values implicit in it. Perhaps the most difficult part of our problem is contained in our failure to develop and effectuate a social philosophy that makes men and women the end rather than the means to social progress. We have yet to develop an adequate philosophy of individualism. Ultimately, we may not be able to "force men to be free" (as Rousseau urges us to do in the *Social Contract*), or delude a child into thinking he is free (as in the *Emile*), or "manufacture" free men (as Ward or Ross might have us do), without paying a heavy price in objectification and depersonalization of human beings.

Perhaps our Enlightenment faith in the progress of humanity was misplaced. A more knowledgeable humanity was not necessarily a more moral humanity. Evil was not always a simple consequence of ignorance. Likewise, the pragmatic ethic of enlightened self-interest did not always seem to work, especially for the children of the oppressed. Education could be used just as easily to repress and to control people for other men's advantage. Progress in knowledge did create power, as Bacon suggested, and it did help develop a wealthy technological civilization, but that power and that wealth were often readily employed for the wholesale destruction of humanity. The most advanced technological civilization seemed incapable of dealing with the great moral issues. Our Enlightenment ideology was, it seems, admirably suited for conquering a wilderness and building a powerful technological state, but dangerously inadequate for facing the moral issues of our times. We have yet to learn how to create social institutions that enhance the dignity of man.[92]

Some of these problems come into sharp focus in our practical day-to-day educational activities when, as educators, we play God with other people's lives, presuming to know what another person is and will become. At that subtle, sensitive, critical point, we lose faith, as Auguste Comte did, in the individual, and we begin to fashion him and his destiny on the "social kneading board." At that critical point, we cease to become teachers of free men and become instead directors for social servitude. Thus, I believe the professional educational expert in the twentieth century often was and is a tragic figure. While repeatedly professing to serve the interests of the student and humanity, he more often served the interest of collective power. His own deep antipathy to violence and conflict inclined him to turn away from injustice with the hope that, by rationalizing the system, he would somehow make the injustices of the system disappear. That myopic vision allowed him to condone, if not justify, the very injustices he ethically deplored.

As professional experts became more securely ensconced as anointed guardians of the social system, the injustices of that social system seem to have faded from their consciousness. Under the circumstances, victims of repression are treated by measuring their failures and calling them heritable, while sincere, honest men can look on a society that is largely structured by wealth, privilege, and status and call it meritocratic.

Notes

1. See Thomas Jefferson, "Bill for the More General Diffusion of Knowledge."

2. Antoine Nicolas de Condorcet, *Sketch for a Historical Picture of the Progress of the Human Mind,* trans. by June Barroclough (New York: Dover Publications, 1955), p. 179.

3. Quoted in J. B. Bury, *The Idea of Progress* (New York: Dover Publications, 1955), p. 282.

4. Edward Bellamy, *Looking Backward* (1887; reprint ed., New York: New American Library, 1963), p. 222. It should be noted that

Bellamy touched a segment of the reform idealism of his day. Within three years of the publication of his book, 162 Bellamy Clubs had been organized in twenty-seven states to spread the message. See Merle Curti, *The Growth of American Thought* (New York: Harper and Row, 1964), p. 610.

5. Mordecai Grossman, *The Philosophy of Helvetius* (New York: Bureau of Publications, Teachers College, Columbia University, 1926), p. 78.

6. Edward A. Ross, *Social Control* (New York: Macmillan, 1906), p. 168. For an extended analysis of the social philosophy of both Edward A. Ross and Charles E. Cooley, see Paul Violas, chap. 3 in *Roots of Crisis: American Education in the Twentieth Century,* by Clarence Karier, Paul Violas, and Joel Spring (Chicago: Rand McNally, 1973).

7. Not only did the total number of immigrants increase from 3.7 million in the period 1891-1900 to 8.8 million in the period 1901-10, but also the percentage coming from northern Europe declined from 44.6 percent in the former period to 21.7 percent in the later period, while the percentage coming from southeastern Europe increased from 51.9 percent to 70.8 percent. See R. Freeman Butts and Lawrence A. Cremin, *A History of Education in American Culture* (New York: Holt, Rinehart and Winston, 1953), p. 308.

8. See Robert H. Wiebe, *The Search for Order, 1877-1920* (New York: Hill and Wang, 1967).

9. Herbert Spencer, quoted in the *Proceedings of the First National Conference on Race Betterment,* Race Betterment Foundation, Battle Creek, Mich., January 8, 1914.

10. Charles Darwin, *The Descent of Man and Selection in Relation to Sex,* 2d ed. rev. (New York: Appleton, 1922), p. 136.

11. See H. H. Laughlin, *Eugenical Sterilization in the United States,* Psychopathic Laboratory of the Municipal Court of Chicago, December 1922.

12. Editorial, *New York Times,* February 22, 1895, p. 4, col. 6. For calling my attention to this quote I am indebted to Chris Shea.

13. Samuel Bowles and Herbert Gintis, in "I.Q. in the U.S. Class Structure," *Social Policy,* January-February 1973, make a persuasive case that, while IQ and cognitive tested skills do not apparently cause hierarchical social stratification, they do serve to legitimize the hierarchical division of labor.

14. Robert Dale Owen, *The Working Man's Advocate,* April 24, 1830, p. 4.

15. Lester Frank Ward, "Education," manuscript dated 1871-73, p. 132, Special Collections Division, Brown University, Providence. I am indebted to Adelia Peters for calling my attention to this manuscript.

16. Ibid., p. 342.

17. Ibid., p. 624.

18. Ibid., p. 312.

19. Ibid., p. 647.

20. Ibid., p. 148.

21. Ibid., p. 149.

22. Ibid.

23. Ibid., p. 152.

24. Ibid., p. 200.

25. Ibid., p. 151.

26. Ibid., p. 15.

27. Richard Herrnstein, "I.Q.," *Atlantic Monthly,* September 1971, p. 64.

28. Ibid.

29. Herrnstein's ideas appear in one sense incredibly naive and in another sense incredibly devastating when leveled against the lower classes. His belief that somehow past revolutions were successful because the lower classes were once more intelligent is nothing short of absurd. By simply ignoring the question of which classes produced leaders for revolutions in the past, as well as ignoring the use of mass communication and efficient police state tactics in putting down revolutionary groups in the modern totalitarian society, he speciously blames the failure of lower-class rebellion on a shortage of intelligence.

30. Herrnstein, "I.Q.," p. 64.

31. Alfred Binet and T. H. Simon, *The Development of Intelligence in Children* (Baltimore: Williams and Wilkins, 1916), p. 266.

32. Ward as quoted by Thomas F. Gossett in *Race: The History of an Idea in America* (New York: Schocken Books, 1968), p. 162.

33. Binet and Simon, *The Development of Intelligence in Children,* p. 318.

34. H. H. Goddard, *Human Efficiency and Levels of Intelligence* (Princeton, N.J.: Princeton University Press, 1920), p. 97.

35. Lewis M. Terman, *Intelligence Tests and School Reorganization* (New York: World Book, 1923), pp. 27-28.

36. Frank N. Freeman, "Sorting the Students," *Educational Review*, November 1924, p. 170.

37. Ibid., p. 171.

38. Ibid., p. 172.

39. Lewis M. Terman, "The Conservation of Talent," *School and Society* 19 (March 29, 1924): 363. It should be noted that late in life Terman seemed to waver from this position. See Karier, Violas, and Spring, *Roots of Crisis,* p. 124.

40. Terman, "The Conservation of Talent," p. 364.

41. Lester F. Ward, *Pure Sociology* (New York: Macmillan, 1903), pp. 359-60. I am indebted to Stephen Yulish for calling my attention to the racial views of Lester F. Ward. Ward's racist views were very much like those of William Shockley, who, in a packed auditorium at Stanford University, invited black students to participate in a "scientific" experiment that would test his hypothesis "that for each one percent of Caucasian ancestry, average I.Q. of American black populations goes up approximately one I.Q. point." "Genetics and Intelligence," *Stanford Observer,* February 1973, p. 8.

42. Terman, "The Conservation of Talent," p. 363.

43. Ibid.

44. See and compare Richard Herrnstein, "I.Q.," pp. 50-53, with Lewis M. Terman, "Were We Born That Way?" *World's Work,* 1922, pp. 657-59.

45. See Terman, "Were We Born That Way?" p. 655.

46. Terman considered himself a New Deal liberal just as Arthur Jensen and Richard Herrnstein today consider themselves liberal.

47. Terman, "Were We Born That Way?" p. 654.

48. I am using the term *racist* here to mean one who believes in the genetic superiority of one race over another and believes that some kind of social action or inaction ought to occur as a result of that alleged superiority or inferiority.

49. Terman, "Were We Born That Way?" p. 655.

50. It should be noted that after he published this work, Brigham began to have second thoughts about the "empirical" basis undergirding his racism. He later repudiated this work, much to the chagrin of men like Thorndike and Terman.

51. Just to make no mistake about who was thought to be really inferior, throughout Brigham's work, the Nordic, Alpine, and Mediterranean races are capitalized, while Negro is not.

52. C. C. Brigham, *A Study of American Intelligence* (Princeton, N.J.: Princeton University Press, 1923), p. 209.

53. David Starr Jordan, "Closed Doors or the Melting Pot," *American Hebrew,* September 26, 1924, p. 538.

54. Ibid., p. 592.

55. Ibid.

56. See William Shockley, "Dysgenics—a Social Problem Reality Evaded by Illusion of Infinite Plasticity of Human Intelligence?" *Phi Delta Kappan,* I-291.5, March 1972.

57. Edward L. Thorndike, *Human Nature and the Social Order* (New York: Macmillan, 1940), p. 957.

58. Edward L. Thorndike, "Intelligence and Its Uses," *Harper's,* January 1920, p. 233.

59. Ibid., p. 235.

60. Ibid.

61. Lester Frank Ward, *Glimpses of the Cosmos,* vol. 4, p. 295.

62. See Lester F. Ward, "Eugenics, Euthenics, and Eudemics," *American Journal of Sociology* 18 (May 1913): 739.

63. Ibid., p. 239. Also see Thorndike's review of Ward's *Applied Sociology* in *Science,* n.s. 24, no. 610: 299.

64. For a more complete picture of the social effects of the differentiated curriculum, see Edward Krug, *The Shaping of the American High School,* vol. 2, *1920-1941* (Madison: University of Wisconsin Press, 1972).

65. For the earlier movement, see Raymond E. Callahan, *Education and the Cult of Efficiency* (Chicago: University of Chicago Press, 1962).

66. Thorndike, *Human Nature and the Social Order,* p. 428. This last work by Thorndike in many ways suggests approaches to social problems that were later developed by such think-tank operations as Rand Corporation and Systems Development Corporation.

67. Ward also suspected this, but then backed away by suggesting that these differences are probably socially produced.

68. A book designed specifically for teachers.

69. Edward L. Thorndike, *Educational Psychology, Briefer Course* (New York: Teacher's College, Columbia University, 1914), pp. 350-51.

70. Edward L. Thorndike, *Individuality* (Boston: Houghton Mifflin, 1911), pp. 30-34.

71. See National Organization for Women, Task Force of the Central New Jersey Chapter, *Dick and Jane as Victims: Sex Stereotyping in Children's Readers,* pamphlet (Princeton, N.J.: Women on Words and Images, 1972), pp. 6-7.

72. Ibid.

73. Edward L. Thorndike, "The Psychology of the Half-Educated Man," *Harper's,* April 1920, p. 670.

74. Ibid.

75. Letter from Edward Ross to Theodore Roosevelt, August 1, 1911, Edward Ross Collection, Wisconsin Historical Library Archives, Madison.

76. Letter from Edward Ross to Mr. Earl M. Rydell, February 9, 1921, Edward Ross Collection, Wisconsin Historical Library Archives, Madison.

77. Gregory Mason, "An Americanization Factory," *Outlook,* February 23, 1916, p. 448.

78. Marion Brown, "Is There a Nationality Problem in Our Schools?" in *N.E.A. Proceedings* (Chicago: University of Chicago Press, 1900), p. 585.

79. Ibid., p. 590.

80. For many insights about this controversy, I am indebted to Russell Marks. See his "Race and Immigration: The Politics of Intelligence Testers" (manuscript, 1973); and "Testers, Trackers and Trustees: The Ideology of the Intelligence Testing Movement in America 1900-1954" (Ph.D. diss., University of Illinois, 1972).

81. While most of the congressional testimony surrounding the immigration restriction law stressed the heredity argument, the large banking and manufacturing interests represented in the National Civic Federation supported closure on grounds of economic advantage. Many of the arguments used by the liberal-dominated Immigration Restriction League leaned heavily on the need for social harmony and Americanization.

82. See Walter Lippmann, series of articles in *The New Republic:* "The Mental Age of Americans," October 25, 1922, pp. 213-15; "The Mystery of the 'A' Men," November 1, 1922, pp. 246-48; "The Reliability of Intelligence Tests," November 8, 1922, pp. 275-77; "The Abuse of the Tests," November 15, 1922, pp. 297-98; "Tests of Hereditary Intelligence," November 22, 1922, pp. 328-30; "A Future for the Tests," November 29, 1922, pp. 9-11; "The Great

Conspiracy," December 27, 1922, pp. 116-20; "The Great Confusion," January 3, 1923, pp. 145-46.

83. See Lippmann, "A Future for the Tests," p. 10.

84. See Allison Davis, "Education and the Conservation of Human Resources," American Association of School Administration, Washington, D.C., May 1949, pp. 74-83.

85. For a perceptive analysis of this shift see Marks, "Race and Immigration."

86. One is reminded here of Le Mettrie's essay, *L'homme machine.*

87. Andrew Hacker, "On Original Sin and Conservatives," *New York Times Magazine,* February 25, 1973, p. 65.

88. Christopher Jencks, Marshall Smith, Henry Acland, Mary Jo Bane, David Cohen, Herbert Gintis, Barbara Heyns, Stephan Michelson, *Inequality: A Reassessment of the Effect of Family and Schooling in America* (New York: Basic Books, 1972).

89. For evidence on the relationship of family income and schooling, which he apparently left out, see Bowles and Gintis, "I.Q. in the U.S. Class Structure."

90. The work is flawed at many points and contains bad logic as well. For two critical reviews, see Gerald Chasin, "Pull the Ladder Up, Jack—I'm on Board," *Nation,* February 19, 1973, and Henry M. Levin, "Schooling and Inequality: The Social Science Objectivity Gap," *Saturday Review.*

91. Godfrey Hodgson, "Do Schools Make a Difference?" *Atlantic Monthly,* February 1973, p. 46.

92. See Clarence J. Karier, "Humanities and the Triumph of the Machine," *Journal of Aesthetic Education* 3, no. 2 (1969). Also see Karier, Spring, and Violas, *Roots of Crisis.*

Faculty Critique

by FRANCIS SCHRAG

Mr. Karier has told us about the social attitudes and ideals held by some eminent social scientists and educators from the Enlightenment to the present. Binet, Terman, Ward, Thorndike, and Jensen are known to students of psychology and sociology for the contributions they have made to the advances of those fields. Mr. Karier is right to call our attention to the social consequences of their work and to the social ideals that animated and inspired that work. These men not only had but *intended* to have an impact on society, and they must be judged by that impact as well as by their work in the laboratory.

What impact did they have? I had hoped to learn this from Mr. Karier's paper, but I cannot say that I am satisfied with his account. His version of social history goes something like this: There was a time prior to the Enlightenment when, despite the hierarchical organization of society, the dignity of all men was recognized. Some Enlightenment thinkers wished to remove the arbitrary inequalities due to caste, class, or privilege. They wished to create a society in which men rose or fell according to their natural talents. This required that children be tested and sorted. The rich and powerful people at the top of the social pyramid did not want their children to be dispossessed by the poor, oppressed people at the bottom. They needed a sorting mechanism that would favor their own children at the expense of the children of the poor. Luckily for them, at that moment a new breed of men emerged—the professional sorters. Some were the paid lackeys of the oppressors. Others were well-intentioned though naive men whose ideas were exploited. These men did their job well. They told the schools how to sort children so that the children of the rich could maintain and even extend their hegemony. They told the schools how to sort children so that the oppressed would not complain or put up a fight. Today we live in a hierarchically ordered social system. Who is responsible for this calamity? The business tycoons and corporate executives? No, those earnest, liberal social thinkers from Ward to Jensen who either were on the oppressor's payroll or provided the benign mask behind which the oppressor could work his foul deeds.

There may be something to this version of how we got to where we are, but one would like some evidence. Take the status of women, for example—one of the many topics Mr. Karier tries to cover. He tells us that Thorndike was a sexist, and I believe him. He tells us that a recent study of children's literature demonstrates bias against women, and I believe him. Moreover, we know that women are, or at least until recently have been, an oppressed group. Does this not prove that Thorndike was among those responsible for the depressed status of women? I don't think so. We need, for example, to link

Thorndike directly to the sex bias in contemporary children's books. How do we do this? Here is Karier's lame attempt:

Thorndike was, perhaps, the most influential shaper of the meritocratic educational state in the early twentieth century. For almost half a century, he held sway at Columbia University, teaching thousands of teachers and administrators, publishing 50 books and 450 monographs and articles. His massive three-volume work *Educational Psychology* (1913) set the tone of that discipline for almost two decades. From his pen flowed a prodigious number of educational maxims, psychological laws, textbooks and scales of achievement for elementary, secondary, and college courses in varied fields, dictionaries for elementary and secondary schools, and teacher's manuals. He not only told the teachers what to teach and how to teach it, but also told them how to evaluate their work. Because he wrote so many of the texts and the tests used in elementary and secondary schools, his impact on American educational practice was both immediate and extended.

This just will not do. Mr. Karier's analysis falls down just where one most needs the concrete, detailed documentation that only the historian can provide. What precisely was the impact of the testers' ideologies on school practices, and what precisely were the social consequences of various school practices such as the differentiated curriculum? Did Thorndike's work, for example, influence the writers of today's children's books? Did Ward's apparently unpublished writings on education and meritocracy influence Terman and Thorndike? Did the introduction of standardized IQ tests have any effect on rates of social mobility? If so, what was the effect? Without answers to these kinds of specific questions, Mr. Karier's version of history is as speculative and probably as biased as the official version he wishes to supplant.

I should like to say a few words about the ideal of meritocracy—an ideal held by all the thinkers Mr. Karier discusses. I take it that, for him, this ideal is ignoble at best and vicious at worst. What does this ideal consist of? Essentially, a belief in four propositions: (1) that men are not equally endowed with talent and intelligence, (2) that the more talented have more to contribute to society, (3) that those with greater talent should be identified and their talent nourished, and (4) that their authority and remuneration should be commensurate with their contribution to society. Now, I would agree with Mr. Karier that a society based on these propositions alone would not be a just society and therefore not a good society. This has been recently argued by John Rawls, who correctly points out that a man is no more responsible for his natural endowment than for the family or social milieu he happens to be born into. But does one give merit no recognition at all? Mr. Karier's own position is not spelled out beyond some unexceptionable rhetoric concerning human dignity and treating men as ends and not means. This, unfortunately, does not take us very far in providing a usable principle for the distribution of scarce resources.

It is hard to defend, indeed even to imagine, a society in which talent and achievement do not yield greater rewards than lack of talent and inactivity or failure. What would such a society look like? Three possibilities may be briefly sketched out. In one, people are tested and judged just as they are now, only the rewards are allocated on a basis inversely proportional to merit. Only students whose scores fall below a maximum on college entrance tests would be admitted to college, only physicians who failed their board exams would be given licenses, only students who wrote shoddy dissertations would receive their degrees, and so forth. It is amusing but not inspiring to tease out the consequences of such a system.

The second possibility is one in which everyone receives an equal allocation of the goods of the society. Everyone receives the same pay, everyone performs an equal share of the unpleasant tasks. Of such a society one must say, first of all, that it has never existed on this planet. Secondly, one might wonder whether even such an extreme attempt at equalization would be successful. Would equalizing pay successfully equalize status or power? I doubt it. Finally, would such a principle of allocation be desirable? Would individuals be willing to undergo long and arduous training, would they seek positions of great responsibility or personal risk without the expectation of special reward or recognition? Would anyone seek the services of a less qualified person if the services of a more qualified person could be obtained at the same cost?

The third possibility is one in which rewards and offices are distributed entirely randomly, perhaps by lottery. Such a system would be fair in a sense, but it is hard to see how anyone—even the most oppressed—would profit. If Mr. Karier is attracted to such a society, I call his attention to the curse Martin Mayer reserved for extreme egalitarians in a recent article:

That they should cross the river on a bridge designed by an engineering school where students were admitted by lottery; and that their injuries should then be treated by a doctor from a medical school where students were admitted by lottery; and that their heirs' malpractice suit should then be tried by a lawyer from a law school where students were admitted by lottery.[1]

Mr. Karier castigates his subjects for not facing up to the difficult problem of social justice. I find him equally evasive. I am not sure whether general philosophical principles like Rawls's principles of justice will provide clear and unequivocal answers to the really difficult questions of the just allocation of goods. I am sure that glib slogans about the dignity of men are of no help at all.

Note

1. Martin Mayer, "Higher Education for All: The Case of Open Admissions," *Commentary,* February 1973, p. 47.

Author's Reply to Faculty Critique

I'd like to make several remarks on your commentary. I'm not sure if you understood what I was saying, especially at the beginning. I was not suggesting that the utopia would be a reflection of some golden age in the past. I have no notion that there ever was such an age. And I would be perfectly willing to assume that we have made and in the future will make progress—in technology, in science, and so on. I would suggest, however, the possibility of developing a society that would encourage people to become engineers, or doctors, for instance, on the basis of values other than financial payoff.

On this question of cause and effect between a man's work and later social policies, we face a difficult problem. I'd like to see a lot more detailed analysis done. I would like to know more about Thorndike, and I would like to make the connections much more specifically.

I don't presume to say that testers are responsible for all the ills of the twentieth century. I'm merely saying that they were part of the process behind those ills, as we are part of it today. And, in spite of the attempt to be objective and scientific, their ideas and their values came through—and came through fairly clearly. In an interesting way, some of their values, for instance on race, came through more clearly in the earlier part of the century than they do now.

I gladly admit that I don't have the answers to the quest for the ideal of meritocracy and social justice in the liberal state.

Audience Discussion

Walberg: Many testers are not aware of the testing movement in ancient China. In the Mandarin testing system, young boys were given mastery tests on the Confucian classics. In order to master these tests, the boys had to do a lot of memorization. All segments of the society—the children of the rich and the children of the poor— had the opportunity to take these exams. They may not have had equal opportunities to prepare for them, but at least they could take them. Some of the people who have studied this system, such as the famous sociologist Max Weber, believe that the stability of the old Chinese civilization was at least in part attributable to the fact that the leaders, the Mandarins, had to go through this extensive system of objective examinations. Thus, testing may have had consequences for the society, making it very stable and to some extent promoting equal opportunity. So I think tests can work in both ways, although, as was pointed out here, it's very important for us to look at some of the historical consequences in this country in this century.

Implicit Values in Evaluation

Q: I'd like to interject something about the positive aspects of studying, like the example just mentioned. It may facilitate social mobility for people from disadvantaged groups to allow them to get scholarships and so forth. Obviously for the individuals involved that's extremely beneficial. But it implies a definition of a social problem that can't be accepted willy-nilly. It implies that the important thing is to skim off the cream—the brightest—from the top. It is not clear to me that it is socially more advantageous to do that than to raise the floor.

Karier: Yes, my perspective is that we, as academics, are too preoccupied with tests and measures of what we think is the highest quality life, whereas we fail to respect a good bricklayer and the wide variety of other talents and abilities that people show on their jobs. We tend to overemphasize this single quality of tests. As much of the research indicates, neither school marks nor IQ nor standardized achievement tests are correlated with the many things we value later on in life. That's what disturbs me about standardized testing: that we tend to gear the curriculum and so much of what we do toward a single, and I fear a kind of unreal, educational goal that is not related to most subsequent experiences.

Q: Is it correct to say that scores on standardized tests are not related to later life outcomes—at least the ones like income and occupation? As I understand the data, the Blau and Duncan data and the research coming out of Johns Hopkins from Muuse, *within* certain educational characteristics, for example, among those who have not graduated from high school, there's hardly any correlation with income; among those who got a B.A., there's hardly any correlation. But if you look *across* those different artificial cutting points in our educational system, the correlation is very, very high.

Karier: Sure. I was thinking in terms of a broader range of adult values.

Q: Perhaps education selects and does not teach.

Karier: Some of the questions that were raised here are important questions for the historian of the twentieth century. For instance, I suspect that studies that are done not in terms of social class but in terms of the tracking in schools miss all kinds of available data. The professional experts are saying these things, trying to make as much connection as possible. But the hard data involving social class are still there and can be worked on.

Biases in Standardized Tests

Q: How do we figure out what ways to measure what things for what reasons?

Karier: I think the movement toward performance testing is probably a healthy thing, even though I criticized it as a way of evading the issue. Performance as a test is probably much healthier in terms of changing people than the kinds of abstractions we've been working on. But I still think we ought to take a look at our tests in terms of the biases of today. For instance the Stanford-Binet still has a heavy racial bias. The last revision of the Stanford-Binet was in 1960. There's a particular sequence showing a person with clearly Negroid features and one with Anglo-Saxon features, and a child at the age of six is asked: "Which picture is prettier?" The next sequence shows, interestingly enough, southern European features against Anglo-Saxon. A black child who has looked at himself in the mirror and has an adequate feeling about himself is going to get that "wrong." But look at the child who gets it right: what has society done to that child? It has really taught him to lie about himself, to play the game that society demands. And the same is true of the southeastern European. Now both of these questions, I suspect, came in with Terman, who did the early revision of the test, although he did not do the 1960 revision. I suspect that sequence has been there ever since. In the early part of the century the southern European immigrant was really considered dirty, as far as this culture was concerned. We've got to look at the primary sources; the evidence is there.

We went through the Army tests of World War I that were standardized at the University of Illinois. Those tests show a lot of interesting values. The tests really reflect the values of the culture. The assumptions that they made about moral character include incredible racial overtones.

Uses of Evaluation Studies

Q: In reading the remarks of some of the people you discussed (which I've never read before), one thing struck me: They seem to be a bit more candid than people were before, about their desire to change the society in certain directions. I was wondering if you thought that was a good idea. Evaluators tend to announce their own values and aspirations to the world before they publish their evaluations. We think in our civilization that men are scientific giants and moral midgets.

Karier: That's an interesting point, you know. What persuades? Thorndike made a case, for instance, for rejecting the classical languages. He made all kinds of tests and studies on mental discipline, and he supposedly proved that Latin didn't make a difference. Now, years later, people in educational psychology go back to those studies and say, "Well, how in the world could he have proved anything with that?" The tests were completely loaded; they had errors running all the way through them. Then we look around at the history of the turn of the century, and we find that a lot of people wanted to get rid of the classical languages for a lot of different reasons. Thorndike was saying it, and people grabbed on, saying, "This is scientific." There are a lot of connections between the process and our conceptions of science, the authority of science, and the educator as scientist.

Walberg: I have the impression that perhaps both humanists and scientists may be suffering under the delusion that evaluation makes a difference. It may be that the social climate of our times determines the results of both scientific and humanistic research. When there's a concern about social inequality, the historians find it. So, we're mixing up the direction of causality here; evaluation may be a function of policy, rather than policy being a function of evaluation. Max Weber pointed it out a long time ago. I think we're still in our adolescence in the field of evaluation. We have a long, long way to go. We haven't even got a clear understanding of the notion of objectivity. I think we've got to look at it from a wide variety of perspectives, and try to avoid picking out bad guys and good guys.

Political Values and Evaluation

Q: The general gist of your paper, Mr. Karier, was that evaluators had certain political and social attitudes. Are political attitudes necessarily imbedded in the craft of evaluation?

Karier: I get in trouble here separating cause and effect. We have a situation in which the economic reward system tends to support those researchers who find supporting evidence for the values and attitudes the system espouses. There's a selective factor here, but I'm not sure when it's operational.

Walberg: My point of view is that there is no such thing as the discipline of evaluation. For instance Levin—he would consider himself an economist. Jensen would consider himself a psychologist. Many other people doing evaluation do not consider themselves primarily evaluators, but rather applied psychologists or applied economists. One of the crises of the field, I believe, is that it doesn't have its own philosophy. So we can get a wide variety of perspectives among people who might be called evaluators, but they have all kinds of political opinions, and they certainly come from all sorts of disciplines, including the humanities.

Q: On the question of whether or not to test, inevitably a certain kind of person holds certain values. What do you think of a person like Allison Davis, who is outside the establishment mainstream and whose tests were intended to do away with the kinds of products you've been discussing?

Karier: I think Davis was honestly trying to come up with a valid testing procedure. However, I also suspect that he was working in the context of a movement toward a more integrated society for efficiency's sake.

Q: It seems to me that, particularly in your paper, you were still questioning whether tests are valid at all. Would you go so far as to suggest that, until we make tests significantly different from what they are, we shouldn't be using them?

Karier: No, I wouldn't go all that way. But I really think that we ought to look much more carefully at the tests we're using and probably throw out some of them, especially those standardized tests in which we're really tracking people. I understood some of the previous speakers to say that we're under the gun today—that we have to make decisions, and we should simply go with whatever information we've got. I suspect that we're not that much under the gun and that there are a lot of decisions that probably shouldn't be made.

The Future of Evaluation

Q: What directions might you suggest for testing in the next decade or so?

Karier: The historian is very bad as a predictor.

Q: Well, how about the historian as a dreamer, then?

Karier: I think the past has a significant part to play in terms of framing our questions in the present. I don't think that the past necessarily controls where we're going in the future or that it should. But I think that it should figure in the present analysis.

There are tremendous philosophical problems present, with regard to ethics, moral behavior, and the way in which we use our knowledge. I'd really like to see philosophers, sociologists, anthropologists, testers, and evaluators working on these problems in this century, because it seems to me that this is the critical area. How do you use that knowledge? It's never absolute. It can't be absolute. Any absolute that you take all the way to the *n*th degree turns into a vice. For instance, I find myself oftentimes advocating academic freedom in a wide variety of ways. I could say, "I'm in favor of total freedom for the scientist to inquire all over the place." Chomsky raises this question in his essay on IQ and class. He asks: What would you think of the tester who wanted to investigate the heritability of usury in Germany in 1939? That's a legitimate scientific question. You know, you could simply investigate that and see if there's any correlation between the Jews as a group and the tendency to practice usury. You might even find some interesting correlations. But you might also recognize the social context—that is, what that research would be used for under National Socialism.

Q: That's more a historical than a scientific question, I think.

Karier: But then I get into a box again. Under my concept of academic freedom, the scientist ought to be free to keep on going under any circumstances, just sifting and winnowing for truth. But when that truth begins to cut people up and burn them in the ovens, then I begin to back off. I begin to say, "No, wait a second. We shouldn't do this." There is a social context, and I don't think any of us escape it. I don't escape it as a historian, and I don't think the psychologist escapes it either. Our work can have a tremendous social impact. The arguments over Jencks and others are having an influence, even though it may be the wrong influence from their standpoint. We may not always control the use of our knowledge, but we are morally responsible for the knowledge we produce. This is the tragic dilemma of our age.